Living in Infamy

Living in Infamy

*Felon Disfranchisement and the
History of American Citizenship*

Pippa Holloway

OXFORD
UNIVERSITY PRESS

OXFORD
UNIVERSITY PRESS

Oxford University Press is a department of the University of Oxford.
It furthers the University's objective of excellence in research, scholarship,
and education by publishing worldwide.

Oxford   New York
Auckland   Cape Town   Dar es Salaam   Hong Kong   Karachi
Kuala Lumpur   Madrid   Melbourne   Mexico City   Nairobi
New Delhi   Shanghai   Taipei   Toronto

With offices in
Argentina   Austria   Brazil   Chile   Czech Republic   France   Greece
Guatemala   Hungary   Italy   Japan   Poland   Portugal   Singapore
South Korea   Switzerland   Thailand   Turkey   Ukraine   Vietnam

Oxford is a registered trademark of Oxford University Press
in the UK and certain other countries.

Published in the United States of America by
Oxford University Press
198 Madison Avenue, New York, NY 10016

Library of Congress Cataloging-in-Publication Data
Holloway, Pippa.
Living in infamy : felon disfranchisement and the history of American citizenship /
Pippa Holloway.
pages cm
Includes bibliographical references and index.
ISBN 978–0–19–997608–9 (hardcover : alk. paper)   1. Political rights, Loss of—
United States—States.   2. Ex-convicts—Suffrage—United States.   3. Election law—United
States—States.   4. African American criminals.   5. Citizenship—United States.   6. Race
discrimination—Law and legislation—United States.   I. Title.
KF9747.H65 2013
324.6'20869270973—dc23
2013017920

1 3 5 7 9 8 6 4 2
Printed in the United States of America
on acid-free paper

For my Dad

CONTENTS

PREFACE

In 1888 Democrats in Richmond, Virginia, came up with a plan to help their incumbent, George Wise, fight off his Republican challenger in a race to represent the state's third district in the U.S. Congress. Aware that African Americans voted predominately for Republican candidates, Richmond Democrats developed a strategy to obstruct their vote and limit their electoral impact. On election day, the party stationed "challengers"—official partisan election monitors—at the city's three predominantly African American precincts in Jackson Ward, where they spent the day questioning voter eligibility. Only African American voters underwent this interrogation. Each time a challenger disputed the credentials of a voter, the accusation had to be evaluated by an attendant panel of bipartisan precinct judges. These judges confirmed with voters their age, the spelling of their name, and their place of residence. The Democratic judges colluded with the Democratic challengers by slowly and carefully verifying the information on the registration lists. Any voter whose credentials were suspect had to swear an oath that he was qualified to vote, and each was informed he faced perjury charges if a later check of his credentials disqualified him.

One particular kind of challenge took a disproportionate amount of time: voters who were accused of having a prior criminal conviction. Under Virginia's constitution, individuals convicted of felonies or misdemeanor larceny could not vote. Prior to election day the precinct judges had received lists of voters made ineligible because of criminal conviction. Upon each challenge, the judges combed through the list of convicts, which contained about two thousand names, searching for that individual's name. Because the segregated precinct had separate lines for the two races, white voting proceeded apace while African American voters waited for hours. Over five hundred black voters were still waiting in line to vote when the polls closed. Many others had given up due to frustration or intimidation.[1]

Defenders of this process said these inquiries were appropriate and no delaying tactics had been used that day in Richmond. It took longer to check the registration of black voters, Democrats claimed, because of African American ignorance and lack of education. Illiterate voters might misstate their addresses and misremember their ages. They might be unable to spell their names, making it difficult to distinguish between individuals with similar names. Democrats also claimed that African Americans were more prone to criminality, making the list of black criminals far longer than the list of white criminals. A largely partisan report later summarized, "The judges of election then, in order to protect the ballot-box from the votes of thieves and felons, were compelled to look carefully to these lists."[2]

The scene in Richmond in 1888 might seem familiar to observers of contemporary elections in the United States, or at least a foreshadowing of things to come. Prior criminal convictions are the primary reason for which adult citizens are excluded from suffrage in the United States today. In 2010 approximately 5.85 million people could not vote due to criminal convictions. While about one-fourth of these disfranchised individuals are incarcerated, the majority are either under correctional supervision (probation or parole) or have fully completed their sentences but remain disfranchised under state laws.[3]

Felon disfranchisement has been described as a "modern day poll tax," a phrase that evokes racially oriented disfranchisement techniques of the past and underscores the racially skewed impact of laws denying the vote to individuals with serious criminal convictions.[4] The racial disparities in the impact of these laws today are indeed stark. African Americans are disfranchised due to criminal convictions at more than four times the national average. In three southern states (Virginia, Kentucky, and Florida) felon disfranchisement laws block electoral participation by over 20 percent of the African American voting age population. Southern states disfranchise more of the total population, across races, too. Six southern states (Alabama, Florida, Kentucky, Mississippi, Virginia, and Tennessee) lead the nation by disfranchising more than 7 percent of the total adult population because of their history of criminal convictions.[5] Although the Twenty-Third Amendment and the 1965 Civil Rights Act eradicated poll taxes, along with other barriers to suffrage such as literacy tests, felon disfranchisement laws have persisted and in fact expanded their reach in recent decades. While men have traditionally had the highest conviction and incarceration rates, African American women are the fastest-growing portion of the prison population and therefore are disfranchised in increasing numbers.[6]

Laws disfranchising for criminal convictions have thus far been immune from the constitutional challenges that outlawed earlier racially motivated disfranchisement techniques. But, amid growing concerns about the vast exclusion of voters this represents, nineteen states have revised their policies since 1997, making restoration of rights easier and, in some cases, automatic after completion of sentence. Nonetheless, the hurdles for restoration of voting rights remain significant or insurmountable for many, and millions of individuals still face lifelong disfranchisement for criminal acts they committed years or even decades earlier. [7]

America woke up to the electoral impact of these policies in the year 2000, when George W. Bush won the presidential election in the state of Florida by 537 votes, giving him the electoral vote margin to become president. A large number of individuals—nearly 10 percent of the voting age population—had been unable to vote in Florida due to a state law that permanently disfranchised anyone with a felony conviction unless pardoned by the governor.[8] In addition, election officials wrongly purged the registration of many individuals who did not have prior felony convictions, preventing them from voting. Newspapers reported that African Americans comprised 44 percent of those removed from the rolls in Florida's pre-election voter purge, although they made up only about 11 percent of the state's voters.[9] Some suggested that these "purge lists" were prepared with partisan intentions. Florida's Republican Secretary of State, Katherine Harris, hired the contractor and oversaw the process. Harris was also, at the time, co-chairwoman of the Bush's presidential campaign in Florida, a connection that added to speculation about partisanship in election law enforcement.[10] Since the individuals who were disfranchised rightly or wrongly through this process were disproportionately African Americans, a population that votes for the Democratic Party by wide margins, these events arguably benefited the Republican Party and gave the presidency to Bush.[11]

The difficult obstacles facing former convicts who seek restoration of voting rights also came to light after the 2000 election. Florida was one of thirteen states with "discretionary, non-automatic restoration systems."[12] Individuals who wished to have their voting rights restored had to petition the governor and Board of Executive Clemency. Those who successfully completed the complicated paperwork necessary to apply faced waiting periods of up to three years, as there was a backlog of over twenty-five thousand petitions. On September 21, 2000—a few weeks before the election—a number of individuals who had been denied restoration of citizenship rights by the clemency board joined a complaint in federal court that became *Johnson v. Bush*. The plaintiffs claimed that the Florida law had a racially discriminatory impact and intent, thereby putting it in violation of the Fourteenth and Fifteenth Amendments and the Voting Rights Act of 1965. This alleged discrimination included the restoration process.[13]

Florida was not the only state with a complicated, slow restoration process that lacked transparency. In recent years many states have worked to streamline their procedures for suffrage restoration, though significant obstacles and delays still exist nationwide.[14]

Each of these three contemporary issues—disproportionate racial impact, partisan enforcement, and obstacles to the restoration of voting rights and citizenship—has historical roots in the post-Civil War South. Understanding this history is particularly important because recent court decisions concerning these laws have factored historical evidence into their verdicts. Even the terminology by which such laws are discussed today has historical antecedents. Today, many refer to these laws as "felon disfranchisement laws," although, as this book demonstrates, few southern states adopted the felony standard until the late nineteenth century, and laws disfranchising for non-felony offenses persisted until the late twentieth century in some states.[15]

Legal challenges have been largely unsuccessful due to the precedent set in a 1974 U.S. Supreme Court decision, *Richardson v. Ramirez*. In this case, the Court heard historical evidence regarding the constitutionality of a California law disfranchising felons who had completed prison sentences and parole time. At issue was the second section of the Fourteenth Amendment, exempting states from the sanction of reduced congressional representation for denying citizens the right to vote if this denial was based on disfranchisement for crime. This constitutional provision had been largely overlooked until 1974, and the Court sought to interpret its meaning and intent. The plaintiffs hoped to convince the Court that Section Two was an "accident of political exigency" and not intended to affirm lifelong bans on felon voting. By their account, Section Two was rooted in the partisan political issues of the 1860s and irrelevant in the present. Defending the law, attorneys for the state of California claimed that Section Two represented a constitutional affirmation of state laws disfranchising individuals for criminal conviction.[16]

The Court sided with the defendants and ruled California's disfranchisement law valid. The majority of the justices construed Section Two as granting states an "affirmative sanction" to disfranchise ex-felons. Felons, according to the Court, did not have a constitutionally guaranteed right to vote. This ruling distinguished felons from other disfranchised populations. Laws disfranchising felons did not have to pass the "strict scrutiny" standard that applied to laws that violated fundamental rights, since voting was not held to be a fundamental right for felons. On the basis of this decision, individuals do not have a claim to substantive due process and equal protection when they are denied suffrage on the basis of prior criminal convictions.[17]

Richardson v. Ramirez did not preclude all successful challenges to laws denying convicted individuals the right to vote. In 1985 the U.S. Supreme Court's decision in *Hunter v. Underwood* declared laws disfranchising for crime that were enacted with a racially discriminatory intent to be unconstitutional. In this case, the Court considered Alabama's disfranchisement scheme, a product of the state's 1901 constitutional convention, which denied the vote to individuals convicted of felonies, infamous crimes, some enumerated misdemeanors, and crimes of moral turpitude.[18] The Court evaluated evidence from historians that the constitution as a whole, and the provision disfranchising for crime in particular, had been adopted with a racially discriminatory purpose. It cited the work of J. Mills Thornton and weighed evidence from Malcolm Cook McMillan's 1955 study, *Constitutional Development in Alabama*.[19] Historian J. Morgan Kousser offered evidence in this case when it had been heard at the appellate level, and the Circuit Court had cited his work and the work of other historians in its decision.[20] To understand the intent of the 1901 convention, the Court heard testimony about speeches made at the convention, the racial agenda of convention members, and turn of the century stereotypes about African American criminality. The justices were persuaded by the historical evidence of racial intent and concluded that the Alabama law was invalid because it violated Section One of the Fourteenth Amendment, the Equal Protection Clause. This clause, the Court ruled, does not permit "purposeful racial discrimination." Establishing that racial discrimination was a motivating factor behind the law changed the burden of proof; once that was demonstrated, those defending the law had to prove that the provisions disfranchising for misdemeanors and crimes of moral turpitude would have been enacted even if there had been no racially discriminatory purpose. The Court found that the intent of the 1901 convention was to disfranchise African Americans, and the provision disfranchising for these particular crimes would not have been adopted were it not for the racial agenda of the convention.[21] Using similar reasoning, the Mississippi Supreme Court overturned that state's law disfranchising those convicted of certain misdemeanors in 1995 in *McGlaughlin v. City of Canton, Mississippi*, ruling that laws targeting minor crimes should come under stricter scrutiny than those that disfranchised ex-felons due to their legacy of racial intent.[22]

The 1965 Voting Rights Act (and its 1982 revision) prohibits voter qualifications that had the original *purpose* of racial discrimination or the *effect* of racial discrimination.[23] However, in the aftermath of *Ramirez*, only restrictions on voting by individuals with criminal convictions that were intended to racially discriminate are subject to equal protection claims. One might expect that identifying discriminatory intent in southern constitutions that were drafted at the height of Jim Crow would be easy enough to do, but two court decisions have made establishing intent in current laws more difficult. In 1998 the Federal Fifth Circuit Court of Appeals heard a petition that originated with two Mississippi inmates, Keith Brown and Jarvious Cotton, who were representing themselves without professional legal council.[24] They claimed that Mississippi's laws disfranchising for felony convictions were established with the intention of discriminating against African American voters and were therefore invalid. In the decision *Cotton v. Fordice* the court agreed that the laws had been enacted with racial intent but that subsequent revisions to the law had allowed it to "overcome its odious origin."[25] This case helped form the basis for another Fifth Circuit case, *Johnson v. Bush*, the case stemming from Florida's 2000 election. Citing *Cotton v. Fordice*, a U.S. district court in Miami ruled that Florida law was constitutional despite its racist origins. "The re-enactment of the felon disfranchisement provision in 1968 cleansed Florida's felon disenfranchisement scheme of any invidious discriminatory purpose that may have prompted its inception in Florida's 1868 constitution."[26]

The decisions in *Cotton* and *Johnson* are striking because they offer a vision and pathway for a kind of statutory rehabilitation.[27] Laws that were tainted by their pasts because they were designed to do racist work and perform unconstitutional acts of racial discrimination can be "cleansed" easily and even unintentionally. In the eyes of the courts, previous legislative intent can be "overcome" by an amendment; a change to one part of a constitutional provision implies a repeal and re-ratification of the entire section. This is precisely the opposite approach taken by laws permanently disfranchising individuals for prior criminal acts. For most of the twentieth century individuals who have committed crimes in the United States were branded "convicts" for life. Even after they served their criminal sentences and were free from court supervision, the contamination of their past affected their civil status, depriving them of the right to vote absent a formal and complicated restoration process. Laws can be reformed and rehabilitated fairly easily, but individuals cannot.

This book explores the development of laws and attitudes concerning felon disfranchisement in the United States. Much of the focus of this book is the post-Civil War South because these laws took on unparalleled importance in the South during this period. Rather than remaining in the background of suffrage requirements as they generally had been up to that point in American history, laws disfranchising for crime became part of the strategy of disfranchising the formerly enslaved, and newly freed,

African Americans. Southern states modified constitutional provisions that governed voting by convicted individuals, revised statutes governing disfranchisement for crime, enforced these laws with renewed vigor at the ballot box, and debated the means by which voting rights could be restored. Growing numbers of voters across the South encountered these laws as obstacles to suffrage.

Through this process, America as a nation began to work out a national consensus on disfranchisement for crime. Congress, faced with evidence of these new practices in the South, chose to look the other way. Others outside the South took note of events in the region and in some cases adapted southern disfranchisement laws to their own political ends. Laws disfranchising individuals on probation and parole became the accepted norm in American states, and states across the country permanently disfranchised individuals with serious criminal convictions. Over the course of the twentieth century, as felony convictions became more common and prison populations expanded, large numbers of Americans from all racial backgrounds lost the right to vote. The operation of these laws nationally came to mirror that of the South because racial minorities and the economically disadvantaged were and are disproportionally incarcerated and disfranchised. So, to understand the nation, we must understand the South.

By limiting the rights of some, America has defined the rights of others. Disfranchising voters because of criminal convictions has promoted the belief that suffrage is only for the morally upright. The current over-hyped concern with fraudulent voter registration and the growing push to require voters to present picture identification are part of the larger ideology that suffrage is an indication of privileged citizenship and that the ballot box must be protected from the criminally minded. Today, as in the past, laws and legislatures define who can be part of the political community. The pages that follow, in an effort to add to our understanding of the right to vote in the United States, offer a detailed examination of the origins and impact of laws disfranchising for criminal convictions.

Living in Infamy

Introduction

This book charts the history of disfranchisement for criminal conviction in order to investigate the legal traditions and ideologies behind the broad range of arguments for denying voting rights. Looking at the origins, development, enforcement, and impact of these laws illuminates important landmarks in the history of suffrage in the United States. While laws disfranchising certain classes of convicted criminals have long been part of the Anglo-European law, in the decades after the Civil War white southern Democrats found ways to use them to disproportionately affect African Americans. Combining beliefs about African American propensity for crime and a racially biased justice system, southern Democrats used statutes disfranchising for crime to impede black electoral participation. As one of the first methods used to disfranchise the newly freed slaves, these laws helped establish the intellectual framework that justified African American disfranchisement. The idea of denying voting rights to those convicted of certain crimes was affirmed and expanded in this period, establishing a system that has affected American democracy ever since.

Historical scholarship on southern disfranchisement in this period has traditionally focused on means and ends. Excellent studies have documented the use of literacy tests, poll taxes, and residency requirements by white southerners in order to deny suffrage to African Americans in the century after Reconstruction.[1] This scholarship has taken the tactics of white southern political leaders at face value, explaining that lawmakers created policies based on their observations of the behavior of African Americans. For example, historians have demonstrated that legislatures made suffrage contingent on the passage of literacy tests. Such tests had racial and partisan implications because African Americans had lower rates of literacy. Historians have agreed that this disfranchisement technique was based on an observed reality that African Americans were disproportionately illiterate. Poll taxes allowed Democrats to turn African American poverty into grounds for disfranchisement. The "grandfather clause" exempted whites from certain suffrage requirements, motivated by the recognition that the grandfathers of African Americans had been disfranchised. But the analysis of the motivations behind disfranchisement techniques generally begins and ends here: white southerners witnessed particular characteristics of African Americans and then used this information to erect racially targeted barriers to suffrage. The fact that these barriers also restricted access to the ballot by lower-class whites was an added benefit for white southern Democrats who, particularly after 1890, worried about challenges from Populists and other interracial alliances of the lower classes.

The problem with this analysis is that it overstates the rationality of the white southern racial agenda and fails to look at the historical roots of the ideologies that guided and justified these disfranchisement strategies. Looking at the racist rhetoric and partisan agenda of southern policymakers in an attempt to understand the logic of suffrage requirements does not tell the whole story. White southerners who hoped to use laws disfranchising for crime to target African American voters in the post-war South were not simply inspired by the facts on the ground or solely acting to preserve the rule of the Democratic Party. Rather they sought political interventions that would interrupt the revolutionary social changes facing the defeated Confederacy. The passage of the Thirteenth and Fourteenth Amendments meant that African Americans could no longer be denied citizenship rights due to their status as slaves because "slave" was no longer a legal category. This change in political status had epic implications not just for elections and governance but for the traditional racial distribution of social power and authority as well. As they fought to preserve the social and political order, white southern political leaders soon realized that the rights of citizenship could still be denied to individuals deemed "infamous" due to their conviction of certain criminal offenses. Infamy had its roots in English common law and legal systems in Continental Europe, but far from being seen as an antiquated designation in the United States, infamy gained increasingly widespread acceptance, particularly in state constitutions in the decades before the Civil War. After 1865 white southern political leaders limited the suffrage rights of African Americans by extending the civil and political degradations of infamy to an increasing portion of the black population.

This book has two central arguments. First, it demonstrates that in the post-Civil War South infamy offered a justification for the denial of citizenship rights to African Americans, a means to disfranchise a portion

of the African American population, and a rationale for making distinctions between different kinds of criminal convictions. White political leaders in the South built on the legal tradition of infamy but added a racial
component, associating African Americans with infamy and linking infamous crimes with African Americans. Since infamous individuals could be
denied the vote, white southerners developed a strategy of using infamy
and criminal convictions to perpetuate and justify the disfranchisement
of African Americans. But this strategy went beyond simply convicting
African Americans of crimes and punishing them with disfranchisement. It
developed into a larger effort to infame and thus disfranchise the race—by
associating African Americans with criminality, degrading them through
legal and extra legal violence, and denying the newly freed slaves the dignity traditionally associated with those deserving of suffrage.

In this way, infamy provided southern whites a blueprint by which
pre-war social and political relations might be reconstructed after 1865.
Similarities between the civil status of slaves and convicts made this
seem like an appropriate response to the perceived problem of African
American citizenship. One can view the battles over the citizenship rights
of African Americans in the post-war South as a battle over whether
African Americans would remain infamous, as infamy was the status that
all enslaved people in the United States had occupied prior to 1865. While
convicting African Americans of infamous crimes could not replace slavery as a justification for the denial of citizenship for all African Americans,
nor could it completely eliminate African American suffrage, it supplied
a framework and a starting point. This narrative reveals the centrality of
infamy to African American disfranchisement and the centrality of race to
felon disfranchisement.

A second key argument of this book concerns the generalization of
infamy and the agreement to disfranchise all who had been held in prison
regardless of race. By the end of the nineteenth century nearly all southern states imposed lifelong disfranchisement on felons.[2] States outside
the South that had previously been more reluctant to endorse the disfranchisement of convicts endorsed this approach as well. This development
stemmed both from changes in the legal definition of infamy and developments in American criminal justice. The inhumane treatment of prisoners,
the expansion of the prison system, the public nature of punishment by
forced labor, and the abandonment of the idea of reform and rehabilitation
of prisoners all contributed to a national consensus on permanent disfranchisement for certain convicted criminals that exists to this day.

An explanation and history of infamy is essential for this study. In the
western legal tradition, infamy has served as a judgment on the civil and

political status of convicted individuals. Infamous individuals experienced civil "degradation"—meaning the loss of the rights of citizenship. Under Greek and Roman law, and then later across early modern Europe, certain kinds of criminal conviction resulted in loss of the status and privileges of citizenship. In addition to the possible punishments of incarceration, forfeiture of property, corporal punishment, and/or banishment, some convicted individuals might lose the right to vote (though not all had suffrage rights to begin with since suffrage was not a universal right). They might also lose the right to testify in court, bring civil prosecution, serve on juries, hold public office, or enlist in the army. Infamy removed an individual's honor and respect as a citizen.[3]

English common law, the legal tradition with the most direct relevance to U.S. law, had a well-defined tradition of infamy. Infamous individuals were disqualified from court testimony, jury service, suffrage, or office-holding. In 1771 William Eden explained the English system in *Principles of Penal Law*, "There are two kinds of infamy: the one founded in the opinions of the people respecting the mode of punishment; the other in the construction of law respecting the future credibility of the delinquent."[4] The former, the most common form of infamy in William Eden's period, might seem strange to readers today. *Infamia juris* or "infamy of law" came when the convict was subjected to a degrading punishment. William Blackstone's roughly contemporaneous *Commentaries on the Laws of England* described infamous punishments as those "that consist principally in their ignominy." Blackstone enumerated infamous punishments as "hard labor, in the house of correction or otherwise, as well as whipping, the pillory, or the stocks."[5] The public nature of the punishment contributed to the infamy brought upon the convict. Public and degrading punishments lowered the social status of such individuals, depriving them of the respect due to citizens. Being subjected to an infamous punishment, then, made you an infamous person.[6]

The latter form of infamy, *infamia facto* or "infamy of fact," is that one that is more easily understood in the contemporary era. Infamy of fact occurred when an individual committed a crime that violated the moral code or exhibited disregard for principles of law, order, and truth. Someone who was infamous in fact had been convicted of a crime for which he lost his reputation and status. One could become infamous of fact through a conviction for certain kinds of crime that evidenced a lack of honor, such as perjury or treason. Infamy could also result from crimes of sexual immorality, such as bigamy or fornication. These crimes brought infamy because they undermined the honor of the individual, what Eden termed loss of "credibility." English common law considered crimes of deceit, such as larceny, to be infamous, but crimes of violence, such as murder or assault, generally were not.[7]

Infamous punishments—those that brought infamy to the recipient— were common in both continental Europe and in England, dating back at least to the early modern period. Not all convicts, though, were susceptible to these penalties. Nobles, clerics, and wealthy men were immune from degrading punishments; these individuals, when convicted, received high-status punishments, primarily imprisonment. Those who received high-status punishments were spared infamy and the loss of citizenship rights.[8]

Legal scholar James Q. Whitman makes an observation that is critical to this study. He points out that over the course of the eighteenth, nineteenth, and twentieth centuries, European punishment "leveled up." Nations gradually eliminated the most degrading punishments, even for lower status individuals. Convicted individuals of all social statuses came to be treated like elites and imprisoned rather than whipped or put in stocks. Degradation through punishment and the accompanying loss of rights slowly disappeared in Europe.[9] In contrast, according to Whitman, the United States "leveled down." In the nineteenth-century United States, convicted individuals were increasingly subjected to low-status punishments, making them degraded and infamous and denying them the rights of citizenship. So, at about the time that Europe was ending a tradition of public whipping, forced labor, and infamy, the United States was endorsing and expanding such punishments and reinvigorating the concept of infamy.[10]

While the prevalence of degrading punishments made *infamia facto* a persistent tradition in the United States, state laws continued to differentiate between infamous and non-infamous crimes in the first decades of the nineteenth century. For example, Tennessee's 1829 code separated crimes into infamous and non-infamous offenses, dividing them according to the traditional categories in English common law. Infamous offenses included a variety of property crimes, arson ("malicious burning"), sex crimes (bigamy, crime against nature, incest, rape, carnal abuse of a female child), counterfeiting, forgery, and perjury. Murder and various kind of assault were not categorized as infamous. In Tennessee, infamy in fact became infamy in law as those who were convicted of infamous crimes lost key rights of citizenship. The 1829 code disqualified infamous individuals from testifying in court in Tennessee (except in their own criminal cases), and six years later the 1835 constitution barred them from voting.[11]

Infamy, indeed, was revitalized nationwide in this period, and in states across the country infamy brought deprivation of the rights of citizenship, which in the United States came to include the right of suffrage (at least for white men). The 1818 Connecticut constitution specified that a conviction for an infamous crime brought about disfranchisement, as did New York's 1821 constitution, Virginia's 1830 constitution, and the 1836 Arkansas constitution.[12] In North Carolina, where common law applied to most crimes in the antebellum era, election officials excluded individuals judged infamous from suffrage.[13] Other state constitutions enumerated some infamous crimes, often substituting the phrase "high crimes and misdemeanors" for "infamous." For example, Mississippi's 1817 constitution and Alabama's 1819 constitution both instructed the legislature to disfranchise for "bribery, perjury, forgery or other high crimes and misdemeanors."[14]

Americans talked about infamy in ways that reflected a persistent understanding that degradation came from the punishment as often as from the conviction of the crime. And they recognized that infamy brought both disgrace and the revocation of citizenship rights, following the tradition that personal degradation brought the degradation of citizenship. When a man in Chowan County, North Carolina, was sentenced to twenty lashes for petit larceny in 1838, a friend petitioned the court on his behalf for leniency and demonstrated his understanding of the impact of an infamous punishment on a man's status: "the infliction of so degrading a punishment .... must have the effect of rendering him infamous."[15] Also common was the belief that the dignity of citizenship must be protected from those who had endured the most humiliating punishments. Evidence of this perspective can be found in an 1830 court case, *Commonwealth v. Fugate*, where a Virginia appeals court held that a convicted felon was disqualified from serving as a justice of the peace. The court wrote, "When the people of Virginia established their constitution, they never intended that the bench of justice should be contaminated by the presence of a convicted and attainted felon."[16] In 1864 North Carolina Governor Zebulon B. Vance explained the social and civil impacts of infamy in this threat to individuals considering desertion from the Confederate army: "If permitted to live in the state at all, you will be infamous. You will be hustled from the polls, insulted in the streets, a jury of your countrymen will not believe you on oath, and honest men will shun you as a pestilence."[17]

It is difficult to draw a clear distinction between understandings of *infamia juris* and *infamia facto* in the nineteenth-century United States. While it was widely held that infamous punishments could bring degradation and infamy, the law continued to distinguish between infamous and non-infamous crimes. The idea that some serious crimes, specifically crimes of violence, did not indicate infamy persisted in the nineteenth century, though it was becoming anachronistic. As late as 1887, though, the

Kentucky Supreme Court offered such a perspective in *Anderson v. Winfree*. In *Anderson* the court defended the exclusion of violent crimes from its catalog of infamous offenses, thereby allowing murderers to vote.[18] The court explained that infamous, disfranchising offenses were crimes "inconsistent with the common principles of honesty and humanity, and convict the perpetrator of depravity and moral turpitude."[19] Murder, the court believed, did not fall into such a category. Of course, an argument might well be made that murder and other violent crimes do in fact reflect moral turpitude, but the Kentucky court, along with many citizens at the time, held that violence did not reflect immorality and that it therefore should not result in the loss of suffrage and citizenship. At the 1890 constitutional convention in Kentucky, John D. Carroll of Henry County defended this position and helped explain why he believed thieves to be less moral than murderers: "Any person who commits a crime that is a felony in sudden heat and passion, no matter what that crime may be, ought not to be debarred of the right of suffrage.... Does it make a man any the less a good citizen?" Central to his argument, and undergirding the opinion in *Anderson*, was the belief that intentionally malicious crimes required premeditation. Carroll and many of his contemporaries believed that an individual who committed forgery or robbery deliberately desired to "do wrong" because he or she planned it ahead of time. In contrast, an individual who committed a crime of sudden violence and passion, it was thought, likely never conceived of such an act before the moment of the act. They also believed that violent crimes had a more limited social impact. Violence, this argument held, affected only one person, while crimes that involved deceit or dishonesty would lower social morality more broadly by encouraging dishonest behavior in others.[20]

The justification of certain violent acts, particularly those committed by white men, was a particularly common phenomenon in the South and may help explain why southern states were somewhat more likely to continue to make legal distinctions between infamous and non-infamous crimes. Historian Bertram Wyatt Brown has written that violence in the South allowed men to "preserve white manhood and personal status in the fraternity of the male tribe." Much of this violence was connected to the defense of personal honor—a right that was, supposedly, the exclusive domain of white men. If white men were the sole possessors of honor, then they were the only ones for whom violence might justify the defense of honor. For white elites, the defense of honor might involve participation in a duel, while lower-class white men fought in taverns and streets. Regardless of the form it took, violence from this perspective was a component of masculine citizenship, not a disqualification.[21]

Also common in the South, but not the exclusive preserve of the region, was the growing belief that blacks, slave or free, were morally and intellectually inferior and a "degraded race." According to historian George M. Fredrickson, whites in both the North and South frequently used the specific word "degraded" to describe African Americans throughout the nineteenth century. Many whites believed African Americans to be morally deficient, lacking in judgment, impetuous, and requiring the discipline of slavery to stifle their immoral tendencies. Defenders of slavery found the roots of degradation in biological, racial inferiority, while those who supported abolition blamed slavery for corrupting African Americans and taking away their humanity.[22]

For both sides, the degradation of slaves, like the degradation of infamous convicts, stemmed from the fact of their incarceration as well as the punishments they received. Slaves and infamous convicts have existed in comparable, though not identical, legal states throughout the western European legal and historical context. Nations in the Euro-American legal tradition denied many rights of citizenship to both slaves and infamous convicts. Both populations were barred from voting, and neither could testify in court nor serve on juries. In colonial Virginia, a 1748 law barred "convicts, as well as negroes, mulattoes, and Indians" from testifying in court.[23] Individuals who were incarcerated experienced a loss of freedom that was in some ways comparable to slavery. In England, certain infamous convicts suffered "corruption of blood." Such "attainted" individuals could not inherit property nor transmit property to descendants, and this degraded status could be inherited.[24] Similarly, slaves passed their slave status to their descendants and lacked property rights.

Both slaves and convicts were seen as dependent and degraded by this dependence—infamous because of the conditions to which they were subjected. In 1830 South Carolina Congressman George McDuffie described slaves as those who "perform the menial and degrading offices of society" in his explanation before Congress as to why African Americans should not be allowed to vote. They were degraded by the fact of their servitude and thus could never function as citizens: "A state of servile dependence is utterly with out political freedom; and by conferring the right of suffrage upon persons in that condition, whatever may be their color, you do not elevate them to the character free men, but degrade liberty to their level."[25]

Degradation was believed to be a characteristic of all African Americans, not just slaves. This conflation supported the logic of depriving free blacks of full citizenship rights. Freedmen and women were assumed to be tainted by their slave past and the conditions of their race. Some specifically connected African American degradation with criminality to argue against granting them suffrage. For example, some whites believed that African Americans, due to their lack of moral character, might be more liable to take bribes in exchange for votes. At the 1835 North Carolina constitutional convention, one delegate described the problem of African American propensity for bribery, "With a little drink, and some trifle, they could be 'bought like a lot of poultry.'"[26]

Scholars have suggested that in the European context, the humiliation and degradation of being incarcerated derived from its similarity to slavery. Friedrich Nietzsche wrote, "Punishment first acquired its insulting and derisive character because certain penalties were associated with the sort of people (slaves, for example) whom one treated with contempt."[27] The American sociologist and penologist Thorsten Sellin has argued that the treatment of criminal offenders, at least in the Western world, stemmed from the treatment of slaves.[28] Gustav Radbruch's study of German law (written as his country was coming under Nazi government) found that "the criminal law bears the traits of its origin in slave punishments....to be punished means to be treated like a slave." According to Radbruch, being treated like a slave renders a convict socially and morally degraded. "The diminution of honor, which ineradicably inheres in punishment to this day, derives from slave punishments."[29] For both slaves and convicts, their degraded conditions and the humiliation of their captivity were incompatible with the honor and dignity of citizenship.[30]

Joan Dayan has argued for a reverse chronology in the United States. Here, she observes, where slavery developed later than in Europe, the legal status of slaves derived from the status of incarcerated convicts. "Strategies of divestment" of rights, modeled on the treatment of convicts, offered a template for the legal status of slaves in the United States. Dayan's work explores the connections between the "civil death" of convicts and the legal system that governed slavery in the United States. Civilly dead individuals, those either awaiting execution or facing life imprisonment, lost all civil and political rights. While her ideas stem primarily from examining those whose humanity and citizenship were fully denied under law (i.e., not only the denial of the right of suffrage), she underscores the importance of examining the post-Civil War decades in which more individuals occupied an intermediate status of "disabled" citizens. After the war, Dayan writes, ex-slaves "were effectively deprived of civil rights and reduced to the status of incomplete citizens...This status was analogous to the status of felons because felons were citizens whose rights to citizenship were disabled or restrained."[31]

Evidence of how the law evaluated the rights of convicts and slaves in relationship to each other in this period can be found in the Thirteenth and Fourteenth Amendments, both of which constructed the rights of free men in opposition to the rights of convicted criminals. The Thirteenth Amendment is best known for outlawing slavery but it sanctioned it in one instance: "Neither slavery nor involuntary servitude, except as a punishment for crime whereof the party shall have been duly convicted, shall exist within the United States, or any place subject to their jurisdiction." After 1865 only convicts could be slaves in the United States.[32]

The Fourteenth Amendment sought to free the former slaves from infamy, pushing back against the Black Codes—post-war state laws limiting the movement and freedoms of black southerners—and constructing a racially neutral definition of citizenship. But the Fourteenth Amendment dealt an even more lasting blow to the rights of convicts than the preceding amendment with a passage that simultaneously opened the door for the denial of political rights to African Americans. The second section of the Fourteenth Amendment required states to grant suffrage to all men, but allowed states to deny this right "for participation in rebellion, or other crime." [33]

Much is at stake in this debate over the origins of Section Two of the Fourteenth Amendment because of the U.S. Supreme Court's reliance on historical evidence in deciding *Richardson v. Ramirez*. The central question is whether Congress intended to authorize disfranchisement for crime and therefore exclude such laws from heightened scrutiny. While the Court's majority answered this question in the affirmative, Justice Thurgood Marshall's dissent suggested that Section Two had no clear mandate and dubious origins. According to Marshall, a draft of the amendment "went to a joint committee containing only the phrase 'participation in rebellion' and emerged with 'or other crime' inexplicably tacked on."[34]

Richard Bourne and Jason Morgan-Foster have considered legal evidence unexamined by the Court in 1974 to construct an explanation of congressional intent that challenges the Court's analysis in *Richardson v. Ramirez*. Concerned that with the end of the Three-Fifths Compromise enumerating the slave population by three-fifths for the purpose of congressional representation, southern states would receive more congressional seats and more political power, Republicans in 1866 looked for ways to limit the power of southern Democrats. Some congressional Republicans pushed for a blanket prohibition on voting by all former Confederate rebels. But this came into conflict with a draft of the amendment that aimed to protect African American voters by punishing states who disfranchised eligible voters by decreasing their congressional representation. States who disfranchised former Confederates would have been punished for disfranchising this group, just as they would have been for disfranchising African

Americans. To avoid this, Congress agreed to a clause that exempted states from the abridgement of congressional representation if they denied the vote "for participation in rebellion."[35]

But how did "or other crime" enter into the amendment? Morgan-Foster argues that that the phrase "or other crime" was added in order to encompass various acts committed by the former Confederate rebels. Drafts of the amendment exempting states from reduced representation for disfranchising former rebels referred to those who had committed the "crimes" of "treason" and "disloyalty" and used such phrases such as "insurrection or rebellion against the United States."[36] The final language of the amendment, "rebellion, or other crime," was simply a combination of the various proposals made, all of which were aimed at punishing the criminal acts of those who had fought against the United States.[37] Section Two was meant to allow states to disfranchise for treason and other crimes of disloyalty, not general criminal acts. It was, "in effect…the culmination of a series of proposals, each meant to except from the count people guilty, *not of crimes generally*, but only of crimes involved in the *rebellion*."[38] The proposed amendment foundered in the Senate, however, with concern that it was too punitive toward the former rebels. A compromise was reached whereby the final language in Section Three barred individuals from holding federal office if they had previously taken the oath to support the United States government and then voluntarily joined the Confederacy. But Section Two remained unchanged.[39]

Similarly, Richard Bourne sketches out a logical argument that corroborates the interpretation that in Section Two Congress was focused on former rebels, not a more general class of convicted criminals:

> Looking at the world from the perspective of people in 1866, at the time the Fourteenth Amendment was drafted, the only classes to whom voting rights might be denied conceivably large enough to affect the non-racial apportionment scheme of Section Two, were (1) the group of black voters that the framers wanted enrolled and (2) the unreconstructed white voters the framers hoped to disfranchise.[40]

The number of incarcerated and formerly incarcerated individuals in the nation at this time was quite small, and their disfranchisement would not have affected congressional representation. African Americans and former rebels, though, were significant parts of the population and their disfranchisement could affect apportionment. Congress gave southern states leeway, therefore, to disfranchise former rebels for a variety of crimes without risking seats in Congress.[41]

A recent article in the *Yale Law Journal* by Richard M. Re and Christopher M. Re draws on historical evidence to reach the opposite conclusion, arguing that Congress did in fact intend to endorse disfranchisement for the conviction of crimes in Section Two. Re and Re uncover what they term "the irony of egalitarian disenfranchisement," by which they mean "the tendency of radical egalitarians in the Reconstruction era to justify the enfranchisement of black Americans by simultaneously defending the disenfranchisement of criminals." Virtue, a characteristic lacking in convicted criminals, was an appealing standard by which to measure the right to suffrage, replacing old arguments based on race. Re and Re review some of the evidence that is also considered in the following chapters in this volume; chapter 2 in particular confirms their point that Congress understood the implications of Section Two when it rejected an opportunity to constitutionally restrict disfranchisement for crime in the Fifteenth Amendment. Re and Re's larger argument will be considered in the Conclusion.[42]

This book expands the historical understanding of Section Two of the Fourteenth Amendment not by searching for intent prior to its passage but by considering its most immediate effects and Congress's reaction to them. In the fall of 1866 Section Two offered an opportunity for southern whites to draw on the legal tradition of infamy to define the political rights of African Americans. Denying African Americans citizenship due to criminal convictions, thereby rendering them legally infamous, was part of the larger effort to save the status quo of white supremacy in the South. Extending the status of infamy to as much of the black population as possible would restrict citizenship in a way that had both precedent and utility, connecting race to the long tradition of denying the vote to infamous individuals. It could make those who had been "infamous in law" under slavery become "infamous in fact" during and after Reconstruction.

A number of factors made infamy an appealing model for the rejection of African American political rights in the post-war South. Infamy followed convicts out of jail and persisted to deprive them of civil rights, offering a model for lifelong denial of citizenship rights beyond the period of slavery. Southern whites believed that the degradation of slavery, like the degradation of incarceration, followed African Americans into freedom. Many whites saw all African Americans, not just those who were enslaved, as degraded.

Infamy is critical to understanding rationales for the denial of suffrage, and it is worth considering how infamy shaped all disfranchisement techniques, not just those focused on convicted criminals. White southern Democrats used poll taxes, literacy tests, and "grandfather clauses" to perform the work of maintaining white political supremacy. All three of these methods reaffirmed the infamous status that southern whites believed blacks to have, and all have historical antecedents in English common law. Poll taxes connected civil rights to economic status, giving suffrage to those with money to pay the tax. Historically, in England wealthy individuals could be spared from infamous punishments, avoiding a loss of civil rights, including the right of suffrage. Wealthy people did not get whipped or put in the stocks; if they committed serious crimes they would be put in prison—which was considered more dignified (and therefore did not result in infamy) because it was a private punishment. Considering wealth as a measure of citizenship rights and a means to avoid the civil status of infamy, then, was not new to the post-war South.

In addition, under English common law infamy could be mitigated by literacy. In England, clerics were exempt from infamous punishments— they could not be whipped, mutilated, or executed. (This is the "benefit of clergy" exemption.) James Q. Whitman argues that a critical stage in the "leveling up" of punishments—that is the gradual elimination of the most degrading punishments—occurred with a "generalization of clerical status" in medieval England. One did not actually have to be a priest to receive the benefit of clergy. Rather, "The test of clerical status...was literacy: people who could read were presumptively clergy, entitled to benefit from relatively mild punishment." From the fourteenth century onward, more and more individuals could claim this exemption. On the first offense, some could even legally feign literacy.[43] In sum, literacy and wealth have historically served as barriers against infamy, and literate individuals were spared infamous punishments. Illiterate individuals and lower-class individuals were, in contrast, more likely to lose their citizenship rights with an infamy designation. Seeing literacy and wealth not just as a measure of citizenship but specifically using them as an antidote to infamy has a history that predates the post-Reconstruction South.

Finally, grandfather clauses were used in some southern states to protect whites who could not meet certain requirements of suffrage, from being denied the vote—it protected them from a degradation of citizenship that made them infamous. Grandfather clauses allowed one to inherit the status of citizen. The corollary was that one, too, might inherit the status of infamy; if your grandfather could not vote because he was a slave (and therefore infamous), then you too could not vote. This harkens back to the medieval idea that infamy was a status that could be inherited. This "corruption of blood" could be passed on to succeeding generations.

An understanding of infamy also helps inform our understanding of the disfranchisement of lower-class southern whites in the late 1890s. Richard Morris's 1954 essay, "The Measure of Bondage in the Slave States," explains that both the Old and New South saw a "virtual continuity of the institutions of compulsory labor." Farm tenancy—the system under which lower-class, landless southerners of both races lived—bore a close resemblance to the labor systems that had come before it. "These forms of compulsion under which white paupers, vagrants, debtors, and tenants worked out their obligations provided the framework for the neo-slavery which the Black Codes of Reconstruction fastened upon the former slaves."[44] Imposing disfranchisement, and therefore infamy, on a population largely comprised of landless debtors already degraded by their dependence fit perfectly into the historical framework of citizenship in the South. This is not to say that the Populist inclinations of lower-class southern whites did not motivate efforts to deny them the vote in the late nineteenth century, but to note the antecedents of disfranchising landless debtors. Lower-class whites and blacks were degraded by their poverty, debt, and dependence; disfranchising white tenant farmers was intellectually and culturally possible in a way that, for example, disfranchising wealthy whites would not have been.

A core principle connected efforts to disfranchise African Americans and the movement to deny suffrage to convicts in the late nineteenth-century South: the idea that awarding the right of suffrage to individuals believed to be degraded due to their race or their infamy would undermine the dignity of the citizenship itself. Allowing a degraded man to vote would degrade those who voted alongside him. Voting in proximity to convicts or slaves degraded other men of privilege. The rhetorical similarities between the two is striking. In 1890 a delegate to the Kentucky constitutional convention described his opposition to convict voting by explaining, "The spectacle of a squad of prisoners, escorted by a jailer or Sheriff, from behind the bars, or from the rock-pile, to the polls [would] degrade rather than elevate the right of suffrage, in the sight of the worthy."[45] Just as voting by infamous convicts might degrade the citizenship of free men in the eyes of that Kentucky delegate, so too, in the eyes of many white southerners, would the suffrage of former slaves. An Alabama newspaper put it this way in 1903, "The ballot in the hands of ex-slaves was in almost every instance... used to despoil, degrade, and humiliate the real citizens of the almost helpless south."[46] Likewise, at the 1898 Louisiana constitutional convention a delegate explained that a goal of the convention was "to eliminate from the electorate the mass of the corrupt and illiterate voters who have during the last quarter of a century degraded our politics."[47]

The history of laws disfranchising for crime offers an opportunity to evaluate the relationship between the law on the one hand and cultural and intellectual traditions on the other. Laws are neither passive reflections of existing social values nor the sole agents of historical change. Laws governing the franchise that were passed in the second half of the nineteenth century were rooted in historical understandings of who is and is not entitled to be part of the political community, while they simultaneously shaped social understandings of citizenship. The Thirteenth, Fourteenth, and Fifteenth Amendments irrevocably connected freedom, citizenship, suffrage, and manhood in the American legal tradition, while offering opportunities for those who sought to limit African American access to the ballot and to restrict black citizenship more generally. One particular subset of these efforts to limit black suffrage, laws disfranchising for crime, had antecedents in older legal traditions but also, as this work demonstrates, generated a set of connections—both legal and cultural—between criminality and suffrage that persist into the present era.

Disfranchisement of African Americans in the late nineteenth-century South was not rooted simply in partisan politics or solely in the value of excluding an inferior race from political power. African American political participation did not merely threaten white political and social dominance. Southern whites believed that suffrage by degraded individuals would undermine the dignity of their own citizenship—an idea with a history that pre-dated African American suffrage and that was embedded in long-held constructions of citizenship itself. White southerners felt punished when the federal government granted African Americans citizenship, not only because this change threatened their electoral majorities but because it devalued their status and citizenship as well.

Suffrage has historically been both a product and an indicator of elite social status in the United States. This right, though, conveys privilege only to the extent that some are denied it. If all exercised the rights of citizenship through truly universal suffrage, then suffrage would not offer evidence of elevated social status; from that perspective, the value of suffrage would be diminished. If suffrage is a privilege only to the extent it is denied to others, then extending suffrage to African American men in the post-war South posed a particular threat to white male privilege. The tradition of infamy offered the possibility of protecting against this threat, first by offering a justification for excluding African Americans from the vote—a reason for perpetuating this division of citizen and non-citizen—and additionally as a method for their disfranchisement. As racial barriers to suffrage were challenged and fell, this binary construction of citizenship continued, although criminal convictions, not race, began to form the basis for this division. White southern Democrats never succeeded in making all African Americans convicts. They did not have to because literacy tests and poll taxes did the primary work of disfranchisement. But one could say they succeeded in making all convicted felons African American through laws and practices that denied civil rights, including suffrage, to prisoners and the formerly incarcerated. Decades later, after race-based disfranchisement has officially ended, laws disfranchising for crime perpetuate this dichotomous construction of suffrage and citizenship.

CHAPTER 1

ↀ

"Not Infamous, nor Subject to Another Man's Will"

At North Carolina's 1835 constitutional convention, delegate Jesse Wilson from Perquimans County made a curious argument against continuing to allow free black men to vote in that state. Wilson asserted that such men should be disfranchised because they were the victims of vigilante violence: "A white man may go to the house of a free black, maltreat and abuse him, and commit any outrage upon his family—for all which the law can not reach him." This violent assault would not be prosecuted because African Americans in North Carolina—slave or free—could not testify against whites in court. This barrier to testimony and the vulnerability to violence that it produced proved to Wilson that such men should be denied the vote. "After this, shall we invest him with the more important rights of a *freeman*—the high privilege of exercising the function of a voter?"[1]

Another delegate, James Bryan of Cartaret County offered a similar perspective. Bryan explained that the different treatment of the two races by the state's criminal justice system justified the disfranchisement of free black men. In North Carolina, free blacks who committed crimes and could not pay the court fine could be "hired out"—essentially enslaved as punishment for crime. Whites, in contrast, could not be treated that way: "If the same policy had been adopted with regard to *free white citizens*, is there a doubt… [that the state's citizens] would have declared that the act was void, and that it was an unconstitutional deprivation of the liberties and privileges of a freeman!"[2] This strengthened Bryan's conviction that free people of color should not be granted suffrage. Men who were so easily enslaved and degraded could not be "freemen" who enjoyed the full rights of citizens.

Both Wilson and Bryan believed that infamy and degradation disqualified men from citizenship. Though they likely would not have used such terminology, they believed that African Americans, as a race, were *infamia juris*—infamous in law. Furthermore, they recognized that whippings and forced labor were infamous punishments whether administered privately or sanctioned by the state. As a result, violence not only terrorized African Americans but, it also operated on an additional conceptual level by denying African Americans the *status* of citizens. Being denied the rights of citizenship therefore indicated infamy. Both Bryan and Wilson believed that free blacks should be denied suffrage and other citizenship rights not simply because of their race but because—due to both law and tradition—they were infamous.

In the first half of the nineteenth century, ideas about infamy, degradation, and race shaped legal and popular understandings of citizenship and the right to the franchise in the United States. The ideological framework that held infamy to be inimical to suffrage shaped the development of state constitutions. Many of those involved in writing these constitutions—primarily white, economically elite, men—believed African Americans to be degraded and certain classes of convicts to be infamous. But while southern lawmakers drew a clear line between degraded individuals—African Americans and infamous convicts—and the franchise, lawmakers outside the region, particularly in the northeast, had more varied and flexible perspectives on who should have the right of suffrage.[3]

The development of public policy with regard to suffrage in the early nineteenth-century United States is a contradictory story of both expansion and contraction of access to the franchise. Alexandar Keyssar's sweeping history of American suffrage points out that most states eliminated property requirements for voting in the first half of the century, so that on the eve of the Civil War no state used property requirements to disfranchise white men. But with property ownership no longer used to evaluate the worth of an individual and his value as a citizen, policymakers turned to an assessment of an individual's actions. In some cities and states African Americans had been able to vote in the late eighteenth century, but states now moved to eliminate such exceptions. Furthermore, most states restricted access to the franchise for the first time for those with certain criminal convictions.[4]

The work of Jeff Manza and Christopher Uggen on felon disfranchisement in the United States concurs with Keyssar, pointing out that in the early to mid-nineteenth century, restrictions on voting by convicts followed "on the heels of the decline of property and other restrictions on white male suffrage." This was because the expansion of the electorate provoked concern among some elites about "undesirable" voters. Individuals convicted of serious crimes were immediate targets of suffrage restriction. In particular, those who committed electoral fraud or other election-related crimes were seen as threatening the purity of the ballot box. Manza and Uggen conclude, "Between 1840 and 1865, all 16 states adopting felon disenfranchisement measures did so *after* establishing full white male suffrage by eliminating property tests." Furthermore, nearly all states that were established after 1850 included provisions disfranchising felons in their constitutions.[5]

In a number of states, racial restrictions on suffrage (limiting the electorate to white men) and constraints on the voting rights of convicts were enacted simultaneously. In Tennessee, for example, the same 1835 constitution that barred infamous convicts from voting also enacted the requirement that all voters be white.[6] Connecticut's 1818 constitution was the first in that state's history to specify that all voters must be white males (except for those black men who possessed the franchise in 1818; i.e., current voters retained their rights). The new constitution also disfranchised for all crimes "for which an infamous punishment is inflicted."[7] New York's 1821 constitution limited African American suffrage for the first time by imposing a property qualification on African American voters but not white voters and denied the vote to individuals convicted of infamous crimes.[8]

Manza and Uggen find that laws in the South disfranchising for felonies came later than in the North and Midwest. Their conclusion is based, in part, by drawing a distinction between earlier provisions in southern states that disfranchised for "bribery, perjury, forgery or any other high crime or misdemeanor" and later provisions (which they date to the post–Civil War era) that targeted all felons. They assert that southern states passed these broader provisions after 1865 in an effort to disfranchise the newly freed slaves.[9] While my work affirms their general point that felon disfranchisement was connected to racial ideologies and had a racial agenda, this chapter offers a different picture of the first half of the nineteenth century by demonstrating that southern states had a greater propensity to punish crime with life-long disfranchisement and other civil penalties before 1865 than non-southern states did. In addition, my analysis of state laws indicates that while southern state constitutions passed prior to 1820 used the "other high crime or misdemeanor" framework, after 1820 most southern states disfranchised for all infamous crimes. Alabama even included larceny in its list of disfranchising crimes in 1827. The larger picture of infamy and punishment in the South presented here suggests that the differences between these suffrage provisions passed in southern states before 1820 and after 1820 mostly indicate semantic differences not a regional reluctance to deny rights of citizenship to individuals convicted of serious crimes. (See Table 1.1)[10]

Table 1.1. ENACTMENT OF CONSTITUTIONAL PROVISIONS
DISFRANCHISING FOR CRIME IN SOUTHERN STATES[11]

State	Date Enacted
Louisiana	1812
Mississippi	1817
Alabama	1819
Missouri	1820
Virginia	1830
Tennessee	1835
North Carolina	1835
Arkansas	1836
Florida	1838
South Carolina	1865
Georgia	1868

Across the nation both African Americans and convicts were the targets of limitations on the franchise in the first half of the nineteenth century because ideas and traditions about infamy shaped public policy toward both of these populations. Convicts were considered degraded due to their punishment and incarceration and therefore unfit for suffrage. The perception of dependence also contributed to infamy of both populations. For example, Thaddeus Stevens (later a well-known Radical Republican congressman but at the time a delegate to the Pennsylvania constitutional convention of 1837) classed convicts with other dependent and degraded subjects—paupers and vagrants. Stevens endorsed a proposed poll tax this way: "No one could be deprived of a vote by this small tax qualification except paupers who were placed on the public charge by the certificate of a magistrate, common vagrants, and convicts in the penitentiary and jails."[12] Men with the right to the franchise were free of dependence and infamy. At Virginia's 1830 constitutional convention, delegate Philip Doddridge from Brooke County explained his view of who should be able to vote this way: "They are males of twenty one years of age and upwards—of sound mind, not infamous, nor subject to another man's will—that is freemen."[13] In contrast to freemen, slaves and convicts were in a constant state of subjection and infamy.

White male political leaders saw African Americans as infamous—due either to the degraded condition of their race under slavery or their biological inferiority—and thus unfit for citizenship and suffrage. Jacob Radcliff, a former New York mayor and state supreme court justice, was

described in 1821 as expressing his opposition to African American suffrage this way: "He considered the principle of exclusion [from suffrage]
to be derived not from the distinction of colour but resorted to as a rule
of designation between those who understand the worth of that privilege and those who are degraded, dependent and unfit to exercise it." The
degradation and dependency of African Americans, in Radcliff's view,
made them unfit to vote even though slavery had been abolished in the
state.[14]

The logic went the other way as well; white men who were disfranchised
became degraded. Virginia's 1830 constitutional convention—the convention that brought disfranchisement for infamous crimes to the state—
debated a complicated proposal that would revoke the suffrage rights of
those who leased land (i.e., those who did not own it) if they did not pay
certain taxes. This idea that a white man might be granted suffrage one year
but denied it the next due to failure to pay a tax incensed delegate John
Rogers Cooke of Frederick because such individuals would be "degraded
from the rank of one of the sovereigns of the country and [become] a member of a disfranchised class."[15]

In the South the dichotomy between infamous men and citizens was
so significant that it could at times even trump race. In 1835 the South
Carolina Supreme Court explained that a man's status "is not to be determined solely by the distinct and visible mixture of negro blood, but by reputation, by his reception in to society, and his having commonly exercised
the privileges of a white man...[A] man of worth, honesty, industry and
respectability should have the rank of a white man." Thus, the court established a standard whereby those who society treated as citizens—those
who "exercised the privileges of a white man"—were neither infamous nor
degraded *nor even black*. Just as disfranchisement and denial of the rights
of citizenship might produce infamy and degradation, the exercise of the
rights of citizenship (of which a key and visible right was suffrage) could
prove the absence of degradation and therefore evidence whiteness.[16]

The distinction between citizens and those who were disfranchised was
often framed in relation to criminality. Disfranchisement meant being
treated by the state like a criminal. For example, at New York's 1821 constitutional convention, an advocate of African American suffrage expressed his
concern with the disfranchisement of this population: "Why, sir, are these
men to be excluded from rights [i.e., suffrage] which they possess in common with their countrymen? What crime have they committed for which
they are to be punished?"[17] Disfranchisement, degradation, criminality,
and infamy all marked a population that was outside the bounds of citizenship. By the 1840s opponents of African American suffrage began to cite

scientific authorities to argue that the race had a predisposition to criminality and therefore should be denied suffrage rights. These pseudo-scientific arguments would continue to have credibility for decades. At New York's 1846 constitutional convention delegate John Kennedy offered statistics to prove that "the relative proportion of infamous crime is nearly thirteen and a half times as great in the colored population as in the white." Blacks had a "criminal disposition," which led Kennedy to oppose any expansion of the franchise to members of this race. The criminality of the race therefore helped justify the disfranchisement of the race.[18]

The conditions of their incarceration separated those convicted of serious crimes (what today would be labeled "felonies") from those convicted of minor, petty offenses (i.e., misdemeanors). The former, under most state laws, faced long incarceration in prisons, whereas the latter likely faced shorter sentences in jails. Policymakers in the early nineteenth century saw clear differences between prisons and jails. Prisons, where those with infamous offenses served time, were considered uniquely degrading. In 1857 the Massachusetts Supreme Court described the distinctive characteristics of state prisons this way: "The convict is placed in a public place of punishment, common to whole State, subject to solitary imprisonment, to have his hair cropped, to be clothed in conspicuous prison dress, subjected to hard labor without pay, to hard fare, coarse and meager food, and to severe discipline." Such individuals were subject to another man's will in a public and visible way that marked them as infamous. The court conceded that individuals in local jails or houses of correction might experience similar conditions but these facilities did not have "the same character of infamy." Anyway, in a kind of circular logic, the court continued, since other ignominious punishments (whipping, branding, and other punishments with a public and degrading character) were no longer used by the state, then "unless this is infamous then there is now no infamous punishment other than capital."[19] More than half a century later the North Carolina Supreme Court echoed this sentiment. The court explained that both felons and misdemeanants might be assigned to hard labor, but felons suffered degradation because they were forced to wear "stripes." Misdemeanants were statutorily protected from such a uniform, so that they might "be spared the humiliation and degradation of stripes."[20] The court's opinion indicated the sense that those who committed the more serious crimes faced degradation by the infamy of their punishment; their exclusion from citizenship was due to their punishment not the immorality of their criminal act.

Disfranchisement, dishonor, and infamy were inseparable, as was reflected in arguments for penalizing dueling with disfranchisement and/or disqualification from office holding. In the nineteenth century a number of states, including Alabama, Mississippi, Tennessee, Louisiana, and Michigan, passed provisions restricting the citizenship rights of duelers. These states did not require a conviction for dueling (which would have likely been covered under existing criminal disfranchisement statutes), but penalized individuals for participating in duels.[21] At Michigan's 1867 constitutional convention delegate Eugene Pringle from Jackson explained succinctly why duelers were targeted with disfranchisement: "This provision is not intended so much to punish such offenders as to discourage the commission of that kind of offenses by making it dishonorable by disfranchising men engaged in it."[22] Duelers, the theory went, would be associated with criminals and paupers because they had been relegated to a degraded punishment through their disfranchisement. Dueling would no longer be associated with honor but with dishonor because it was penalized with disfranchisement. The punishment brought infamy and degradation, not the crime.

This perspective underscores that the link between disfranchising criminals and disfranchising African Americans was not simply the idea that crime and bad behavior disqualified one from certain privileges. Rather, the logic of the time was that if one was infamous one could not enjoy the full rights of citizenship. Infamy might be produced by the law or it might be reflected in one's status before the law.

Despite these national ideological agreements with regard to race, crime, degradation, and infamy, northeastern and southern states differed in an important way. Delegates to constitutional conventions in the northeast evidenced a distinct degree of unease with permanently disfranchising individuals convicted of crimes in the early to mid-nineteenth century. While some northeastern states did disfranchise for crime, others in the region rejected such provisions entirely; in other cases, constitutional conventions limited the impact or extent of these provisions to protect the rights of those with criminal convictions. In contrast, southern states uniformly enacted sweeping provisions permanently disfranchising for infamous or major crimes in this period, and there is little evidence of dissent or debate over this punishment in the South.[23]

Some at northeastern constitutional conventions who questioned the value of lifelong disfranchisement for crime suggested that such a penalty would not have any deterrent value but in fact might encourage crime. Others posed logistical questions, suggesting that such laws would be difficult if not impossible to enforce fairly. But most common were those who demonstrated a belief in the potential rehabilitation of criminals. Permanent disfranchisement did not make sense to those who believed that incarceration would result in rehabilitation.

Some New England colonies had given courts the authority to disfranchise certain individuals but other New Englanders sought to limit this punishment. The Connecticut Colony's 1662 charter specified that, "[I]n case any freeman shall walk scandalously, or commit any scandalous offence, and be legally convicted thereof, he shall be disfranchised by any of the civil courts." A revision in 1672 restricted the power to disfranchise so that only the Court of Assistants had this authority, thereby limiting the judicial bodies that had this power. It also gave this court the ability to restore suffrage to those who demonstrated "good behaviour."[24] After statehood, the Connecticut legislature enacted a similar statute in 1804.[25] Vermont allowed for disfranchisement of certain offenders in the early days of statehood, but criticism of this practice soon emerged. A 1797 statute had permitted the state supreme court to disfranchise individuals convicted of bribery, corruption, or any "evil practice" that rendered him "notoriously scandalous."[26] Three years later, the state's Third Council of Censors met and recommended that the legislature repeal the act and limit disfranchisement to those convicted of election offenses.[27] The council believed that the law went "against the letter and spirit of the eighth article of the bill of rights" and contradicted the intent of the constitution's framers who "contemplated to preserve inviolate the right of suffrage to every freeman, unless he should in fact forfeit the right, by acting wickedly and corruptly, relating only to that estimable privilege."[28] The legislature finally adopted the council's recommendation in 1832, and convicts in Vermont have enjoyed suffrage ever since.[29]

In Maine in 1819 a proposal to disfranchise for crime met with unyielding opposition at the state's constitutional convention. There, political leaders debated a proposal to exclude "those who have been convicted of any infamous crime and not pardoned from being an elector." Many men rose to speak against the proposal and question the enforcement of such a provision. The first, Josiah Thacher from Gorham, asked whether anyone, including judges, understood the distinction between infamous and non-infamous crimes. He also cast doubt on how the law would be enforced, suggesting that it was simply too complicated. What if the individual was convicted in a foreign country, would it still serve to disfranchise? What if someone was disfranchised based on a forged record of conviction? But, most importantly, Thatcher suggested that those convicted of infamous crimes might someday be rehabilitated: "Suppose a lad eight, nine or ten years of age, should in fact be convicted before a Justice of the Peace of felony on a nest of hen's eggs, or some trifling piece of property; and afterwards become a good and worthy member of society, will this Convention declare him forever after unworthy the privilege of voting in these elections?" Daniel Coney of Hallowell agreed, saying convicted individuals might repent and be reformed. Oliver Phelps from Weld expressed concern the proposal might cause "inconveniences in town meetings." He asked, "How are we to decide at the time of elections, whether a person has been convicted or not? He may not always have the evidence of his pardon with him, or a town the evidence of his conviction. If a vote were given by him, and it were afterwards ascertained that he was not entitled to vote, the election might be considered illegal." Only one man spoke in support of the idea, Ether Shepley of Saco, who proposed it. He said the proposal would not only aid the purity of elections, but would also have other favorable side effects. "Young persons would be more cautious of committing crimes, and Courts would be more careful of convictions, when they saw such consequences as the result." Following these discussions, the assembly rejected the plan to disfranchise infamous convicts.[30]

Almost two decades later Pennsylvania, too, declined to enact a proposal to disfranchise for just one infamous crime—dueling. No other crime in Pennsylvania carried the penalty of disfranchisement, but some delegates at the state's 1838 constitutional convention felt that dueling was a sufficiently odious practice that it should be punished with an additional penalty.[31] Delegates first considered a provision to disfranchise individuals convicted of dueling for a period of seven years. But many spoke out against the plan. Some believed that a man who was "shunned and denounced" with this penalty would be likely to engage again in criminal behavior. Charles Brown of Philadelphia explained, "How could he live among you as a good citizen? Would he not be rendered misanthropic and desperate? Would he not hold blood as cheap as the waters of yonder stream?" Others, too, emphasized the transformational potential of incarceration and complained that punishments that extended beyond incarceration failed to take this into account. James Porter of Northampton explained that "reformation and repentance" would "wipe away his guilt." Therefore, an extended period of disfranchisement, beyond incarceration, was "directly contrary" to that principle. Ultimately, the convention decided that duelers should be punished by disqualification from holding elected office, though the governor could remit this disqualification with a pardon.[32]

Pennsylvanians again took up the idea of a lifelong disfranchisement for certain crimes at the state's constitutional convention in 1873. The discussion began with a proposal to disfranchise individuals convicted of violating election laws. George Lear of Bucks County suggested extending disfranchisement to those convicted of any infamous crime. Lear seemed well-versed in the issue, explaining that he wanted to disfranchise all individuals convicted of infamous felonies as well as those convicted of forgery and perjury, which were infamous crimes but misdemeanors. "It seems to me to be very proper that we should disfranchise the thieves and burglars and pickpockets and the infamous characters who have been convicted and sentenced for criminal conduct. Not that we should include in our sweeping prohibition all men who have been convicted in criminal court at all, for instance, as to assault and battery, but all these infamous characters who have been the pest of the community." Lear's comments indicated that he held to the old notion of infamous crimes as excluding acts of violence. Responding to Lear was delegate Samuel M. Wherry from Cumberland County, who may have given one of the most comprehensive and impassioned rebuttals of disfranchising convicts ever spoken. Wherry offered four arguments. First, he asserted that any individual valued and respected enough to live freely in society should have the right of the franchise. Only men who were dangerous criminals and denied freedom by incarceration should be also denied suffrage. Second, he believed that disfranchisement was an unfair punishment because it lacked "variability." All individuals, regardless of the crime they committed, faced the same sanction. He saw this as unjust. Third, since "men are most likely to under rate it as a punishment" it lacked a "deterrent force" and was ineffective as a tool of public policy. Finally, disfranchised men faced a level of alienation from society that made them likely to offend again. Denying them the vote made them dangerously anti-social. Wherry concluded:

> Now I ask the committee, is disfranchisement a good kind of punishment? Does it possess the qualities of a good punishment? Has it variability? Has it certainty? Has it applicability? Has it deterrent power? It does not possess a single one of these qualities. And what is left to it? Nothing but the miserable sham of analogy, and the wicked, absolutely wicked spirit of vengeance. That is all.... Can the Commonwealth of Pennsylvania, or any other free Commonwealth, afford to create in her midst a class of exiles not exiled? Can we afford to set apart an ostracized class in our very midst, who will be forever plotting against the peace of the state?[33]

Ultimately the convention decided that individuals who violated election law should be disfranchised for four years; those convicted of infamous crimes, bribery, perjury, or embezzlement should be permanently barred from holding elected office but still permitted to vote.[34]

Maryland's 1850 constitutional convention decided, after much debate, to disfranchise for some criminal convictions but opted to put limits on the extent of these measures. A proposal disfranchising for infamous crimes produced quite a bit of dissent and, in particular, opposition based on a belief in the rehabilitative impacts of incarceration. One delegate, Robert Brent from the city of Baltimore, argued against what he called "perpetual disfranchisement." He believed that an individual who had served his sentence should be free of all penalties. Another, Thomas R. Stewart from Caroline County, insisted that many who had served prison time had been "reformed by punishment." He too "was averse to putting an indelible mark of infamy on convicts." Ultimately, the convention passed a law disfranchising for infamous crimes and larceny, but limited this to convictions after the age of twenty-one years and made provisions for a governor's pardon.[35]

In 1864, with another constitutional convention underway, Maryland political leaders again debated whether individuals should be permanently disfranchised due to criminal convictions. Joseph M. Cushing from the city of Baltimore proposed an amendment automatically restoring suffrage rights to individuals who had completed their incarceration, explaining, "If a man is convicted of any crime, and is sentenced, that sentence is decided...to be a sufficient punishment...I see no reason why there should be added to that a disfranchisement for all time, debarring the man for all time of all chance of reform, and all opportunity of becoming again a good and respectable citizen." Cushing's fellow delegate from Baltimore, John L. Thomas, Jr., supported this position. Thomas asserted that if convicted individuals experienced a loss of suffrage after release from incarceration, they might offend again, even if they had been rehabilitated while in prison. "But as soon as he comes out of the doors of the penitentiary, he is met in his very teeth with another stigma flung in his face, saying to him you are still a felon....that in itself is enough to crush the exertions, and energies, and good intentions of any man." The proposal, however, did not pass, and Maryland continued to disfranchise those who had not been pardoned.[36]

Opinions on Cushing's proposal for automatic restoration turned on the issue of reform. Archibald Stirling Jr. from the city of Baltimore argued that most convicts should be disfranchised for life. He believed them to be "among the most reckless and degraded of the community" and rarely rehabilitated by their time in prison. "I have known only one or two instances in which any man ever sent to the penitentiary has reformed." In contrast, delegate Cushing had such faith in the possibility of reform through incarceration that he believed that those who served in the penitentiary were more deserving of citizenship than those who had been punished for minor offenses in jails. He explained:

The influences of the penitentiary and the influences of the jail are two very different things. A man in the penitentiary is not forced to herd with other felons.

He is kept at hard work and is not allowed to speak to the people that are near him. It is mainly a reformatory power. It gives him time for reflection and under the present system tends to his improvement.

Yet those who had served time in jail had no such opportunities: "[I]n most of the jails of the State they are herded together, and the influence of the jail is very different."[37]

At neither of the Maryland conventions did those opposed to permanent disfranchisement succeed in halting these measures. The majority of delegates held that convictions for infamous crimes should bring lifelong disfranchisement. But those who opposed lifelong disfranchisement for infamous convicts put up a serious fight. Their arguments reflected a deep belief in the possibility of reform that led them to reject the idea that incarceration brought infamy.

Michigan's 1850 constitutional convention saw a short debate over disfranchisement for crime that also reflected these competing beliefs about infamy and rehabilitation. Proponents of disfranchisement saw criminals as infamous both because of their crime and because of their incarceration. Delegate H. T. Backus from Detroit asked, "Is a man who has been steeped in crime and who has come out of the State prison a fit person to participate with us at the ballot box to make our judges and our constituted State authorities? I think not." Those on the other side believed in reform and rehabilitation: "The object of punishment [is] the reformation of crime. If it does produce that effect we ought not to place odium upon him after he has had the wholesome lesson of instruction imparted to him." They believed convicted and incarcerated individuals should not face disfranchisement for life because they likely had been reformed by incarceration. In the end, the assembly decided not to disfranchise individuals for criminal convictions.[38]

How do we account for these regional differences in attitudes toward disfranchisement for crime in the mid-nineteenth century United States? The historical literature on criminal justice suggests that northern and southern states have had different histories of criminal justice and corrections, in particular divergent approaches to incarceration, rehabilitation, and corporal punishment. Beginning in the nineteenth century, northern states built prisons that focused on rehabilitation of offenders. Eastern State Penitentiary in Philadelphia, modeled on the idea that labor and solitude could result in penitence and reform, was perhaps the most famous. In New York, Auburn Penitentiary reflected a different approach that also valued silence and housed prisoners in isolated cells but saw communal labor as conducive to rehabilitation.[39] In contrast, incarceration in the

South was aimed more at punishment than rehabilitation. Southern states relied heavily on convict leasing, gaining private and public economic benefit from prison labor, and built fewer prisons before 1900. The reformation and rehabilitation of prisoners was not a significant part of the agenda of southern correctional systems.[40]

Also relevant to the regional differences are the divergent historical trajectories of corporal punishment—and of course slavery. States outside the South, particularly northern states, outlawed corporal punishment in the first few decades of the nineteenth century.[41] Northeastern states had abolished slavery by this time as well. In contrast the South relied longer on corporal punishments, and these punishments became racialized. Over the first decades of the nineteenth century, southern courts increasingly spared white men from whippings as punishment for crime, to such an extent that the rare whipping of white men met with opposition and protest.[42] Slaves continued to receive whippings until the institution of slavery itself was eradicated. With infamous punishments increasingly reserved for blacks, the connection between race and infamy became more absolute in southern states at the same time it was weakening in the North.

Robert Perkinson's history of Texas prisons looks to the legacy of slavery and Jim Crow to understand regional differences in incarceration and punishment. Confirming other scholarship that documents regional differences in the history of criminal justice, he finds that prisons in Texas and other southern states focused on punishment rather than rehabilitation. The system of convict labor, a direct heir of the legacy of slavery, meant that extracting labor from prisoners was also a priority of the criminal justice system. In the nineteenth century, white southerners believed that a "stable democracy" required that "no white man entrusted with the vote be dependent on another and that degradation be concentrated exclusively among utterly dependent slaves....The notion of locking up white men and making them toil amounted to an intolerable inversion of a divinely ordained social hierarchy." Perkinson concludes that racial differences in punishment were, thus, derived from racial hierarchies, and racial disparities in the criminal justice system today are rooted in a past where the criminal justice system targeted African Americans and spared whites.[43]

The ideology of infamy, too, developed differently in the North and South in the nineteenth century. Northeastern states in this period moved away from this idea that infamy came from punishment (partly because of the decline of ignominious punishments) and toward the idea that infamy came from committing serious crimes. This change was at times explicitly stated. For example, in 1836 the Vermont Supreme Court wrote, "The old notion that infamy depended upon the nature of the punishment is long since abandoned."[44] In 1849 the New York code commission explained, "For a long time the infamous character of a crime was supposed to result rather from the mode of punishment than from the nature of the offence. The law in this respect has gradually changed and it now appears to be finally settled in the English courts that the infamy arises not from the punishment nor from the judgment but from the nature of the crime."[45] Northern states appear to have been following the evolving European model more closely and phasing out infamy.

This development was important because it allowed for the possibility of reformation and was likely connected to development of rehabilitative penology. Someone degraded by the infamous punishment would always be degraded. But someone who repented and reformed might have the mark of infamy lifted. A system that sought to reform convicts through incarceration—the system implemented in the northern states—counteracted the tradition of permanent infamy, degradation, and thus disfranchisement.

In the pre-Civil War South questions of social status and race were quite literally black and white. The system of racial slavery fixed social hierarchies, entrenched an order where one was either a citizen or infamous slave, and mitigated narratives of reformation and rehabilitation. Corporal punishments—whippings or forced labor—were primarily meted out to African Americans, slave or free. Such punishment then left the mark of infamy (possibly even a physical mark, evidence of whipping) on all who received it, because it signified degradation and enslavement. If you were infamous and degraded by virtue of your race and/or punishment, you had no privileges of citizenship. Slaves and infamous individuals were infamous for life; free blacks, while not utterly dependent as slaves were, were nonetheless seen as infamed by their race. They joined those outside the boundaries of citizenship—debtors, vagrants, the insane, and women. White men who were not infamous held a respected status and exercised full rights of citizenship. "Respectable" men who ran afoul of the law could seek pardons and reprieves, but as a whole there were few opportunities for those who were excluded to move into the status of "citizen."

The North was simultaneously moving the other way—abandoning the idea of permanent infamy. One's status as a criminal was no longer necessarily fixed; individuals could be redeemed. In the eyes of some northern policymakers, even African Americans might be redeemed in some instances from the degradation of their blackness and granted the rights of citizens. New York's provision allowing African American property holders to vote is an example of this. Property ownership elevated some African American men out of degradation and into the ranks of citizenship, as one of the proponents of this exemption was reported to have explained at the convention: "It was true, that the blacks were in some respects a degraded portion of the community, but he was unwilling to see them disfranchised, and the door eternally barred against them. The proviso [allowing suffrage by black property owners] would not cut them off from all hope, and might in some degree alleviate the wrongs we had done them. It would have a tendency to make them industrious and frugal, with the prospect of participating in the right of suffrage."[46] Just as prisoners could be redeemed—perhaps by learning industry and frugality—so too might African Americans property owners become elevated in the eyes of some white northerners.

After 1865, southern whites faced a crisis. The emancipation of slaves and the Fourteenth Amendment's guarantee of citizenship undermined their assertion that citizenship was for whites only. The clear line between citizens and infamous non-citizens, between whites who ruled and blacks who were ruled, was suddenly vulnerable. Southern whites responded by seeking to buttress this distinction by affirming African American infamy as best they could. They could no longer designate the former slaves as non-citizens, but imposing disabilities on their rights that limited their access to full citizenship, the sort of disabilities that both indicated and produced infamy, was a goal that was in reach. Within months of the war's end, the newly passed Black Codes not only would regulate the behavior of the former slaves but would also regulate their status by maintaining their infamy. Congressional Reconstruction was still a year away, and white Democrats who governed state legislatures passed laws that restricted the liberty of the former slaves. Before the war, only free people of color had their inferior status affirmed by the law; now the Black Codes would continue that work. Black Codes perpetuated the legal infamy blacks experienced in the slave era, denying the former slaves the rights of citizenship that were already denied to infamous criminals and barring them from testifying in court against whites, jury service, and suffrage. Laws restricting the ability of African Americans to purchase land and homes in certain towns restricted their right to property. Black Codes also forced African Americans to labor and constrained their freedom of movement. Individuals not under control of whites through labor contracts became criminals, put under the control of the convict labor system; this was permitted because the Thirteenth Amendment sanctioned enslavement as punishment for crime.[47]

Perpetuating the infamy of African Americans became a key part of the South's effort to defend dichotomies of citizenship in the wake of expanded federal authority. The Black Codes preserved the infamy of this population in multiple ways. Those who stepped out of line became actual convicts, infamous under law. But perhaps more importantly, under the logic of the day, Black Codes infamed the entire race. Just as members of North Carolina's 1835 convention understood that differential treatment under the law degraded African Americans, so too did legislatures passing Black Codes understand these laws to be maintaining the infamy of the former slaves. The fact that any African American not contracted to work could be essentially re-enslaved made all African Americans degraded—just as the speakers at North Carolina's 1835 constitutional convention had imagined it. Being subject to state-sanctioned violence and failing to be protected from private acts of terrorism indicated infamy. Barriers to jury service, court testimony, and suffrage were not just evidence of infamy *but also causes of it.*

The Black Codes were the first of a series of efforts, described in the following chapters, to use the weapon of infamy to contest African American claims to suffrage and full citizenship. This strategy enabled white southerners to exploit their control over the criminal justice system as a means to enforce their ideas about citizenship in the region. This was part of a larger effort to maintain white political and social authority, defining whites as privileged citizens and excluding African Americans from political authority, while degrading the status of the black race.

CHAPTER 2

✺

"Disqualified in Advance"

In the fall of 1866 white Democrats in North Carolina spotted a gap in the text of the proposed Fourteenth Amendment. The amendment had not yet been ratified. Indeed it had only passed Congress a few months earlier. But in anticipation of the amendment's passage and its unprecedented provisions giving citizenship to the newly freed slaves, a group of Democrats in North Carolina embarked on an unusual campaign to blunt its impact. They undertook mass whippings of African Americans across the state. An outraged U.S. Army officer overseeing Reconstruction in North Carolina, Robert Avery, wrote to his superiors in Washington to explain the situation. According to Avery, individuals in North Carolina whipped as punishment for petty crime lost the right to vote. Across the state, white former rebels conspired to "seize negroes, procure convictions for petty offenses punishable at the whipping post, and thus disqualify them forever from voting in North Carolina." Avery wrote that, although blacks were not yet enfranchised in the state, whites anticipated that they soon would be sought to disqualify as many as possible. In one county, he had heard reports that whites "whipped over sixty at the last term of the County Court, and by next spring they would have disqualified about all of them." While wary of second-hand information, Avery had any lingering skepticism about the rumors resolved when he overheard a discussion among several members of the state legislature who were celebrating the fact that whipping African American men enabled them to "head off Congress from making the negroes voters." One of the men stated, "We are licking them in our part of the State and if we keep on we can lick them all by next year, and none of them can vote."[1]

The national press soon learned of Avery's report, and news of the events spread across the country. An article in *Harper's Weekly* described a courthouse in Raleigh where a crowd of five hundred watched "the public whipping of colored men as fast as they were convicted and sentenced." The article explained that "whipping in North Carolina operates as a civil disqualification," so individuals who were whipped were permanently barred from suffrage. Due to the whipping campaign, which reportedly was carried out daily for an entire month, many African American men were "disqualified in advance."[2] The *Atlantic Monthly* also recounted the incident: "The public whipping of negroes for paltry offences is carried on in North Carolina on a large scale, for the reason that by the laws of that State every man who has been publicly whipped is excluded from the right of voting." This would allow southern states to "evade" the Fourteenth Amendment.[3]

The *Atlantic Monthly* was correct to identify both local and national causes of the whipping campaign undertaken in North Carolina. Under state law, individuals convicted of infamous crimes faced disfranchisement and the loss of other rights of citizenship. If southern states could no longer deny citizenship to African Americans because they were slaves, making African Americans infamous could serve the same purpose. Whipping made individuals infamous because infamy, under English common law, could result either from the commission of an infamous crime or from the receipt of an infamous punishment such as whipping. This explains why disfranchisement for prior criminal convictions was among the first strategies employed to block African American suffrage in North Carolina, even before the Fourteenth Amendment guaranteed them citizenship. Those in North Carolina who whipped African Americans to "disqualify them in advance" were following the basic principle that infamous men did not have the rights of citizens. Whipping them did not fundamentally change their status because these white southerners already believed that African Americans were degraded and infamous. Whipping *restored* them to this status. Whipping transformed African American men from ex-slaves into criminals, defying the new constitutional amendment that made them citizens. It was an obvious solution to the perceived threat of black citizenship because it reestablished their infamy, thereby reaffirming their lack of citizenship.

On the national level, presidential action contributed to these developments in North Carolina. Andrew Johnson's plan for Reconstruction permitted states to re-establish local courts. Although the Freedmen's Bureau and the army also set up judicial tribunals where African Americans were more likely to receive justice and fair trials, local courts now operated across the region with Johnson's consent. These local courts—sometimes referred to in this context as "civil courts"—enforced the Black Codes (until they were outlawed), mandated corporal punishment for small crimes, and channeled African American defendants into the convict lease system.[4] In North Carolina, apparently, they also cooperated in the December 1866 whipping campaign by convicting and punishing as many African American men as possible for minor or possibly even fabricated charges.

The growing battle between Johnson and Congress over the direction of Reconstruction soon extended to the issue of corporal punishment in the South. Reconstruction administrators, acting under congressional authority, outlawed whipping in North Carolina in mid-1866. But soon after, Johnson issued a statement invalidating these orders and allowing local courts to authorize whipping for convicted individuals. Colonel James V. Bomford, commander of the military post in Raleigh, wrote to Washington to express frustration at the confusing and contradictory instructions. "Am I to consider [the president's reinstatement of corporal punishment] an official order to me? For previous to the receipt of this communication I had already interfered to prevent punishments by the Civil Courts."[5] Bomford hoped his letter would point out what was at stake in North Carolina by underscoring the impact that whipping would have on electoral politics. The attention paid to the issue in the national press indicated that some had understood his message.

The Fourteenth Amendment, passed just a few months earlier and now under ratification by the states, also played a key role in inspiring the whipping campaign. The amendment would guarantee rights to all citizens, but it did not specify that suffrage was a right of citizenship. Rather it offered a series of weak protections for suffrage. Section Two of the amendment allowed states to deny suffrage for any reason, but those that did so faced a loss of congressional representation unless suffrage was denied for "participation in rebellion, or other crime."[6] This apparent sanctioning of disfranchisement for any kind of criminal conviction did not escape the notice of white Democrats in North Carolina; in fact, it inspired them to begin their whipping campaign.

From the perspective of protecting the rights of individuals with criminal convictions, the Fourteenth Amendment represented a step backward from the Thirteenth Amendment. The Thirteenth Amendment, known most famously for outlawing slavery, did permit slavery or involuntary servitude as punishment for crime. However, the amendment specified that enslavement could only follow a proper conviction: "Neither slavery nor involuntary servitude, except as a punishment for crime whereof the party shall have been duly convicted, shall exist within the United States, or any place subject to their jurisdiction." In contrast, the Fourteenth Amendment did not offer any guidance on the conditions surrounding criminal conviction and simply allowed states to outlaw voting by those considered criminals (or rebels) without any restriction. This distinction supports the argument that this section of the Fourteenth Amendment was aimed at allowing the states to restrict the voting rights of former rebels, not those who committed "other crime[s]" of any variety. Many of the offenses for which these rebels might be accused were not ones for which convictions might be secured in court. The greater flexibility of the Fourteenth Amendment's language would have allowed states to disfranchise individuals who participated in criminal acts related to the rebellion without first convicting them of crimes.

Democrats in North Carolina were not alone in envisioning ways that allegations of crime and criminal conviction could keep African Americans from the ballot box, even before they were granted citizenship rights. In December 1865 the South Carolina legislature enacted a law, part of the state's Black Codes, that classified as felonies many kinds of petty theft that had formerly been considered misdemeanors, including the theft of livestock or crops or theft that involved breaking into any kind of dwelling or enclosure. The legislature also specified that among the punishments for a felony, at the discretion of the court, was disfranchisement for between ten and twenty years.[7] The newly enacted constitution of 1865 backed up this legislation by giving the General Assembly the right to "impose disqualification to vote as punishment for crime."[8]

Is it possible that the authors of South Carolina's constitution and criminal code had black suffrage in their sights, despite the fact that the newly freed slaves had not yet been granted citizenship or voting rights?[9] One contemporary witness claimed this was the case. Thomas J. Robertson, a white South Carolina businessman who temporarily chaired the 1868 South Carolina constitutional convention at its opening session, explained that one of the goals of the Black Codes had been to deny the right of suffrage to African Americans. Democrats, anticipating that the newly freed slaves would be granted citizenship rights, created these criminal penalties to target black voters. He told the convention, "The intent of those laws was to deprive every colored man of their right of citizenship" because the laws "made the most trivial offense a felony."[10]

News of the whipping campaign in North Carolina prompted a response by Republican leaders in Congress. Having seized control of the post-war planning from President Johnson, Congress was now on the brink of passing the Reconstruction Act that would set the terms for fully restoring the former Confederate states to the Union. Just weeks after Avery's report reached Washington, Republican congressman Thaddeus Stevens proposed an amendment to the pending bill that would have prevented states under Reconstruction from disfranchising individuals for any crime other than insurrection or treason. When southern states revised the suffrage provisions of their constitutions at constitutional conventions to be held in the following year, the new documents would have to comply with this requirement (as well as others).[11] A contemporary account said that Stevens was motivated by reports from North Carolina. "He gave as a reason for proposing this amendment that in North Carolina, and other States where punishment at the whipping-post deprives a person of the right to vote, they were every day whipping negroes for trivial offenses. He had heard of one county where authorities had whipped every adult negro they knew of."[12] Stevens hoped that his proposal would prevent states from convicting and whipping African Americans for petty crimes as a means of disfranchising them.[13]

Other Republicans in Congress, though, were uneasy about requiring southern states to enfranchise such a wide range of former convicts. Illinois Representative Jehu Baker warned that under Stevens's proposal "the penitentiaries of these states might disgorge their inmates upon the polls." [14] Representative Thomas D. Eliot from Massachusetts who would soon chair the Committee on Freedmen's Affairs, similarly argued against this element of Stevens's plan, explaining, "I do not think we want to admit to vote those who have been disfranchised by reasons of crimes heretofore committed, such as murder, robbery, etc."[15] But Ohio Republican John Bingham—known as the primary author of the Fourteenth Amendment—made the most vehement objections:

> What is this but asking this Congress to say in advance, if the insurgent States shall so frame their constitutions of state government, that thieves, robbers and assassins shall never be deprived of the right of the elective franchise it will be approved; otherwise their constitutions will be rejected.[16]

Denying citizenship to individuals with serious criminal convictions had widespread, national acceptance. Although congressional Republicans recognized Stevens's concerns that disfranchisement for crime could achieve partisan ends, they insisted that the right of states to disfranchise for crime be preserved.[17]

Ultimately Congress acknowledged Stevens's concern and voted to place some restrictions on the ability of southern states to disfranchise convicted individuals. The first Reconstruction Act, passed March 2, 1867, required southern states to allow all male residents over twenty-one years of age to vote, "except such as may be disfranchised for participation in the rebellion or for felony at common law." Congress hoped that limiting disfranchisement to felonies, thereby reversing the broad permission given for this practice under the Fourteenth Amendment, would protect against further efforts to disfranchise African Americans for minor crimes.[18] North Carolina could no longer whip African American men for petty crimes to "disqualify them in advance," and South Carolina could not deny the vote to former slaves convicted of minor agricultural theft.

In the subsequent months leading up to the 1867 election, in which voters would select delegates to state constitutional conventions, issues of crime and criminal conviction headlined debates over suffrage rights. The central and most public aspect of this debate were questions over which (if any) former Confederates could vote in the upcoming election, but issues concerning the voting rights of individuals with criminal convictions also surfaced in this context. If suffrage was to be denied to individuals who "participated in rebellion," how were registrars to determine what constituted "participation?" The loyalty oath required of all voters, passed in the March 23 Reconstruction Act, denied the vote to Confederates who had held public office before the war, and it required prospective voters to swear that they were not disqualified due to rebellion or felony conviction.[19] But what of those who took the required loyalty oath but whose claims to suffrage rights were disputed?

In response to these uncertainties, President Johnson authorized the War Department to issue a memorandum clarifying who might be legally denied registration for suffrage. According to this memorandum "actual participation in rebellion, or the actual commission of a felony" did not bring about disfranchisement. Rather, "the sort of disfranchisement here meant is that which is declared by law passed by competent authority, or which has been fixed upon the criminal by the sentence of the court which tried him for the crime." The bottom line was that mere accusation could not result in disfranchisement for rebellion or felony. Registrars should only deny the vote to those with actual convictions.[20]

The War Department issued this clarification because of suggestions that the opposite would happen. Some Republicans schemed to broadly interpret the "rebellion" provision of the Reconstruction Act in order to deny suffrage to former Confederates. Johnson's alignment with southern Democrats made him careful to protect the voting rights of these former rebels as much as possible—a stance that was already bringing him into conflict with Republicans in Congress. But Johnson's order also, perhaps unwittingly, offered some protection to individuals facing disfranchisement for allegations of crimes other than rebellion. No one should be disfranchised on the basis of an accusation absent conviction. Despite this, some southern Democrats would still try to find ways to selectively disfranchise African Americans due to prior criminal acts in the 1867 election.

This later effort was part of a larger effort by southern Democrats to block African American voting in 1867 despite the federal protection.

White southern Democrats hoping to restrict black voting saw the opportunity to deny them suffrage through allegations of prior criminal convictions. They counted on assistance from local registrars who opposed African American suffrage. On the other side, Republicans in Congress claimed growing authority over Reconstruction and worked to protect African Americans from such abridgements of their rights. Federal Reconstruction administrators tried to anticipate strategies Democrats would use and attempted to narrow the range of crimes for which individuals, particularly African American men, could be denied suffrage. They also reined in registrars who failed to correctly enforce the Reconstruction Act's provisions regarding registration and suffrage.

Late in the summer of 1867, registration for the election began, a process that Congress demanded be completed by September 1.[21] Concerned that criminal allegations would be used to limit the black vote, Reconstruction officials in Charleston, South Carolina, began to look for ways to further narrow the scope of the "felony" disfranchisement standard established just a few months earlier in the Reconstruction Act. In other words, while the Reconstruction Act allowed states to disfranchise individuals convicted of felonies, federal officials in Charleston did their best to limit the number of individuals affected by this restriction on felon voting.

First, in August federal officials in Charleston published "General Instructions to Officers of Registration, for their Information in Revising the Lists of Voters." Reconstruction administrators circulated this order across the Second Military District, which was comprised of North Carolina and South Carolina. Among these instructions was the proviso that individuals could be disqualified from voting only if they had been "disfranchised by the sentence of a competent judicial tribunal for felony."[22] This established a standard for the court in which the conviction occurred, limiting the judicial bodies that could disfranchise. Though the order did not clarify what constituted a "competent judicial tribunal," it is likely that federal officials were concerned about the power of convictions levied in more informal venues of justice—the kinds of venues where slaves or even former slaves might have stood trial—to disfranchise.

By October registration was complete and the election just weeks away. Local registrars were now revising and finalizing registration lists. For the second time, federal officials in Charleston issued an order instructing registrars on the suffrage rights of former convicts, this time with specific directives concerning the revision of voter registration lists. When individuals were disqualified for a conviction, registrars were required to note in the registration book the reason for disqualification. The only legitimate grounds for disqualification, the order stressed, was conviction of a "felony by a court of competent jurisdiction." Registrars had to strictly follow the language of the Reconstruction Act. Apparently, registrars had been disqualifying voters for an array of other reasons, including some that were inappropriate.[23]

To even further clarify federal orders, the document quoted language directly from voter registration books as examples of such inappropriate disqualifications. Some of these illegitimate grounds for rejection were unrelated to criminal activity. For example, some voters had been crossed off registration lists for being "too old." But a number of these illegitimate challenges concerned crimes and allegations of criminal convictions. Individuals could not be disqualified "for seducing a white woman (said to be deficient in intellect)," evidence that a registrar had tried to disqualify someone for this very reason. Nor was it appropriate to deny the vote to those "convicted of trading with negroes before the war." Slaveholders had struggled to stop whites, usually lower class non-slaveholders, from conducting commercial transactions with slaves, and many elites saw such commerce as a threat to their authority and power over slaves.[24] South Carolina had passed a law in 1857 allowing for the whipping of those who traded illegally with slaves. Whipping white men meant punishing them—and therefore treating them—as slaves, causing some to protest that a white man should not be subjected to such degradation.[25] But trading with slaves was seen as such a serious crime that it justified this infamous punishment. After the war white individuals convicted of this crime might not only be seen as a political threat by Democrats—i.e., likely to vote Republican— but also as having achieved a kind of infamy and removal from the body politic of white male citizens due to this crime and punishment. Those who had traded with slaves might thus be considered infamous and targeted for disfranchisement. Other criminal convictions that Reconstruction officials warned were inappropriate reasons for denying the vote included: "fugitive from justice," "publicly whipped," "disloyalty," "sentenced to nine months imprisonment," "convicted of murder and pardoned by the Governor," "tried and convicted; granted a new trial because of plaintiff's son having been on jury," and "convicted of petty larceny."[26]

Finally, the order indicated that some registrars were disqualifying people who may, in fact, have been correctly disqualified. However, the grounds for disqualification were not properly documented in the registration books. For example, some registrars had written "felony" or "convicted of stealing" to justify disfranchisement. Other examples included "convicted of rape," "convicted of grand larceny," "accused of larceny," "concealing stolen property," "larceny," "manslaughter," "charged with willful perjury," and "convicted of murder." These were legitimate reasons for disqualification, the order explained, but they were inappropriately notated. The only formula that served as sufficient grounds for rejection was "convicted of felony by a court of competent jurisdiction." The order demanded registrars reproduce this exact language in their registration books when disqualifying voters for criminal conviction.[27]

Despite the work of federal officials, when election day came in November, Democrats in some districts still tried to disqualify African American voters because of prior, alleged criminal activities. Evidence of their efforts can be found in the reports and actions of the constitutional conventions that followed. In some southern states, experiences from the 1867 election prompted Republicans to revise their state constitutions so as to place greater restrictions on disfranchisement for criminal conviction than the federal standard set out in the Reconstruction Act.

In South Carolina, two members of the 1868 constitutional convention described partisan and racial biases in the enforcement of disfranchisement provisions at the 1867 election. White Republican Thomas J. Robertson from Columbia, explained how judges and police had conspired to target African Americans with laws disfranchising for crime: "If a colored man struck a white man, all [the latter] had to do was go before an officer of the law and declare that the colored man struck him with intent to kill and that offense, according to the law of 1865 constituted a felony." Robertson explained that this was part of an effort to deny suffrage to African American men.[28] Another white South Carolina Republican, Simon Corley of Lexington, charged that, in some districts, African Americans had been denied registration and suffrage due to crimes they had committed as slaves. Corley explained that some South Carolina registrars had employed a very broad definition of "felony," disfranchising former slaves for petty offenses if they had been "punished as felons."[29]

To prevent ex-slaves from being denied the vote this way in future elections Corley proposed amending the state's constitution to read, "No offences heretofore committed by a slave, nor punishment inflicted on the same, can now be held as coming within the intent and meaning of the reconstruction laws in reference to felony." Any voter registrars who failed to follow this directive were to be reported to the commander of the military district.[30] A revised version of Corley's proposal was enacted in the final 1868 South Carolina constitution: "No person shall be disfranchised for felony, or other crimes committed while such person was a slave."[31] A critic of Reconstruction ridiculed these efforts to protect the voting rights of former slaves by saying, "No person is to be disfranchised for felony committed when a slave, which gives a negro homicide, house-burner, rav-isher, or robber the franchise, when a white man convicted of like offenses loses it."[32] Those elected in 1867 in South Carolina and charged with writ-ing the new constitution applied lessons learned in that election, including lessons about potential manipulation of laws disfranchising for criminal convictions, to the new constitution.[33]

While Corley and his allies in Columbia were primarily concerned with protecting the political rights of former slaves, they were prescient in iden-tifying an evidentiary issue that would allow for racial and partisan manip-ulation of these laws for decades to come. Many southern courts in this era—not just slave courts—failed to keep formal records. Inferior courts adjudicated disputes in rural areas and small towns. Referred to variously as "magistrates' courts," "trial justices' courts," or, in cities and towns as "mayor's courts" and "police courts," these courts operated below the level of circuit courts; the circuit court served as the first court of appeals for their decisions. In rural Florida, some referred to them informally as "wire-grass courts." A local citizen served as judge, often someone with no formal legal training but with a degree of respect and prominence in the community. These courts traditionally lacked a set venue for hearing cases; instead, rural magistrates heard cases wherever they were when approached by dis-puting parties and in whatever spaces were available and convenient. This resulted in hearings that were conducted in locations such as post offices, fields, taverns, country stores, front porches, and town squares.[34]

With no written records of court proceedings, fair and impartial enforce-ment of suffrage laws was impossible, even for the best-intentioned elec-tion officials. Lack of court documentation could affect white voters as well. In 1876, for example, a white man named Charley Jones was barred from voting in Lake City in Columbia County, Florida, when Democrats accused him of having been convicted of a crime and serving time in prison at the end of the Civil War. A Republican poll-watcher disputed Jones's disfran-chisement. He said that Jones had not been arrested but had been held instead by soldiers. Jones was never confined to a jail but "kept in a guard house." No record could be found of his conviction or incarceration, and the matter was never resolved.[35] That same year in Virginia some mem-bers of the General Assembly questioned the ability of convictions in infe-rior courts to permanently disfranchise. In 1876, Senator James H. Allan, who represented James City and York Counties, asked that the Senate Committee for Courts of Justice investigate whether a person convicted of petit larceny in a Justice of the Peace court could be disfranchised despite the absence of a jury trial. However, the General Assembly failed to legis-late on the matter.[36]

Delegates to the 1868 constitutional conventions in North Carolina and Virginia expressed similar concerns that a dearth of evidence, past biases, and inconsistencies in the criminal justice system might bring about wrongful disfranchisement. In North Carolina two Republicans on the suffrage committee sought to protect African Americans from being labeled infamous criminals for convictions and punishments received as slaves by specifying that individuals who had been convicted of infamous crimes be disfranchised only if the conviction had occurred "since becoming citizens of the United States." Under this proposal, individuals convicted of infamous crimes (or punished as infamous criminals, i.e., whipped) while they were slaves would retain their voting rights.[37] In contrast to South Carolina, however, their plan did not attract support from the full convention and did not appear in the final constitution. Another unsuccessful effort to limit the reach of laws disfranchising for crime in an 1868 constitutional convention occurred in Virginia. William H. Andrews, an African American Republican from New Jersey representing Isle of Wight and Surry Counties, proposed limiting disfranchisement to felony convictions from "reconstruction courts." Andrews pointed out that it is "well known that there is a large class of prisoners now committed unjustly" by the courts of Virginia's secession government. He argued that convictions under the Confederate government should be invalidated, since the government had been illegal. His proposal did not pass.[38]

The Virginia constitutional convention also considered restoring suffrage to a white man whose conviction and punishment in the past outraged some supporters of civil rights. Republican John Hawxhurst offered a resolution calling attention to the case of John A. Blevins. In 1848 a Virginia court had convicted Blevins of "teaching colored people to read." He had been incarcerated for a grueling fourteen years and was finally released by the Union Army when Richmond fell. Hawxhurst proposed that Blevins be "relieved from all civil and political disabilities created by said charges, conviction, or imprisonment." He also proposed that the disabilities be removed "of all other persons created in like manner." Finally, Hawxhurst asked the committee to inquire and report "as to the expedience of relieving all political disabilities arising out of any charges, conviction, or imprisonment that have taken place, or shall hereafter take place, under the illegal governments of this State since the passage of the ordinance of secession and before the state is admitted to the Union, under the acts of Congress."[39] The full convention, however, failed to act on the issue.

The most radical proposals aimed at protecting those with prior convictions from disfranchisement came at conventions in Alabama and Florida where delegates offered plans to eliminate disfranchisement for crime completely. At Alabama's 1868 convention two Republican delegates, likely cognizant of the partisan manipulation of the felony disfranchisement standard in the 1867 elections, sought to prevent any individual from being disfranchised for any criminal conviction. The first came from Thomas Peters, who offered a suffrage proposal with no provision disfranchising for any crimes at all. Peters had been a prominent white Unionist who advocated for penal reform and expanded access to education at the convention. This may have motivated his opposition to disfranchising for criminal convictions.[40] James T. Rapier, an African American man from Lauderdale who had attended law school in Canada and would later represent Alabama in the U.S. Congress, also proposed a broadly inclusive suffrage provision that did not disfranchise any convicted individuals.[41] However, delegates to the Alabama convention rejected these very liberal measures, choosing instead to continue to follow the parameters of the Reconstruction Act and disfranchise for certain serious crimes.

In Florida, radical and moderate Republicans competed for dominance at the 1868 convention, and the two sides presented draft constitutions with stark differences on suffrage. A group of Radical delegates—the majority of whom were African American—offered a constitution that contained no provision at all disfranchising for criminal convictions. Their proposal did not carry the day, however, and instead the convention approved the suffrage plan put forth by the moderate Republicans. The 1868 Florida constitution was the most conservative one approved that year with regard to suffrage. It allowed all former Confederates to vote, made allowances for a literacy test after 1880, and reapportioned legislative districts to minimize the power of African American votes. Though the previous constitution had disfranchised individuals convicted of bribery, perjury, or other infamous crimes, the new constitution added larceny along with all felonies to the list of disfranchising offenses.[42]

This evidence from the 1867 elections and 1868 constitutional conventions makes several things clear. One is that southern Democrats had in the course of the 1867 elections tested the limits set in the Reconstruction Act by trying to disqualify individuals for crimes who should have been permitted to vote. This was part of the strategy to disfranchise African Americans by extending disqualification for criminal convictions to the largest section of the black population possible. Second, federal administrators became aware of their plans and pushed back, trying to assert control of the registration process and protect African American voters from being targeted by these techniques. Limiting the venue of conviction to "courts of competent jurisdiction" and monitoring the grounds for disfranchisement noted in registration books both represented ways that Reconstruction administrators sought to restrict the reach of conviction-based disfranchisement techniques.

Finally, efforts by Republicans to revise state constitutions in order to head off the manipulation of these laws in future elections met with limited success. This is partly because restricting the citizenship rights of criminals had a long history; a baseline of general support for disfranchising convicted individuals is not difficult to explain. But politics and partisanship played important roles as well. The composition of these state constitutional conventions, and in particular the political strength of Radical Republicans, both black and white, varied from state to state. Protecting the voting rights of African Americans was not the highest priority issue for some conventions, particularly those dominated by white moderate Republicans. South Carolina's convention had a particularly significant level of African American participation, both in number and political authority, so it is not surprising that this state went the furthest to protect African Americans from being targeted with laws disfranchising for prior criminal convictions. In Florida, Alabama, and Virginia, efforts to pass such provisions came from Radical Republicans, but they failed to attract wider support. The failure of North Carolina, the state said to have produced the most "republican constitution," to protect African Americans from being disfranchised for crimes committed as slaves is more difficult to explain.[43] Overall, splits between Radical and conservative Republicans were evident in their approaches to suffrage generally and their approach to disfranchisement for crime in particular. Most Radical delegates, who sought the maximum protection for African American votes, would disfranchise for few, if any, crimes.[44]

Also at issue at the 1868 conventions were the political rights of those who had fought against the Union. These individuals had been accused, and sometimes convicted, of treason. While it is fair to assume that the disfranchisement of former Confederates was largely separate from the issue of disfranchising common criminals, these issues were not entirely disconnected. Congress had been clear in the Fourteenth Amendment that certain Confederates lost the right to vote or hold office, unless they received a congressional pardon. But the voting rights of other Confederates were left open to the states; states could disfranchise for "participation in rebellion or other crimes" without sanction under Section Two of the Fourteenth Amendment. Thus, states could pass additional laws limiting the voting rights of former rebels. In some states, debates over the political rights of rebels included discussions of whether "other crimes" that were related to the rebellion also brought about disfranchisement. A resolution at Alabama's 1868 constitutional convention noted that many men in the state had been "principles or accessories" in the murder of Union men. If they had been tried in court, they would have been convicted but "through the default of solicitors and grand juries [they were] in the possession of all civil rights." The resolution's author, Samuel S. Gardner of Butler, asked the Committee on Elective Franchise to look into a means of disfranchising such individuals.[45] Several states added treason to their disfranchising standards in this era, but this action alone did not answer all the relevant questions about how criminal disloyalty should be punished. Some conventions engaged in long discussions of what exactly defined treason.[46] Because all of these issues were contained in the suffrage planks of constitutions, discussions of these two classes of offense—criminal acts and crimes of disloyalty—at the conventions often occurred one after the other. As conventions weighed the impact of these two kinds of crimes on citizenship, the treatment of convicted criminals informed discussions of the treatment of loyalty offenses and wartime conduct, and vice versa.

When southern constitutional conventions met in 1868 one of the most common revisions of the provisions disfranchising for crime was the addition of treason to the list of disfranchising offenses. Four states, Alabama, Arkansas, Louisiana, South Carolina, and Virginia changed their constitutions to deny the vote for treason.[47] But this was not a uniform trend across the region. Several states did not specify that treason disfranchised—including Mississippi and Florida.[48]

Some framers sought to expand the disfranchisement of former rebels by denying citizenship rights to those who had crossed lines in their wartime behavior—lines not only of national loyalty but also criminal activity. In other words, by defining certain kinds of wartime behavior as criminal, radicals justified extending disfranchisement to these classes of rebels. For example, in Alabama the convention considered ways to punish former Confederates who had committed war-related crimes under proposals expanding the disfranchisement of former Confederates for crimes they committed during wartime. The convention discussed proposals that would disfranchise individuals who signed the ordinance of secession, those who "killed or otherwise abused" Alabamians loyal to the Union, those who abused Union prisoners, those who gave aid or comfort to the enemies of the United States, those who murdered freedmen, and more. Ultimately the group settled on a provision barring from voting or holding office those individuals who harmed any member of the U.S. military or who "violated the rules of civilized warfare." John Keffer, the chair of the suffrage committee, explained that this kept from power "the incarnate fiends, whose atrocious conduct during the late war shocked the moral susceptibilities of the civilized world."[49] Louisiana too disfranchised those who had aided the rebellion in a variety of ways including those who "wrote or published newspaper articles or preached sermons" advocating treason.[50]

Two members of the North Carolina convention proposed punishing those who committed (again, absent a conviction) crimes against voters. Thomas J. Candler of Buncombe County and Abraham Congleton of Carteret County sought to disfranchise "those who have prevented, or endeavored to prevent any voter from the free exercise of the elective franchise by threats, violence or bribery." These two men were Republicans, and most likely they aimed to use these measures both to punish Democrats and protect Republicans. The convention rejected their plan, however.[51]

The activities of southern constitutional conventions in the wake of the Fourteenth Amendment do not offer definitive evidence of what Congress meant by "other crimes" in Section Two of the amendment. However, they do support the notion that the phrase "other crimes" in the new amendment was interpreted by Republicans at the state constitutional conventions to mean crimes committed by former Confederates. It also explains why those who sought to use diverse crimes to punish former Confederates avoided the language of the Thirteenth Amendment requiring due conviction when drafting the Fourteenth. Finding ways to deny political power to the former rebels was a priority for Republicans in the North and South. In many southern states, Republicans considered ways to expand the reach of Section Three of the amendment—a fairly narrow provision that punished only former federal or state officeholders who joined the Confederacy—in order to deny voting rights to a larger group of the former rebels based on their wartime conduct. They likely saw Section Two's reference to "other crimes" as a means of accomplishing this. This, then, may offer insight into the original intent of Section Two—at least from the perspective of some members of Congress. These men may have hoped that allowing states to disfranchise for a broad range of unspecified crimes would enable Republicans in the South to disqualify a greater number of former rebels if they chose to do so without facing penalty for it. While it is difficult to know what different members of Congress had in mind when approving the amendment, it is clear that this is how the provision was construed by Republicans in southern constitutional conventions a short time later.

The political rights of disloyal southerners and those of convicted criminals further intersected around the issue of pardons at the South Carolina convention. This convention, like several others, heard petitions for action by the convention. A number of men who had lost their voting rights due to participation in the rebellion petitioned for the restoration of their citizenship.[52] But one man caused some confusion when he asked for relief from punishment for a criminal offense. Thomas Owens sought removal of civil disabilities not for treason but for a felony conviction.

Standard procedure for petitions for restoration was for the convention to send them to the Committee on Petitions. The committee would recommend to the full body whether they should be admitted or denied. Delegate J. J. Wright, on hearing Owens's request, suggested immediately denying it, even before the committee could weigh in on the matter. Wright argued that "it is not the province of this body to ask relief from punishment for a person convicted of felony or criminal offense." B. F. Randolph disagreed, responding that while he did not know Owens himself, other delegates had represented him as a worthy man. So, why not let the Committee on Petitions evaluate his request?[53]

At this point someone spoke who was familiar with the case. Delegate Y. J. P. Owens represented Thomas Owens's district, Laurens County, and knew the petitioner, who shared his last name. Delegate Owens said that petitioner Owens had been a loyalist and "worked faithfully for reconstruction." He had been disfranchised following a conviction for accidentally killing his brother. Following this explanation, the matter was referred to the Committee on Petitions.[54]

When the committee reported back three days later it recommended that his petition be granted. The group was "satisfied of the loyalty of the petitioner." So, rather than judging the petition on his merits—i.e., restoring Owens's rights because the killing was accidental—they viewed his pardon through the same lens as other restorations. He was a loyalist, not a rebel, and therefore his citizenship rights should be restored.[55]

By 1868 all the southern states under Reconstruction had drafted and approved constitutions that complied with federal mandates. These new constitutions followed the provisions of the Reconstruction Act, and therefore southern states disfranchised only for felonies.[56] For example, Alabama's 1868 constitution disfranchised for "treason, embezzlement of public funds, malfeasance in office, crime punishable by law with imprisonment in the penitentiary, or bribery."[57] This list of serious crimes met the Reconstruction Act standard of "felony"—generally understood to be synonymous with penitentiary crimes. Virginia's 1868 "Underwood Constitution" followed the federal directive even more closely, denying the vote to "persons convicted of bribery in any election, embezzlement of public funds, treason, or felony."[58]

Some Republicans in Congress were apparently still wary that Democrats in southern states would find their way around the restrictions on disfranchisement for crime contained in the Reconstruction Act, as they had tried to do in 1867. They persuaded Congress to further limit the ability of southern political leaders to disfranchise for crime in the Readmission Acts passed in 1868 and 1870. These acts reiterated the language of the Reconstruction Act, noting that these states could never amend their constitutions to disfranchise for any crime except felonies. But they took the added precaution of specifying that disfranchisement for felonies could apply only to individuals who "have been duly convicted, under laws equally applicable to all the inhabitants of said State."[59] This revision echoed the language of the Thirteenth Amendment that similarly required due conviction of a crime as the sole condition for slavery or involuntary servitude.[60] It also indicated an abandonment of Republican efforts to disfranchise white southern Confederates with accusations of disfranchising criminal acts— or at least a sense that protecting the voting rights of African Americans had higher priority than eroding the suffrage of former Confederates. The language of the Readmission Acts signaled a concern with the judicial process in southern states and indicated a fear that African Americans might be unfairly convicted of crimes in an effort to disfranchise them. Some in Congress remained concerned that white southerners would continue to try to manipulate these laws, aided by a judicial system with partisan and racial bias, to disfranchise African Americans. But they failed to convince their colleagues that the threat was sufficient to include such restrictions in the Fifteenth Amendment.[61]

In 1869 Congress acted to protect voting rights across the nation through the Fifteenth Amendment. In the course of the debate over the proposed amendment, some in Congress pushed to give the limits on disfranchisement for crime in the Reconstruction and Readmission Acts the force and scope of a constitutional mandate. Several men in the House of Representatives sought to limit disfranchisement under the Fifteenth Amendment to serious offenses. While much of the congressional debate over the amendment centered on the voting rights of former Confederates, some remained concerned abut the issue of disfranchisement for crime, and they proposed language that would have limited the ability of states to do this. These proposals, if passed, would have applied the standards established in the Reconstruction and Readmission Acts to the whole nation. Ohio Republican John A. Bingham proposed an amendment that would have allowed disfranchisement for crimes only if the individual was "duly convicted" and would have limited disfranchising crimes to treason or other infamous crimes.[62] Ohio Republican Samuel Shellabarger offered a plan that restricted criminal disfranchisement to "those duly convicted of treason, felony, or other infamous crime."[63] Neither of these passed the House. If they had become law, they would have limited the power of states across the nation considerably—superseding the Fourteenth Amendment's

language allowing disfranchisement for "any crime," by adding the requirement of "duly convicted" and permitting states to disfranchise for felonies
and/or infamous crimes only.

A similar process played out in the Senate. Republican Willard Warner,
a native Ohioan and Union officer who served as a senator from Alabama,
proposed an amendment that limited disfranchisement for crime to treason, felony, or other infamous crime.[64] South Carolina Republican Frederick
A. Sawyer suggested omitting "felony" from the list, as did Tennessee
Republican Joseph S. Fowler who created a list that matched Bingham's
in the House.[65] None of these plans passed. Congress rejected all efforts to
restrict the crimes for which states across the nation could disfranchise,
thereby affirming the right of states to disfranchise for any crimes they
chose.[66]

Shortly before the final congressional vote on the Fifteenth Amendment,
Wisconsin Republican James R. Doolittle put forward a provision that
read, "Nor shall any citizen be denied by reason of any alleged crime unless
duly convicted thereof according to law." Doolittle opposed black suffrage
and Chinese suffrage and sought to maximize white access to the vote since
African Americans suffrage now seemed to be guaranteed. He hoped this
provision would protect the voting rights of former rebels by putting a stop
to test oaths and bills of attainder. This amendment would have allowed
disfranchisement for any crime, including petty crimes, but the requirement of a criminal conviction would have limited disfranchisement of former rebels to those who were not convicted of any actual crime. The Senate
voted it down.[67]

With the exception of Doolittle's plan, the proposals in the House
and Senate were authored by Republicans who sought to expand African
American suffrage and protect voters from what they viewed to be unjust
disfranchisement techniques. These congressmen were dedicated supporters of African American voting rights and were deeply engaged with the
politics of Reconstruction. Though African American voters in the South
received protection from disfranchisement for petty crimes with the
Reconstruction and Readmission Acts, proposals to restrict the extent of
disfranchisement for crime under the Fifteenth Amendment would have
given such protections more authority and permanence, and they would
have made these limitations on disfranchisement for crime national
in scope.

Between 1866 and 1870 Congress had several opportunities to limit
the ability of states to disfranchise for crime. They chose to confine these
restrictions to southern states, voting down language in the Fifteenth
Amendment that would restrict the ability of non-southern states to

disfranchise for criminal convictions. The outright refusal of Congress to include any restrictions on disfranchisement for crime in the Fifteenth Amendment indicates that the congressional majority was perfectly willing to allow non-southern states to disfranchise for crimes large and small, including petty theft, if they so chose. Members of Congress may have been unaware of this possibility in 1867 when Section Two was drafted, as some scholars have suggested, but a year later the implications of Section Two had become clear. Of course Congress could not have known in 1868 and 1869, when the Fifteenth Amendment was being debated, that the Reconstruction and Readmission Acts would soon have no authority. But the Reconstruction and Readmission Acts applied only to a limited number of states. Yet Congress knowingly and intentionally gave broad leeway in the Fifteenth Amendment for states to disfranchise for criminal acts.

Congress's failure to include a provision in the Fifteenth Amendment limiting disfranchisement for crime nationwide bolsters the case of scholars who have argued that Congress hoped to minimize federal intrusions on the state regulation of the franchise in non-southern states. Qualms about encroaching on the authority of states (particularly those outside the South) to define standards for suffrage, coupled with a general support for disfranchising for criminal conviction, led to the failure of such efforts. Many states across the nation disfranchised individuals for the conviction of certain crimes, and members of Congress would have been understandably reluctant to invalidate this aspect of suffrage requirements in states across the nation; there was simply no constituency for such a change beyond a handful of congressional Republicans concerned about the potential racial implications of these statutes in the South. Those who were so committed to the belief that incarceration might bring rehabilitation of convicts, and who therefore were opposed to lifelong civil punishments for formerly incarcerated individuals, never had a solid majority except in a handful of New England states and were certainly the minority in Congress in this period. Support for punishing convicts with disfranchisement even seemed to be on the rise outside the South. Legislators in New York, for example, began to consider ways to use laws disfranchising for crime to limit the black electorate in this period. In 1872 the state of New York extended equal suffrage rights to African Americans as required under the newly passed Fifteenth Amendment. But that same legislative session made disfranchisement for the conviction of bribery, larceny, or infamous crimes a statewide requirement, not a county option. Erika Wood and Liz Budnitz's study of disfranchisement in New York argues that the New York law was part of a pattern "of circumventing the Reconstruction Amendments and suppressing black voters."[68]

Opposition to polygamy in Utah may also have motivated those who rejected proposals limiting disfranchisement to serious offenses and requiring due process for disfranchisement in the Fifteenth Amendment. At the same time that Congress was debating the proposed Fifteenth Amendment, an effort was underway to limit the political rights of polygamous Mormons in the western territories. Motivated by religious prejudice and competition for political power in the new western states, many non-Mormons worked to prevent the growing Mormon populations in the West from gaining influence over state governments and getting a foothold in national politics. This effort produced the Cullom Bill of 1870, which would have used test oaths to impose civil disabilities, including disfranchisement, on polygamists. The Cullom Bill failed to become law but a decade later similar restrictions on the citizenship rights of polygamists were passed in the Edmunds Act of 1882, which disfranchised any individual convicted of polygamy.[69] Opponents of Mormonism and polygamy in Congress may have hoped to protect these options for disciplining polygamists and politically marginalizing Mormons by opposing restrictions on disfranchisement for criminal convictions.

In this critical period when black southerners gained U.S. citizenship and secured their voting rights, white southern political leaders pushed back, hoping to deny this population both citizenship and political power by designating all or many of them infamous. Before a single African American voted in the post–Civil War South, they faced disfranchisement through the manipulation of laws disfranchising for crime. The events in North Carolina referenced at the beginning of this chapter indicate that this strategy was connected to the simultaneous emergence of political violence. Whipping to "disqualify in advance" in North Carolina was a sign of things to come. Instances of using violence for racial and partisan objectives would accelerate throughout the period of Reconstruction and Redemption, most dramatically with the emergence of the Ku Klux Klan.[70]

The 1867 election exposed a gap in the suffrage protections offered by the Fourteenth Amendment that allowed laws disfranchising for crime to be manipulated so as to target particular individuals or groups. But, although congressional Republicans sought to protect African American voters in the South, racial and partisan agendas beyond the region, combined with a more general desire to limit federal authority over states, stalled efforts to restrict the scope of disfranchisement for crime in the Fifteenth Amendment. In short, the nation did not learn the lessons about the limitations of the Fourteenth Amendment that it might have from the whipping campaign in North Carolina in 1866 and the events that followed during the election of 1867.

In the South, access to the ballot by African Americans would continue to erode. Congress backed off protection for African American suffrage in the 1870s, and then the Supreme Court further undermined the enforcement of suffrage protections in *United States vs. Reese* and *United States vs. Cruikshank.*[71] In the next four years, white southern opponents of African American suffrage would capitalize on the fragility of federal suffrage protections and revise laws disfranchising for crime in ways that violated the Reconstruction and Readmission Acts as part of their attack on black suffrage in the South. As federal authority in the South waned in the 1870s, violence and allegations of criminality would continue to serve as impediments to voting by African Americans.

CHAPTER 3

✧

"A Chicken-Stealer Shall Lose His Vote"

In 1880 in Ocala, Florida, an African American man named Cuffie Washington tried to vote in the congressional election. When he entered the polling station, Democrats challenged his right to vote because, they said, he had stolen three oranges. Washington conceded that he had been convicted of such a crime about a month before the election. Such charges, he said, had become more frequent "because the election was close on hand."[1] Like Washington, several other African American men in Ocala and Marion County were disfranchised that day for having stolen a gold button, a case of oranges, hogs, oats, six fish (worth twelve cents), and a cowhide. Allen Green, one of the alleged hog thieves confirmed Washington's analysis, agreeing that petit larceny charges had increased prior to the election: "It was a pretty general thing to convict colored men in that precinct just before an election; they had more cases about election time than at any other time."[2]

For white Democrats seeking to regain political power in the South after Reconstruction, these events in Florida demonstrated the success of a new scheme to disfranchise African Americans: denying the vote to individuals convicted of minor criminal acts. Between 1874 and 1882 a number of southern states amended their constitutions and revised their laws to disfranchise for petty theft as part of a larger effort to disfranchise African American voters and to restore the Democratic Party to political dominance in the region. These new laws enabled Democrats to prohibit Republicans from voting in some of the most tightly contested elections of this period, expanding the number of African American men who were infamous and disfranchised.

Cuffie Washington's experience was shared by others across the South. On the eve of the same election day in Marengo County, Alabama, a white

Democratic Party worker named Ed Williams and an African American man named Silas Green had a heated conversation about whether Green would be allowed to vote. As several of Green's friends looked on, Williams read Green the section of the Alabama constitution disfranchising for crime and reminded Green that he had previously been arrested and that, consequently, he could not vote. Green argued back, denying that he had never been convicted and insisting on his right to vote. He told Williams that "it was just a charge they made up" and that he had been acquitted in court. Despite his protestations of innocence, Green did not attempt to cast a ballot the following day.[3]

Two years later in Staunton, Virginia, an African American man named James McGuffin entered the courthouse to vote in an election there. Before he could cast a ballot, a white Democrat who was observing the proceedings stepped in to challenge him, saying McGuffin had been convicted of petit larceny the previous year and was thus ineligible to vote. McGuffin denied it. The judge allowed McGuffin to vote, but as soon as he cast his ballot a police officer arrested him for illegal voting.[4] Richard Harris, an illiterate African American man, also tried to vote that day in Gloucester County, Virginia. At the polls, a precinct judge asked Harris if he had ever been convicted of petit larceny. When Harris replied in the affirmative, the judge refused to let him vote. Later, in a deposition submitted for a congressional investigation, the Gloucester County court clerk testified that there was no record of Harris's conviction for any kind of larceny. He had been indicted for felonious assault, but the charges were dropped before the case went to trial.[5]

During the 1870s, in light of diminishing federal willingness to enforce the post-war civil rights amendments and legislative provisions protecting African Americans in the South, increasingly emboldened southern Democrats sought to regain political dominance. Extralegal efforts such as violence and fraud were the predominant techniques used by Democrats to deter Republican voters and diminish the party's strength in the 1870s. African Americans, who voted disproportionately for the Republican Party, were the Democrats' primary targets.[6] But with Reconstruction essentially over, southern Democrats also began making small statutory and constitutional changes that could be used to erode the electoral power of the Republican Party. Many states gerrymandered districts to limit the electoral power of Republican voters. Georgia passed a cumulative poll tax.[7] And, as detailed below, every southern state under Reconstruction, except Texas, changed laws to deny the vote to individuals convicted of petty theft.[8]

Scholars studying laws disfranchising for crime have overlooked these changes to laws restricting the voting rights of those convicted of larceny made in the 1870s and instead highlighted constitutional revisions made across the South between 1890 and 1908. Political scientist Alec C. Ewald writes, "Mississippi's 1890 constitutional convention was the first to take aim at those alleged 'peculiar characteristics'"—in other words, the propensity of African Americans to commit certain crimes.[9] But these laws were preceded by an effort in the 1870s to diminish the African American vote by disfranchising for minor property crimes.

The scholarly focus on the constitutional changes made after 1890 has led to an underestimation of the impact that earlier laws disfranchising for criminal conviction had on African American voters and southern elections. Historians who have noted the existence of laws disfranchising for petty theft in a few states in the 1870s have failed to identify them as part of a larger regional pattern unique to this decade. There also has been an underestimation of their impact on elections. Historian J. Morgan Kousser has written that the effect of laws disfranchising for crime is "unclear, since many were apparently adopted primarily as insurance if courts stuck down more blatantly unconstitutional clauses." Although Kousser offers some evidence that Virginia's law disfranchising for petty larceny reduced the black vote in that state, he observes that such "insurance" was rarely needed because alternative approaches were so effective in restricting the electorate.[10] Indeed, laws disfranchising for crime had little partisan impact after 1890 because Democratic dominance in that era was safeguarded by literacy tests, poll taxes, and white primaries. While convicted individuals were still denied the vote, African American disfranchisement was so extensive and Democratic rule so complete that disfranchising these individuals contributed little to the larger racial and partisan agenda.

But a previous generation of measures disfranchising for larceny conviction passed in the 1870s did contribute to an effort by Democrats to reestablish their authority in the South. These measures targeted African American voters and thereby deprived the Republican Party of electoral support. While Democrats had an interest in disfranchising Republicans of both races, historical evidence about the impact of these laws indicates that they were aimed primarily at African Americans.[11] In addition to correcting the historical understanding of disfranchisement techniques used in the 1870s and 1880s, chronicling the effort to disfranchise for petty theft and exploring the opposition these initiatives generated offer a view on how ideas about criminality shaped the construction of American citizenship in this critical period. Historical studies of voting rights have found resistance to other forms of disfranchisement throughout this period, but until the late twentieth century few voices appear in the historical narrative advocating the political rights of convicted individuals. Just as rare

are historical accounts of convicted individuals who asserted their political rights. In the 1870s and 1880s, however, measures disfranchising for property crimes generated a great deal of protest, opposition, and controversy. Republican leaders in this period identified a partisan agenda at work in these new laws and worked to stop their passage and to protest their implementation for partisan and racial ends.

The expansion of disfranchisement in the 1870s and 1880s to include minor property crimes took a number of forms. Some southern states changed their laws to upgrade misdemeanor property crimes to felonies; felonies were already disfranchising offenses in most of these states. Several states amended or revised their constitutions to expand disfranchisement to include larceny and/or petit larceny. South Carolina, a state with no provision disfranchising for crimes, amended its constitution to establish this penalty for the first time. North Carolina added disfranchisement for crime to its constitution for the first time, codifying what had likely been a long practice. Finally, southern courts interpreted existing laws to include misdemeanor-grade offenses as disfranchising crimes. The path that each state followed varied and involved a complex mix of legal changes. But ultimately this combination of statutory revision, constitutional amendment, and judicial action forms a region wide pattern of expanded punishment for petty theft that was identified at the time as intended to disfranchise African Americans.[12]

The previous chapter noted that Florida's 1868 constitution was the first to disfranchise for larceny, well in advance of other southern states. The 1868 constitutional convention in Florida differed from other states because splits in the convention gave conservatives a good deal more power there.[13] The Florida convention was a harbinger of changes Democrats would make in state after state in the South as they regained political power.

Between 1874 and 1876 four southern states significantly expanded the definition of felony to include property offenses previously defined by statute as misdemeanors. In three of these four states, conviction under these new laws also brought disfranchisement; the fourth added this penalty two years later. Mississippi's 1876 "Pig Law" is perhaps the best known of these. Before 1876, Mississippi law had defined grand larceny (a felony) as the theft of anything valued at more than twenty-five dollars. The Pig Law expanded the definition of grand larceny by reducing to ten dollars the value of stolen goods needed to trigger this felony-grade offense. In addition, the new law defined the theft of certain livestock as grand larceny, even if the property was worth less than ten dollars. The law covered "any hog, pig, shoat, cow, calf, yearling, steer, bull, sheep, lamb, goat, or kid of the value of one dollar or more".[14] Grand larceny was a felony, and

conviction resulted in a sentence to the state prison; the Mississippi constitution disfranchised for "infamous" offenses, a somewhat ambiguous and
evolving term, though one that had come to include most felonies, including larceny.[15]

Alabama leaders acted to change both the statutes and the constitution
in 1875 to permanently disfranchise those convicted of any one of a list
of petty agricultural thefts. In February, Democrats introduced changes to
the penal code that expanded the number of crimes punishable by imprisonment in the penitentiary, that is, felonies. The 1868 state constitution
had denied the vote to individuals convicted of crimes punishable by law
with imprisonment in the penitentiary.[16] The 1875 statutory change rede-
fined several small crimes, previously classified by statute as misdemeanors, as grand larceny. Although horses had formerly been the only livestock
whose theft was a felony offense, the new law added other livestock and
certain crops to the list. Theft of a "cow, or animal of the cow kind, hog,
sheep, goat, or any part of any outstanding crop of corn or cotton" was
now grand larceny—punishable by from two to five years of prison time.[17]
Furthermore, the legislature expanded the definition of burglary (a felony)
to go beyond entering buildings to include breaking into any "structure or
inclosure" near a dwelling.[18] A conviction for any of these newly designated
felonies brought prison time and thus disfranchisement. Later that year,
when the state assembled a constitutional convention, delegates added
"larceny" to the list of disfranchising offenses. At the time, the amendment
was redundant since any felony conviction already led to disfranchisement
in Alabama, but the utility of this change would soon be clear.[19]

Arkansas also expanded the penalties for small larcenies to make more
thefts felony offenses. The 1874–1875 session of the Arkansas legislature
defined theft of items worth over two dollars as grand larceny. These crimes
could now be punished by imprisonment in the penitentiary.[20] The 1868
Arkansas constitution had previously disfranchised individuals convicted
of crimes punishable by imprisonment in the penitentiary, so now the theft
of anything worth more than two dollars meant disfranchisement.[21] In
1881 the Arkansas legislature backed off somewhat, raising the minimum
for grand larceny to ten dollars, so crimes against property of less than that
value were no longer felonies and thus not disfranchising offenses.[22] But at
the next legislative session Arkansas legislators made theft of a cow, of any
value, grand larceny.[23]

Georgia followed a similar approach. Georgia's 1868 constitution disfranchised for treason, embezzlement of public funds, malfeasance in
office, crime punishable by law with imprisonment in the penitentiary, or
bribery.[24] In 1875 the Georgia legislature passed a law making hog-stealing

a felony rather than a misdemeanor. Hog-stealing was now punished the same as cattle-stealing, and both were now disfranchising offenses.[25] Two years later Georgia's so-called Redeemer constitution of 1877, best known for its new, cumulative poll tax, added larceny to the list, as well as "any crime involving moral turpitude."[26] Now theft of any agricultural product, not just cattle and hogs, was a disfranchising offense.[27]

Most historical scholarship on these laws expanding punishment for petty theft have focused on their implications for controlling agricultural labor and property.[28] Landowners were concerned about petty theft not only because of the losses they incurred but also because agricultural theft gave landless laborers independence. Individuals who could survive on their own did not need to depend on their employers for income and food. Laws allowing for prosecution for petty theft gave landlords more power over tenants or sharecroppers who, without the landowners' permission, tried to consume some of the crops they grew.[29]

Studies of Mississippi's Pig Law—the statute that has received the most scholarly attention of this group—have found its most significant impact to be the expansion of the convict lease system. Vernon Lane Wharton wrote in 1947 that the Pig Law "made of the convict lease system a big business enterprise" by generating a large number of prisoners to be leased to employers.[30] Wharton's analysis has been cited favorably in a number of other discussions of the Pig Law, but none of these accounts consider its impact on voting rights.[31] Matthew J. Mancini has challenged Wharton's interpretation by claiming that the rise and fall of prison populations in Mississippi does not fit the chronology Wharton identifies. Mancini does agree that the Pig Law contributed to an increase in the number of convicts available to be leased out.[32]

In addition to reining in labor and fueling the convict lease system, the Pig Law and other similar statutes offered southern Democrats political benefits. Highlighting the problem of theft during the period of Republican rule was a way of demonstrating the failure of Republican governments to maintain law and order. And the Pig Law might also help Democrats' efforts to secure the allegiance of lower-class whites. Livestock theft was a threat to small landholders because families depended on these animals as a source of protein, and Democrats hoped that these laws would be seen as offering a protection for this class. The *Copiahan* newspaper, published in Hazlehurst, Mississippi, helped spin the Pig Law in this manner, suggesting the new legislation would help "the poorer class whose property consist[ed] principally of stock of the kind referred to."[33] Finally, an interest in expanding the pool of prisoners available to be leased out may indeed have been a factor that motivated some of the support for these laws.

However, when viewed in a larger regional context and in connection with related measures, it becomes clear that one of the intended functions of the Pig Law and its ilk was to increase the number of disfranchised African Americans. Making statutory changes to reclassify petty thefts was the first step in the expansion of criminal disfranchisement laws for a combination of reasons. First, these state constitutions lacked provisions allowing disfranchisement for larceny, but they did permit disfranchisement for felonies or penitentiary offenses. Thus, by increasing the number of larcenies that were felonies, states increased the number of disfranchising offenses without changing the constitution. This change offered immediate electoral advantages because statutory changes could be made much more quickly than constitutional changes. A second reason to classify small thefts as felonies was to avoid the restrictions on disfranchisement set out in the Reconstruction Act and Readmission Acts. While federal authority in the South was waning at this point, it was not yet clear that states could basically disregard federal mandates. Congress had restricted southern disfranchisement to felonies, so these states reclassified crimes that had previously been misdemeanors to make them felony offenses. They could now expand the number of individuals disfranchised for crime without violating congressional orders. And these legal changes would receive less congressional scrutiny, since the Readmission Acts put clear restrictions on constitutions but had less authority over statutes.[34]

While legislative intent and the difference between intent and impact are often difficult to discern precisely, Republican leaders at the time believed that lowering the bar at which point larceny became a felony was motivated by disfranchisement. Different legislators might have had diverse reasons for supporting the changes, but Republicans immediately condemned these revisions in penalties for larceny as an effort to limit suffrage.[35] When the bill creating the Pig Law first passed the Mississippi legislature in 1876, Governor Adelbert Ames, a Republican, vetoed it. In his accompanying message he explained the reasons for his veto: "Should this bill become a law, persons convicted of stealing any animal therein mentioned, of not more than one or two dollars in value, may be sent to the Penitentiary, perhaps for a term of years. Even if sent for a short time, the person so sentenced is disfranchised."[36] At this time, relations between Ames and the legislature were extremely tense; his lieutenant governor was facing impeachment, and Democrats had plans to impeach Ames as well.[37] The state senate tried to pass the bill over Ames's veto but failed to get enough votes to override.[38] About three weeks after Ames left office, the legislature passed the bill again, and the new governor, Democrat John Stone, signed it.[39]

In Alabama, Republicans also believed that classifying misdemeanor thefts as felonies was politically motivated. In 1875, a group of Republican legislators from Alabama petitioned the U.S. Congress, protesting the pending legislation expanding grand larceny. They told Congress that they had discovered the "ulterior purposes" of the increased penalties for petty theft. According to the legislators, these new laws offered white Democrats a means to "persecute and oppress" African Americans by making small crimes punishable by incarceration and disfranchisement. The petitioners believed that the political ascendancy that the Democrats had just obtained through violence and fraud would be secured by this expansion of criminal penalties. Convictions for petty crimes, including charges with little or no evidence to back them, could result in a lifetime of disfranchisement. Not only were more convicted individuals excluded from citizenship, but also convictions could easily be secured against African Americans who sought to vote or challenged white authority in any way. The petitioner charged that "Whenever the colored man is indisposed to submit to the dictation of this class, or seeks to exercise his rights as a citizen and voter in an independent manner, these men will be apt to trump up some charge against him, and, with ignorant or corrupt magistrates, can hurry him off to jail."[40]

The expansion of criminal penalties for livestock theft was only part of a coordinated regional agenda that used disfranchisement for criminal conviction to aid the Democratic Party as it sought political dominance in the South. Several southern states also passed new constitutions (or amended existing constitutions) to allow for or expand disfranchisement for larceny. Meanwhile, the chorus of voices warning that these changes were motivated by race and partisanship grew louder.

At the 1874–1875 session of the Virginia General Assembly, conservative legislators pushed through a proposed constitutional amendment that restricted access to voting in a number of ways. In addition to a new poll tax (which Readjusters would abolish in 1882), the assembly proposed disfranchising individuals who had been convicted of petit larceny.[41] Virginia citizens ratified these constitutional amendments in an election the following year.[42] Among the most prominent and outspoken critics of these new provisions was Elizabeth Van Lew. Van Lew was a white woman who served as a Union spy in Civil War Richmond; after the war she was a fearless advocate for African American civil rights and Republican Party activist. Van Lew spoke out against disfranchising individuals convicted of petit larceny on the eve of the 1876 vote on the amendments. She pointed out that disfranchising African Americans for petty crimes strengthened the Democratic Party by eliminating Republican voters. She also pointed out that not only were African American Republicans more likely to commit acts of theft out of desperation and hunger, but also partisan police and judges were more likely to convict them. Judges were biased, and many individuals were willing to testify falsely against Republicans, black and white, for partisan gain.[43] The Democratic Richmond *Daily Dispatch* responded by describing Van Lew's comments as "denouncing the people of this city."[44]

North Carolina amended its 1868 constitution in 1875 to specify which crimes brought criminal conviction.[45] Prior to 1875 the state had followed the common law tradition. Courts conferred infamy judgments but neither the constitution nor statutes explicitly authorized this process.[46] After 1875, the constitution specified that individuals convicted of felonies and infamous offenses lost the right to vote. In 1877 the General Assembly increased its power over the judiciary. Local magistrates, formerly chosen at the local level, were thereafter to be chosen by the General Assembly.[47] The change in the composition of the judiciary, coupled with this enhanced judicial power and the expanded disfranchisement provision, added up to an increase in the number of Democratic judges able to deny the vote to individuals convicted of minor property crimes.[48] The *New York Times* wrote at the time that the "evident purpose" of these changes to the state's court system "is to prevent colored men and poor white men from exercising the right of suffrage."[49]

Between 1878 and 1882, three states moved to disfranchise for larceny directly, rather than subsuming larceny into felony or infamy standards. Louisiana's 1879 constitution revised the state's list of disfranchising crimes; among these changes was the addition of larceny to the list of offenses.[50] In Mississippi, the legislature headed off any confusion about whether larceny was an infamous offense by amending the code to disfranchise for conviction of grand larceny; grand larceny became a disfranchising offense in its own right and not dependent on an "infamous" designation.[51]

Finally, South Carolina moved from being one of the more liberal states with regard to convict voting to being in line with others in the region. South Carolina's 1868 constitution had been one of the South's most lenient toward the voting rights of convicted individuals, disfranchising only for treason, murder, robbery, and dueling.[52] In 1878 the General Assembly increased the punishment for animal theft. Thereafter, "any person found guilty of the larceny of any horse, mule, cow, hog or any other live stock, shall suffer imprisonment in the state penitentiary."[53] That change alone did not expand disfranchisement because South Carolina still did not disfranchise for felony or penitentiary offenses. But in 1882 the General Assembly passed a series of constitutional amendments aimed at restricting suffrage. In addition to creating the widely known "Eight Box Law" (so called because voters had up to eight ballots, each of which they had to deposit in the correct ballot box, a complicated process intended as an obstacle to participation by illiterate voters), the South Carolina legislature added burglary, larceny, perjury, forgery, and any infamous crime to the list of offenses for which one would be disfranchised if convicted.[54]

Building on this success in revising constitutions to disfranchise for larceny, increasingly emboldened southern Democrats sought to deny the vote to individuals convicted of misdemeanor thefts as well, while a handful of federal authorities tried to call attention to the problem and halt this trend. Under the requirements of Reconstruction, the provisions disfranchising for larceny had applied only to felonies, but southern Democrats had begun to disregard this restriction. Evidence that Democrats had been disfranchising for petit (misdemeanor) larceny in Alabama can be found as early as 1877. That year, during a congressional investigation into southern elections, Marengo County Democratic lawyer Henry Woolf testified before Congress that petit larceny did fall within the bounds of the disfranchisement statute. An incredulous (unidentified) senator asked for clarification: "For instance, if a man steals this pen...worth one cent, and is convicted of it, he is disqualified from voting under the constitution of Alabama?" Woolf reiterated his position and informed the committee that the law had been enforced that way in his county.[55]

In 1882 a federal election monitor in Alabama sought to force election officials to allow individuals convicted of misdemeanor larceny to vote, but his efforts backfired. The conflict began when Washington Anderson, an African American man who had been convicted of petit larceny, tried to vote in Mobile County. Local election officials turned him away, saying his conviction had disfranchised him. Two federal officials—the local U.S. attorney and a federal election supervisor—stepped in, telling Anderson that he should vote because his misdemeanor conviction did not disqualify him. Anderson returned to the polls, signed a sworn statement that he was qualified to vote, and cast his ballot. He was immediately arrested and soon tried and convicted for illegal voting. The court sentenced him to two years in the penitentiary. On appeal, the Alabama Supreme Court ruled that disfranchisement for petit larceny was permitted in the state. This settled the issue, to the delight of Alabama Democrats. Mobile, Alabama, attorney F. B. Clark wrote to Democratic governor Emmet O'Neal that the case "has been the instrument in settling a grave question of constitutional law which was tending to become an element of collision between the state and federal authorities."[56]

For Alabama Republicans, the decision in the *Anderson* case confirmed their suspicion that Democrats were moving to disfranchise for ever-smaller property offenses, even ones that were not felonies. The

Southwestern Christian Advocate, a biracial publication of the Methodist Episcopal Church, wrote, "The decision of the Supreme Court of Alabama in a test case confirms the opinion that the framers of the new constitution intended to disqualify from voting those who have been convicted of even the smallest grades of petit larceny." The Mobile *Gazette,* an African American newspaper, wrote that the case proved that the constitutional provision disfranchising for larceny had been a "political trick to disfranchise poor men for committing petty offenses."[57]

Florida, like Alabama, moved to expand disfranchisement to include misdemeanor larcenies. At the time the state's 1868 document was drafted, disfranchisement for larceny applied only to felony larcenies, in accordance with federal requirements. In 1880 Florida governor George F. Drew asked state Attorney General George P. Raney to decide whether misdemeanor larcenies caused disfranchisement as well. Raney replied that in his opinion conviction for petit larceny should result in disfranchisement because, in his view, larceny could mean "larceny of any grade."[58] A year later, the Florida Supreme Court confirmed the attorney general's opinion in *State v. Buckman.* This case originated when a man named Richard Jordan was convicted of theft and fined ten cents plus court costs. When Jordan tried to vote, election officials refused to let him because of this prior conviction. The Florida Supreme Court held that the county had been correct in denying Jordan the right to vote, saying, "A conviction of petty larceny disqualifies a person from voting in this State."[59]

Georgia was the only southern state to place a limit on disfranchisement to crimes that specifically violated Georgia law. Some members of the 1877 convention had expressed concern that individuals living in Georgia might be disfranchised for crimes that were felonies in other states but not in Georgia.[60] The original proposal from the Committee on Elective Franchise at the constitutional convention had limited disfranchisement to individuals convicted of felonies by Georgia courts. Members of the convention expressed a variety of concerns about this limitation, and an intense, two-day debate over the matter ensued. A major issue was the possibility that individuals convicted in other states might come to Georgia to vote. Nathan Bass, from Floyd County, explained that this would "put the criminals of other states upon a better footing than our own." Realizing this, convicts would flock to Georgia to enjoy the right of suffrage. Bass warned, "If we adopt that section as it stands it will make of Georgia a Botany Bay for the scum and off-scourings of all the other states."[61] Robert Toombs, from Wilkes County and a leader of secession, argued back by explaining that the committee had restricted the provision to in-state convictions because what was a felony in one state might not be a felony in another.

The recent Civil War, he pointed out, had underscored the variations in state laws. Before the war southerners who went north to claim escaped slaves risked arrest. Staking a claim to one's own (slave) property might be considered a crime outside the South. Thus a man could lose his vote for conviction in an out-of-state court for an offense that was not even a crime in Georgia.[62] John M. Guerrard offered another defense of this provision by saying that since the United States did not punish individuals who committed treason against other countries, why should Georgia punish those who did so against other states?[63]

Other members expressed concern that under the committee recommendation, individuals convicted in federal courts would not lose their voting rights. Toombs replied that this was a reasonable distinction; disfranchisement was a "high act" and Georgia's courts alone should have the authority to disfranchise Georgia's citizens. Toombs concluded, "The right of disfranchisement should not depend upon the decrees of any foreign tribunal."[64] J. R. Brown, who represented Cherokee County, offered a more practical explanation for excluding federal crimes, saying that, "If it is extended to the United State courts, it will disfranchise about half the citizens of north Georgia who have been convicted in them of making illicit whisky."[65]

As a result of these debates Georgia's constitution specified that for the crime of treason to disfranchise, it must be treason "against the State." Furthermore, disfranchising crimes had to be "punishable by the laws of this State with imprisonment in the penitentiary."[66] This language was unique and not replicated in any other state in the region.

Once laws, constitutional provisions, and court decisions were in place that expanded disfranchisement to include petty property crimes, the impact on elections soon became obvious to black voters and their white Republican allies across the South. In 1880 the U.S. Senate held hearings to investigate the causes of African American migration from the South. One witness interviewed by the committee was Charles N. Otey, an African American attorney, originally from Raleigh but residing in Washington, D.C., where he edited the *Argus* newspaper.[67] Committee members asked Otey what grievances African Americans had with life in North Carolina that were causing them to leave the state. Among the complaints he reported was that African Americans were disfranchised for the conviction of petty crimes, including chicken theft: "Up North they do not send people to the penitentiary for petit larceny, but they do down there. I believe myself, as a Republican, that the law was made for the purpose of disfranchising colored men. If a colored man steals a chicken he is pretty liable to be sent to the penitentiary.... If they are sent to the penitentiary, unless they are pardoned out, it takes away their right to vote."[68]

Later in the hearing Senator Zebulon B. Vance of North Carolina disputed Otey's interpretation and tried to suggest that increased incarceration was actually due to the Republican Party's abolition of whipping, a punishment that had been ubiquitous under slavery. Because whipping was no longer permitted, more petty criminals faced prison time. Otey held his ground: "The law making a felony out of a petty crime was made by the Democratic party.... It was not always the law to put them into the penitentiary for stealing every little thing." Vance asked again if Otey really believed that disfranchisement was the goal of petit larceny convictions. Otey insisted that it was. Vance then suggested that the real reason might be the convict lease system. Might the law really be for "appropriating the avails of their labors, for very slight offenses"? Otey denied that this was the case. Otey remained firm in his conviction that minor larceny convictions were on the rise in order to deny black men the vote.[69]

After states expanded disfranchising offenses to include petty crimes, African American voters faced disfranchisement for alleged convictions at polling places across the South. Individuals of any race could be disfranchised for criminal conviction, but the historical evidence demonstrates that in close elections, Democrats stepped up the enforcement of these laws on African American voters in particular. Lower-class white voters may have also been affected by laws disfranchising for petty theft, as they would have been more likely to have been convicted of theft than would middle- and upper-class whites and since they were more likely than whites from upper classes to vote Republican; but there is little evidence of selective enforcement of these laws against lower-class white voters.[70] Mississippi Republican James W. Lee spoke to this issue directly when he pointed out, on the one hand, that he knew "a number of white men, who had before been sent to the penitentiary, and who did register and vote." On the other hand, "quite a number" of African American men convicted of small offenses were denied the franchise.[71]

Democratic election officials, however, might look the other way and let a convicted African American man vote if he supported their party. Silas Green, the Alabama man whose argument over voting rights was chronicled earlier, claimed to have voted in the past without any trouble. Democrats had allowed Green to vote previously because he supported the Democratic Party. Because Green had changed his party affiliation prior to the 1880 election, Democratic officials threatened to use the law to stop him from voting for a Republican candidate.[72]

Laws disfranchising for conviction of a crime were particularly effective because they offered Democrats a flexible way to manipulate the vote when a close race was at hand. In this period, Democratic rule was ascendant but not absolute. When the outcome of a race could turn on a small number of votes, these laws provided Democrats a way to gain political advantage from their control over police, election officials, and the judiciary at the local level. Before a close election, Democratic election officials publicized their intention to crack down on black Republican voters with prior convictions. Party leaders also worked with local police and judges to increase arrests and convictions for disfranchising offenses. On election day partisan challengers accused African American voters of having criminal pasts, election officials upheld these accusations, and cooperative police arrested and jailed individuals who insisted on casting their ballots, charging them with "illegal voting." The value of such arrests extended beyond preventing that individual from voting, as the threat of arrest likely made some reluctant to even attempt to vote, particularly those unsure of the details of the law. Other disfranchisement techniques were deployed in these years as well, but disfranchisement for petty theft conviction factored into the experiences of voter after voter in state after state. Black voters who witnessed or experienced such disfranchisement were convinced of the partisan agenda of these laws. White Republicans, too, saw a partisan scheme afoot.

A few surviving documents confirm that laws disfranchising for larceny were enforced with partisan and racial impacts in mind. Two examples come from North Carolina, where printed lists of convicted, disfranchised voters from Iredell County in 1888 and Granville County in 1892, housed in the North Carolina Collection at the University of North Carolina, show that the bulk of voters disfranchised in those two counties were disfranchised for larceny and were African American.[73] In Iredell, of the 122 disqualified voters listed, 114 were identified as "colored." As for the crimes committed by these 122 men, all but 10 were convicted of larceny. Iredell County's list does not indicate race. However, in this county, too, larceny was the predominant reason for disfranchisement. Of 175 voters listed, 145 were convicted of larceny.[74]

Another list of disfranchised voters is held at the Special Collections Library at the University of Virginia. Titled "Official Lists of Dead, Lunatic, and Convicted Colored Males who are thereby Disfranchised," the volume lists African American men convicted in Richmond's Hustings Court (the term used to describe municipal courts in Virginia) between 1870 and 1892; those who had died in the city between 1886 and 1889; those who died at or were confined at the Central Lunatic Asylum at Petersburg or the Pinel Hospital in Henrico County; and those convicted of petit larceny at the Richmond Police Court between 1877 and 1892. Two things are notable about these documents. First, they list only African American men. Anyone compiling lists of convicted voters would have had no reason to omit white voters from such a list unless it was intended to solely target African American voters. A list of *all* convicted voters would have been more useful if election officials were truly interested in enforcing the law across the races. The fact that this volume, instead, lists only African American voters adds to the evidence that the enforcement of this law in Virginia during this period was aimed primarily at disfranchising African Americans. Also notable is the number of individuals listed. Over 2,100 names appear among the lists of convicts in the two courts. In a city with a total African American population of 32,330, two thousand disfranchised men represented a significant percentage of the population of voting-age men.[75]

Other evidence of the racial intent and partisan impact of these disfranchisement techniques comes from testimony before Congress, both general inquiries into election irregularities and investigations of specific contested elections. In eight contested elections held between 1876 and 1888 in three southern states, Congress heard testimony that included charges that the electoral outcome had been affected by improper enforcement of laws disfranchising for crime.[76] Congress also heard claims that voters were wrongly charged with having prior convictions and were therefore denied the vote, and a few claims that election officials failed to disfranchise convicted voters. Contestants presented allegations of wrongful disfranchisement for other reasons as well (enforcement of registration laws was particularly at issue). Not all contested election hearings from southern races involved charges of improper criminal disfranchisement, but disfranchisement for crime was one of several common justifications for challenging election results. To be sure, those answering questions before Congress had an agenda—to expose techniques that they believed had wrongly affected electoral outcomes. But the vast amount of similar testimony, from many states, districts, and precincts, offers a convincing picture of the impact of these new laws on southern voters and southern elections.

Just as Florida Republicans reported a rise in convictions of African American men prior to elections, Republicans in South Carolina testified to similar experiences.[77] In the wake of the 1884 election, one South Carolina Republican reported that, "Negroes are frequently arraigned before petty magistrates on the most trivial charges of larceny, and a conviction in these petty courts is sufficient to disfranchise them forever. This conviction is readily obtained, and the whole proceedings clearly indicate, in many cases, that the prosecution is merely a pretext to deprive the negro of his vote."[78]

Individuals also risked losing the right to vote because of convictions that should not have brought about disfranchisement. James Lee, the

Mississippi man quoted previously, told Congress that African American voters had seen their registration blocked because of allegations of all kinds of criminal convictions. While he was serving as county sheriff, African American citizens "came to [him] constantly" charging their voter registration had been refused "because they had been convicted of petty larceny, of assault, or of assault and battery, or of a misdemeanor, or for actionable words, or malicious mischief—for anything whatever." He added that, "If they had ever been before a magistrate they were denied registration." Lee had complained to the chairman of the county election board and argued that convictions for these "small offenses" should not have curtailed voting rights. The official replied that these crimes were all considered infamous and insisted that he was correct in denying these individuals the right to vote. Lee retorted that many individuals were turned away from the polls for misdemeanor convictions that were not infamous crimes. The official told him the matter was not up for debate.[79]

Democrats were able to take advantage of the fact that the laws were complicated, making it difficult for illiterate and uneducated voters to understand the details of the regulations. In Selma, Alabama, in 1877, "the democrats went around...and told the colored men if they had ever been in jail for anything they could not vote."[80] Richard Harris, whose experience was recounted at the beginning of this chapter, seemed unsure of the meaning of the terms "larceny" and "felonious assault" and of the difference between an indictment and a conviction. His lack of knowledge and his uncertainty, combined perhaps with a fear of violent retaliation, kept him from asserting his rights.[81]

In the face of these challenges to their voting rights, some African American voters fought back. When A. Y. A. Wallace tried to vote in Lauderdale County, Alabama, a challenger stepped forward and accused him of having been convicted of larceny. Wallace, an African American schoolteacher, rejected the accusation and insisted on casting his ballot. A stalemate ensued. After a short time, the judge allowed him to vote.[82] African American parents also defended the voting rights of their children. In New Hope, Virginia, in 1882, Dudley Thompson faced disfranchisement when a white police officer monitoring the election attested that Thompson had been convicted of petit larceny. Thompson's father, who had accompanied his son to the polls, protested, saying Dudley had indeed been convicted at one point but this had all occurred before his son was twenty-one years old. Based on his father's sworn statement, Thompson was allowed to vote.[83]

Republican Party officials also tried to help voters rebut charges of prior disfranchising convictions. In Lynchburg, Virginia, in 1884, a Democratic precinct judge questioned a voter about a former assault charge: "Are you the same man that was arrested for an assault in Liberty when Robinson's circus was there?" When the voter responded in the affirmative, the judge said that the conviction for assault deprived the man of the right to vote. But a Republican election monitor standing by insisted that assault was not a disfranchising offense. The judge relented, and the voter cast his ballot provisionally.[84]

While the impact of these laws on the experience of convicted individuals (and those accused of having prior convictions) was significant, even more dramatic was the statutes' contribution to delays for large numbers of African American voters on election day. In a number of key races, Democrats interrogated African American voters at length about a variety of issues, including their criminal history. Democrats also checked the names of African American voters against long lists of convicts. Long, slow-moving lines frustrated some voters who did not have time to wait for hours, and many did not get to vote before precincts closed. These practices further eroded the Republican vote.

The best documented instance of criminal disfranchisement laws aiding these delaying tactics comes from a contest between Republican Edmund Waddill Jr. and Democrat George D. Wise, held on November 6, 1888, in Virginia. This election was to decide who would represent Virginia's Third District in Congress. Several Third District precincts were located in Jackson Ward, an area of Richmond with a large number of African American voters. When the votes were counted, the incumbent Wise seemed the winner by a 261-vote margin. But the Republican challenger, Waddill, asserted that 722 African American voters had been denied the opportunity to vote, including 557 African American voters who been waiting in line to vote when the precincts closed. If these predominantly Republican voters had been allowed to cast their ballots, Waddill claimed, he would have won the election.[85]

According to Waddill, Democratic Party workers serving as challengers in Jackson Ward had blocked African American votes by keeping voters waiting in line as long as possible. African Americans and whites voted in separate lines, so white voters proceeded efficiently through the polls while black voters stood in line for hours. Democratic challengers at the polls delayed the processing of individual black voters, challenging their eligibility and prompting the precinct judges to question voters extensively. They used accusations of prior convictions, as well as other issues, both to dissuade individual voters and to slow the electoral procedure so that many African American voters were unable to vote before the polls closed.[86]

Precinct judges in Jackson Ward had received lists, prior to the election, that contained the names of individuals convicted of felonies or petit larceny in Richmond in previous decades. Whenever a challenger asserted that a voter had a prior conviction, judges had to search the list for that voter's name. This took up quite a bit of time, as the list had about two thousand names on it:

> From the time the polls were opened until they closed at night nearly every colored voter was challenged. When they came to the polls to vote they would give their names, and if their name was found on the poll-book, and if the parties holding the poll-book would say it was all right, the challenger would say, "Hold on, judge. I challenge that vote." After looking over the disfranchised list they would say, "All right; go on." All this time the judge of election would be holding the ballot in his hands, and he never deposited any ballot until the challengers were satisfied.[87]

Eligible voters who had names similar to former convicts often found themselves denied the right to vote. In these cases, voters could sign a statement swearing that they had no prior convictions. Charles Robinson described his experience this way: "When I got up to the window Mr. [Preston] Belvin attacked me then, and said, 'Hold on; don't vote him yet,' just in that manner. He asked me, 'Chas., how old are you?' I told him I was going on 32 years old. He says, 'Have you ever been up before court; you ever been convicted of the penitentiary?' I said, 'No, sir,' and he said, 'I've got you down here disfranchised,' and I says, 'Oh, no, sir. Let me swear my name in then.'" After Robinson had signed a statement swearing that he had never been convicted, Belvin challenged the location of his residence.[88] In these kinds of challenges, voters would cite their residence at one address, but the Democratic challenger would then assert that the address was incorrect. Sometimes, precinct judges would send voters back to their homes to double-check their street address. Others were challenged on account of age; they were asked to demonstrate or swear that they were over twenty-one years old—even gray-haired men who had not been twenty-one for a long time. Some questions were entirely unrelated to eligibility to vote; officials asked black voters how many children they had, the names of their parents, and if they had ever left the country. Questions could be deliberately humiliating. One man testified that in "many cases I heard them ask them who was their master's name."[89]

A congressional committee launched an extensive investigation in to the election, interviewing hundreds of witnesses. The committee's report concluded that 722 legal voters had been prevented from casting their ballots through fraudulent means. As a result, Congress voted to declare Waddill victorious and seat him in the House of Representatives.

Republicans, black and white, identified the racial agenda at work in the expansion of larceny disfranchisement across the region and fought back against this expansion of disfranchisement in a variety of ways, most of which were unsuccessful. Governor Ames's 1875 veto of Mississippi's Pig Law delayed the legislation only a few weeks. Pleas that same year by Alabama Republicans for Congress to intervene brought no significant results. The 1884 Conference of the Leading Colored Men in Florida identified disfranchisement for petit larceny as a key concern at their annual meeting.[90] In Virginia, Republican political leaders tried to defeat the constitutional amendment disfranchising for petit larceny in the 1876 election. At the 1875 Colored State Convention in Richmond, delegates from across the state denounced the plan to disfranchise for petit larceny conviction as well as the proposed poll tax.[91]

White Republicans in Virginia explicitly warned that disfranchising for petit larceny was a means of targeting African American voters. Elizabeth Van Lew remarked in 1872 that there were two hundred African Americans in the state penitentiary who were incarcerated primarily because of their political affiliation. All these men would be barred from voting. She accused judges of being particularly biased against prominent African American political leaders.[92] Other Republicans echoed this argument, claiming that corrupt and partisan judges would disproportionately target Republican voters in an effort to disfranchise them.[93]

Democratic newspapers in Virginia tried to frame the opposition to disfranchisement for petit larceny as a defense of criminal behavior by the Republicans. An editorial in the Richmond *Daily Whig* observed, "As to the amendment disfranchising convicted thieves, we presume that those only in sympathy with this class can object to it."[94] Two days later the same newspaper suggested these disfranchisement measures might deter crime and save the state money: "Ever since the war the criminal expenses of the Commonwealth have been annually increasing because of this species of crime, which, during the winter season, furnishes to the criminals warm quarters and clothing in our overflowing jails. Adopt this amendment and the criminal expenses will be diminished from a third to half."[95]

Virginia Republicans suggested, in contrast, that these amendments would have negative economic consequences. The Alexandria *Sentinel* argued that both of the new disfranchising amendments to the constitution—the poll tax and the provision regarding petit larceny—would hurt poor citizens, black and white. Such regressive measures would also damage the reputation of the state and discourage immigration: "They will *most surely* cause Virginia to be shunned and avoided by the liberty-seeking exiles of the old world and the free citizens of the North, looking for locations for their homes and the investment of their capital and enterprise."[96]

Livestock theft and, more particularly, chicken theft became a key focus for individuals on both sides of the debate over the suffrage rights of individuals convicted of petty theft. The ability to vote was a key component of citizenship, and Democrats insisted that a propensity for theft demonstrated that African Americans were unfit to assume the rights and responsibilities of citizenship. But Democrats also appealed to a growing sense that continence and self-control were valuable qualities of citizens. A race with a propensity for theft lacked self-control and was unsuited for full citizenship in the nation; this logic helped rationalize efforts at disfranchisement.[97] Republicans, on the other hand, tried to counter the Democratic rhetoric of black criminality with their own analysis that defended the behavior and fitness for citizenship of individuals who committed petty thefts. For Republicans, livestock theft represented an act of survival by these new citizens of the nation.

African American leaders and their Republican allies emphasized the small and desperate nature of livestock theft and the disproportionality of the sanction of disfranchisement in their arguments against these new laws. Chicken theft figured prominently as a symbol of a minor, justifiable crime.[98] Speaking at the Colored State Convention meeting, Norfolk resident and former city council member Joseph T. Wilson raised the issue of chicken stealing before the assembled group. Denouncing the pending amendment disfranchising for petit larceny, he exclaimed, "And now they want to disfranchise a colored man because he takes a chicken when he is hungry."[99] Elizabeth Van Lew offered a similar view: "There is a proposition now before the people to amend the Constitution so that the theft of a chicken shall disqualify forever a man as a voter."[100] For Wilson and Van Lew, the idea that permanent disfranchisement would result from a relatively minor crime, such as chicken theft, was outrageous.

In rationalizing and excusing the theft of livestock to feed a hungry family, African American politicians were not only defending acts born out of hunger and the need for survival but also suggesting that such acts were proof of black men's qualification for citizenship, not evidence against it. In the nineteenth-century South, men were responsible for providing for their families. Indeed, bearing such responsibility was a component of masculine citizenship.[101] Individuals who stole animals to feed their families were acting as patriarchal heads of household. When Republicans defended African American men as providers, they were defending them as worthy citizens. Providers should not be stripped of the rights and responsibilities of citizenship; indeed, they should be granted them.

Challenging disfranchisement for larceny countered efforts to extend the penalties of infamy to African American convicts and rebutted the association of infamy with blackness. English common law had considered larceny an infamous crime, and so disfranchisement for larceny was built on long-standing legal traditions.[102] On the other hand, the imposition of the civil penalty of disfranchisement on those convicted of petit larceny was not a settled issue. The Florida court had to rule on the question in *State v. Buckman*, and the matter was debated in states outside the South as well.[103] Claiming chicken-stealers as citizens represented an assertion of their rights as individuals, but also an assertion that petty crimes committed in desperation might indeed be honorable, not evidence of degradation. African American leaders contested the assumption that convicted criminals should be denied political rights and resisted the expansion of infamy to include those who committed small acts of theft.

Democrats in turn made chicken theft into a racist joke. On its editorial page the Richmond *Daily Dispatch*, which had published a series of mocking reports on the Colored State Convention, responded to Wilson's comments: "A sapient member of the negro convention in this city is shocked at the idea that a chicken-stealer shall lose his vote." The editorial continued by ridiculing black morality: "Why should not sheep-stealing be also classed among the harmless pursuits that should in no wise affect a man's political rights? It is time that the wayward morality of other days should be squelched, and that gentlemen chicken- and sheep-stealers be looked upon as patriots determined not to die for the want of food."[104]

This tactic, of upping the ante from chicken stealing to sheep stealing, was echoed in an editorial in the same Richmond paper a year later, on the eve of the vote on the amendments. Commenting on a report of a chicken thief in Halifax, Virginia, the article asked, "What sort of claim to participation in the matter of governing the country has a 'chicken-thief'? It is an insult to the people entitled to vote that they should march up to the polls with chicken-thieves and sheep-stealers."[105] From this perspective, chicken thieves were individuals who were so poor that they were unable to provide their family with basic sustenance. Chicken thieves lacked economic citizenship and therefore were undeserving of political citizenship.

Stephen Kantrowitz has written that as African Americans moved to assume the responsibilities of masculine citizenship in this era—including the role of patriarchal head of household—"they were depicted sometimes as comical and ignorant."[106] This observation rings true, as white Democrats seized on the image of the African American chicken thief as a source of ridicule. Resorting to chicken thievery also suggested failed masculinity. An African American man who was unable to provide for his family and had to turn to theft was not really a man and thus not really a citizen. The idea of chicken thieves graduating to sheep stealing also suggested another racist stereotype that confirmed black unfitness for citizenship: a tendency to excess. A chicken might feed a desperate hungry family for a meal, but a sheep? A sheep was a luxury that would make several meals, and therefore sheep stealing further indicated black intemperance.

Chicken theft also represented a lack of self-control. An individual might see a chicken and instinctively grab it. White Democrats suggested that for African Americans, the temptation of chicken was too strong to resist. This proved to racist whites that African Americans were creatures of desire and emotion, not men of morals and restraint. Those privileged to vote and assume the full responsibilities of citizenship, including suffrage, should be controlled and rational, not impetuous. As a result, chicken theft became an important racial trope. In an article on Mississippi's Pig Law, the Greenville *Times* joked that the legislation would deprive Republicans of "fresh meat." But, according to the paper, one "omission" offered some hope: "Bless the Lord, they haven't said a word about Chickens!" The new law, the paper explained, still contained "some pervisions [*sic*]...for the colored people."[107]

In some instances, Republicans, sensing the irony of the situation, tried to fight back with humor as well. In Bullock County, Alabama, an African American man told of cautioning a farmer to move two turkeys that were sitting on a fence adjacent to a public road: "Jest by...telling 'em to drive them turkeys off that road, I saved two Republican votes."[108] Someone would have been blamed for the missing turkeys, and that individual would likely have been an African American Republican who would, consequently, lose his right to vote. This incident is also further evidence of the widespread belief that laws disfranchising for livestock theft were aimed at suppressing the black vote.

Beliefs about the reasons for petty livestock theft and the judgments drawn about criminal acts committed by African Americans were shifting in the post–Civil War period and continued to change through the end of the century. Many slaves had considered theft of the master's property an excusable act.[109] An English traveler who recorded his observations about his visit to the South explained how black southerners interpreted livestock theft in the slave era: "A slave used, it is said, to reason thus: 'I am my master's, so is this chicken. If I catch and eat the chicken I take nothing from my master.'"[110] For Booker T. Washington, theft by slaves was part of a noble effort to survive in dire circumstances. He wrote, "One of my earliest recollections is that of my mother cooking a chicken late at night, and awakening her children for the purpose of feeding them. How or where she got it I do not know. I presume, however, it was procured from our owner's farm. Some people may call this theft.... But taking place at the time it did, and for the reason that it did, no one could ever make me believe that my mother was guilty of thieving. She was simply a victim of the system of slavery."[111]

After the Civil War, competing voices argued over how to interpret a perceived rise in African American theft. In response to Democratic efforts to justify disfranchisement with stereotypes of black criminality, Republicans underscored the criminal behavior of middle-class and wealthy whites. Virginia state senator George Teamoh, an African American Republican who represented Norfolk County and Portsmouth and had been a member of the 1867–1868 constitutional convention, sounded this note in 1871 in his comments on the proposed amendment disfranchising for petit larceny: "The rich man never, or but rarely, steals on a small scale." Comparing minor black crimes with larger white crimes, Teamoh found wealthy whites to be far more depraved.[112] Similarly, the Mobile *Gazette* in its critique of the *Anderson* decision, which upheld disfranchisement for misdemeanor larceny, compared the disfranchisement that resulted from petty offenses with the crimes of the rich. While minor thefts were punished by imprisonment and disfranchisement, "a State treasurer who steals two or three hundred dollars from the treasury, manages to avoid arrest and escape punishment."[113]

The Richmond *Virginia Star*, an African American newspaper, used chicken theft to question Democrats' definition of criminality and its relationship to race and class. Arguing against disfranchisement for small crimes, the editorial board claimed that "The African robs hen roosts. What does the white man rob? Does he not rob banks, corporations, stores, widows and orphans, star routes, syndicates, and corners, and bulls and bears the markets?" In this formulation, white theft stemmed from greed, while African Americans stole because of injustices perpetrated against them. "In nine cases out of ten, the African robs a hen [roost] from necessity. He is paid such small wages, that he cannot procure enough of the necessities of life." Rich politicians also engaged in a form of theft, the theft of labor without fair compensation: "How many in that Congress are paying their servants what they should?"[114]

Other African American leaders offered similar comparisons of black and white crime. In the 1880 Senate hearings on black migration a witness commented on the relative criminality of African American and white individuals. John O. Kelly, a black business owner from Raleigh, discussed the treatment of the two races before the courts. Asked why African Americans were more likely to steal, Kelly replied that "[sic] negro men is better in some respects in that kind of doing than a white man; if he goes to steal he don't try to steal all you have got and the white man does."[115] Kelly sought not to defend black criminals, but to contextualize and reframe ideas about the criminality of the race.

Teamoh, Kelly, and other African American Republicans offered an expansive analysis of citizenship that endorsed the suffrage rights of those who committed small acts of theft. They challenged the idea that minor theft constituted an infamous crime and a disfranchising offense. This view was characteristic of African American political thought in the emancipation period, but a different perspective came to dominate by the end of the century. In the coming decades, fighting desperately to maintain even minimal political power, African American leaders would try another strategy. They challenged efforts to infame the whole race by separating members of the deserving middle class from the undeserving, potentially criminal masses.

Historian Kevin K. Gaines has argued that the "broader vision of uplift" in the Reconstruction period gave way to a "limited, conditional claim to equality, citizenship, and human rights," favored by African American leaders at the end of the nineteenth century.[116] In the late nineteenth century, elite African American leaders increasingly relied on a strategy of racial advancement that emphasized class distinctions within the black community. Facing diminishing political options, leaders sought to distinguish themselves from the poor black masses, thereby hoping to prove to the white gatekeepers of citizenship that some members of the race were qualified to vote because they had adopted bourgeois values. As part of this plan, greater emphasis was placed on proving that African Americans were capable of temperance, thrift, chastity, and civility.[117]

In contrast, those who defended the voting rights of chicken thieves defended a class of voters lacking bourgeois values and insisted on their honor and manhood. These activists recognized the poverty and difficulties the former slaves faced. Desperate people, committed to surviving and raising a family in a nearly impossible situation, might steal a chicken; this act should not, however, be a basis for denying them the fundamental rights of citizenship. African American leaders found support in the Republican Party for this unpopular position—defending the rights of convicted criminals has rarely been popular—because these new laws disfranchising for petty theft were passed and enforced in such overtly partisan ways.

The legal and cultural prominence given to the idea of African Americans as a thieving race in the 1870s and 1880s worked on another level to justify the larger scheme of racial disfranchisement. Black men who had not stolen chickens were still believed to have the propensity for theft and were therefore unworthy of the privileges of suffrage and full citizenship. The disparate treatment of African Americans before the law marked the whole race as infamous. Racially biased obstacles to suffrage, disparate treatment in the courts, and even statutory segregation measures validated the notion that blacks were not legally assigned the respect given to citizens. Those treated by the law as infamous did not, by tradition, deserve the privileges of citizenship. Consider the examples that began this chapter. If, in advance of an election, white political leaders charged African American men with minor thefts in a concerted effort to disfranchise them, African Americans were not equal citizens. A population that was degraded and humiliated by the courts and political system was not truly equal and not worthy of equal suffrage. Laws passed by white Democrats as part of a partisan agenda, coupled with biased enforcement and an unequal justice system, helped produce and maintain hierarchies of citizenship.

The story that unfolded in these two decades also demonstrates the shifting and interrelated definitions of infamy. Understandings of both *infamia juris* and *infamia facto* were at work in the post-Reconstruction South. White southerners sought to utilize the more anachronistic definition of infamy—infamy for committing an infamous crime—in order to target African Americans for disfranchisement. The commission of minor larcenies might not have resulted in prison time, and therefore might not have guaranteed that such convicts were infamous in law. However, because larceny was traditionally an infamous offense, those who committed it were infamous in fact. The two kinds of infamy might even be contradictory. If one committed a crime that was not infamous, such as murder, and was subjected to a degrading punishment, was one infamous or not? However, this kind of ambiguity served the white elites who held political power. White elites use multiple definitions of infamy to disfranchise those who they wanted to disfranchise and protect those they wished to protect. These multiple paths to infamy could degrade individuals and degrade a race.

By the mid-1880s nearly every southern state had expanded its laws disfranchising for crime to include a far greater array of minor property crimes. The two southern states that had no legislative or constitutional provisions allowing disfranchisement for crime in the past now had laws allowing them to do so. The legal changes made in this era remained on the books for decades to come, and they could be utilized for partisan gain far into the future. Experiences from the 1870s and 1880s demonstrate that partisan advantage can be obtained from laws disfranchising for crime, particularly when election officials with a partisan agenda exploit racially imbalanced rates of conviction and incarceration.

CHAPTER 4

cℕ℈

Furtive Offenses and Robust Crimes

The Mississippi Supreme Court's 1896 opinion in *Ratliff v. Beale* contains a remarkable explanation of the racial motivations behind the suffrage provisions in the state's 1890 constitution. *Ratliff v. Beale* originated when Hinds County sheriff William Thomas Ratliff seized some furniture from the house of an African American man named Ambus Beale because Beale failed to pay his poll tax. Beale challenged the action, saying in effect that the state had never meant to collect the tax from citizens who failed to voluntarily pay it since the tax was intended to be an impediment to suffrage. The court agreed that the tax was a "mere pretense" and "not to be enforced." Why, then, had the state established a tax that citizens were not required to pay? Because, when the constitution was drafted, Mississippi had been in great danger, under threat from "[g]rave and permeating forces for evil." Unstated but implied was that the "threat" was African American suffrage. Although the Fourteenth and Fifteenth Amendments tied the hands of white southern Democrats, members of the constitutional convention had found a way to limit the black vote. The Mississippi court explained in its opinion, "Within the field of permissible action under the limitations imposed by the Federal Constitution, the convention swept the circle of expedients to obstruct the exercise of the franchise by the negro race." These "expedients" involved a number of measures, including the poll tax. Ambus Beale was right. The authors of the suffrage provision had hoped that men like him would fail to pay the tax and be barred from voting.[1]

The genius of these racially motivated but constitutionally permitted measures, the court wrote, was that they omitted mention of race yet disfranchised for "the habits of temperament, and of character" of African

Americans. African Americans were often landless and supposedly care-
less, so the framers instituted a poll tax with very detailed requirements
that could easily be overlooked or confused. They were migratory (primarily because they were landless), so the constitution contained a residency
requirement. Finally, they were supposedly prone to crime—but only certain types of crime. According to the court, since members of the convention believed African Americans to be prone to "furtive offenses" rather
than the "robust crimes of whites," they chose to disfranchise for criminal
offenses that they believed to be characteristic of African Americans. The
court explained, "Burglary, theft, arson, and obtaining money under false
pretenses were declared to be disqualifications, while robbery and murder
and other crimes in which violence was the principal ingredient were not."[2]

The court's opinion in *Ratliff* suggested that the suffrage provision was
drafted with political expediency and African American disfranchisement
in mind. But in order to fully understand the Mississippi constitution and
the explanation offered in the *Ratliff* decision, both should be considered
in a historical context of race, criminality, and citizenship. Two questions
need to be answered. First, how did the court and the convention decide
which crimes were "robust" and which were "furtive and weak?" Second,
why did Mississippians (assuming the court's historical account of the
Mississippi convention is correct) associate "furtive" crimes with African
Americans and "robust" crimes with whites? African Americans are not
"furtive and weak." White people are not disproportionately prone to violence. Labeling murder and assault "robust" crimes is a statement of opinion, not of fact.[3] Failing to contextualize the categorization of these crimes
risks making them appear to be trans-historical facts.

In fact, the court that decided *Ratliff v. Beale* got its history backwards.
Those drafting the constitution's suffrage provision started with a framework that defined the moral implications of criminal acts, which they used
to justify the division of crimes into "black" and "white." The list of disfranchising crimes enumerated by the Mississippi constitutional convention was simply a list of infamous crimes. "Furtive crimes" was essentially
a synonym for infamous crimes under English common law. Crimes that
did not deprive suffrage in Mississippi's new constitution ("robust crimes")
were those not historically considered infamous. The convention members could easily persuade their constituencies that African Americans, a
population considered unworthy of suffrage, were mostly likely to commit
crimes that evidenced a lack of fitness for suffrage and that, conversely,
whites were more likely to commit the crimes that did not demonstrate
degradation of citizenship rights. White Mississippians would believe that
disfranchising for particular offenses offered a special way to limit the

voting population by race due to long-standing beliefs about the infamous crimes, not, as the court suggested, due to beliefs about African American criminal propensities.

Mississippi's was one of many states across the nation to revise its constitution in the 1890s, and this drive for constitutional revision was prompted by numerous circumstances. In the South, white political leaders sought to fully and permanently remove African Americans from the political equation in this period. Persistent efforts by blacks to vote had allowed them to remain a threat to white Democratic dominance, as their votes were potentially available to Republicans, Populists, rival Democratic factions, or other politically insurgent groups.[4] Nationally, a growing concern with immigrant suffrage and electoral corruption motivated political leaders in diverse states to seek ways to efficiently and legally turn African Americans and lower-class whites away from the ballot box.[5] In southern states, all this led to calls for constitutional revisions aimed at dramatically contracting access to the franchise. Among the modifications to suffrage provisions—in addition to literacy tests, poll taxes, and registration requirements—were changes in the kinds of crimes that resulted in disfranchisement.

The court's forthrightness in *Ratliff* has wrongly inflated the importance of Mississippi's constitution in the history of criminal disfranchisement. It has led scholars, policymakers, and courts to identify Mississippi as playing a unique leadership role as the first state to differentiate between black and white crimes in order to target African Americans for disfranchisement.[6] It is certainly true that Mississippi was the first southern state to initiate an effort to permanently end African American suffrage through constitutional revision after the end of Reconstruction. This "Second Mississippi Plan" served in many ways as a model for other southern states and included a poll tax, a secret ballot, a literacy test, a complicated registration scheme, and disfranchisement for a specified list of crimes.[7]

The focus on the trajectory of disfranchisement for crime in Mississippi (as well as South Carolina) in the 1890s has obscured the development of a broader trend across many other southern states. The majority of southern states revised their laws to deny the vote to all incarcerated felons in this period. This expansion of criminal disfranchisement—and infamy—to include lower-class whites both aided the political agenda of elite southern whites and reflected the growing degradation of convicted individuals due to the convict lease system. This change had regional as well as national implications.

There are several problems with using Mississippi's 1890 constitution and the analysis in *Ratliff v. Beal* to draw general conclusions about the history of disfranchisement for criminal conviction in the South in this decade. The first problem is that, as demonstrated in the preceding pages, efforts to disfranchise African Americans by expanding provisions disfranchising for crime had begun much earlier in the South. The second issue overlooked by the focus on Mississippi is that southern states implemented diverse constitutional provisions addressing disfranchisement for crime in the 1890s and early 1900s. Some states followed Mississippi and crafted lists of specific crimes aimed at affecting primarily black voters. But other states took a different approach by constructing or maintaining broader provisions disfranchising for all felonies that would affect both races. Only a state-by-state examination of changes made to constitutional suffrage provisions can illuminate the varied forms of disfranchisement for crime in this period.

Finally, the court's explanation in *Ratliff* and the subsequent privileging of this analysis oversimplifies the reasoning and overstates the rationality of the constitutional framers in Mississippi and other states that followed Mississippi's model. Courts and legal scholars often cite Malcolm Cook McMillan's 1955 study, *Constitutional Development in Alabama*, to explain why Mississippi's leaders selected particular crimes for disfranchisement. McMillan describes the logic of the framers this way: "Most of the crimes contained in the report of the suffrage committee came from an ordinance by John Fielding Burns, a Black Belt planter. The crimes he listed were those he had taken cognizance of for years in his justice of the peace court....where nearly all his cases involved Negroes." According to McMillan, Burns claimed, "the crime of wife beating alone would disqualify sixty percent of the Negroes."[8] McMillan's analysis, like the court in *Ratliff*, implies the application of a rational calculation of black criminal propensity and/or beliefs about such propensities. Southern lawmakers, he suggests, based their decisions on facts and observations about African Americans and crime. This chapter, however, identifies the larger context that shaped the composition of lists of disfranchising crimes, finding that ideologies of race, criminality, manhood, and morality—all rooted in the historical tradition of infamy—informed the construction of such lists of "black" crimes across the South.

Looking at the diversity of provisions disfranchising for crime in southern constitutions and digging into the question of why southern constitutional conventions disfranchised for the crimes they did connects laws disfranchising for crime more precisely to larger intellectual and political currents of the nineteenth century. The historic relationship between race, infamy, and citizenship offers a genealogy of the Mississippi law that extends well beyond John Fielding Burns. Furthermore, understanding the political context behind the constitutional conventions of this period underscores how different approaches to disfranchisement for crime stemmed from the politics of each state. Michael Perman's scholarship on southern disfranchising conventions has demonstrated that white southern political leaders had varied agendas for disfranchisement after 1890. Democrats in Mississippi and South Carolina faced pressure to disfranchise blacks in such a way as to protect the voting rights of white men, while leaders in other states that disfranchised constitutionally in this period had few qualms about limiting the white, lower-class electorate as well. This chapter shows that laws disfranchising for crime were crafted to follow these larger agendas. The differing priorities of the constitutional conventions that Perman identifies are reflected in state constitutional provisions disfranchising for crime.[9]

Mississippi's 1890 constitutional convention was led by men determined to eliminate African American suffrage, and they planned to use laws disfranchising for crime to further this agenda.[10] The state's 1868 constitution had disfranchised for bribery, perjury, or other infamous crimes. In 1871 legislators clarified by statutorily defining "infamous" as synonymous with "felony."[11] At the 1890 gathering in Jackson, delegates considered proposals to amend this broad standard, restricting the kinds of felonies that brought about disfranchisement in order to specifically affect African American voters.

Plans to amend laws disfranchising for criminal conviction came to the floor of the convention as parts of broader revisions of the entire suffrage article. The first such proposal came on the fourth day of the convention and was put forth by Solomon S. Calhoon. Calhoon had been elected president of the convention, and upon his election had spoken of his desire to restore white rule to the state. He offered a series of amendments, all of which were referred to the appropriate committees. Among his suggestions was disfranchising individuals convicted of "any felony" or petit larceny.[12] Later that day, delegate Charles K. Reagan, who would chair the Committee on the Elective Franchise, put forth his suffrage proposal. His list of disfranchising offenses was similar—burglary, larceny, or any felony.[13] These proposals were not unique and would have simply put Mississippi in line with changes made in other southern states over the previous decade and a half. That is, they omitted the ambiguous and dated "high crimes and misdemeanors" and "infamous" criteria, replacing them with the more standard "felony." And they focused on property crimes—"black" crimes that other state constitutions had been targeting since the mid-1870s. Calhoon's and Reagan's proposals were referred to the Committee on Elective Franchise for further study.[14]

The first really unique proposal came three days later, when Anselm J. McLaurin proposed an amendment that would disfranchise any man convicted of beating his wife. This, too, was referred to the Committee on Elective Franchise.[15] The racial intent of McLaurin's provision was clear to those who were present because whites in the late nineteenth century associated wife beating with racial and ethnic minorities, including African Americans and immigrants. In the South, African American men were more likely to be prosecuted for this crime than were white men.[16] A decade and a half later, a white Mississippi political leader confirmed the racial intent of Mississippi's wife-beating provision. In testimony before the Committee on Ways and Means of the U.S. House of Representatives, W. C. Welborn, a former Mississippi State University professor of Agriculture, demonstrated his knowledge of the racial purpose of this provision with an anecdote:

> When I was rather a young man Mississippi was trying to get up some sort of con-stitution that would get rid of the ignorant negro vote. Of course they had to get up something entirely fair on all hands, and they seriously discussed the desir-ability of putting in a clause to disfranchise a man for whipping his wife. I had lived in the white belt when I was young and was living in the black belt then. I said to an old negro that I knew, "Uncle Jeff, is it true that nearly all colored men whip their wives?" He scratched his head a moment and then said: "Well I believes dey all gives dem a little now and then when dey need it."[17]

When the Committee on Elective Franchise offered its proposal to the full assembly, the members did not recommend disfranchisement for wife beating. But they did propose disfranchising for crimes that could be seen, as the court did in *Ratliff*, as stereotypically black crimes. The disfranchis-ing offenses suggested by the committee, and ultimately adopted in the final constitution, consisted of bribery, burglary, theft, arson, obtaining money or goods under false pretenses, perjury, forgery, embezzlement, and bigamy.[18]

The minutes of the Committee on Elective Franchise give little informa-tion about how members crafted the list of disfranchising offenses, and the historical record does not offer any direct confirmation that the commit-tee viewed these particular crimes as "black" crimes. But there is one clue about the path that the committee's deliberations took. The minute book of the committee contains a handwritten draft of the suffrage provision. The list of disfranchising crimes in this draft is identical to the commit-tee's final report—the list of crimes even appears in the same order as the final report. But with one exception: murder was in the handwritten draft but the final report substituted bigamy for murder.[19] At some point, then, the committee must have decided that one should lose the vote for bigamy but not murder. Given the fact that murder, by nearly any standard, is a far more serious crime than bigamy, there must have been a reason for this revision. The reasoning articulated in *Ratliff* offers one explanation. Bigamy was a "furtive" crime and thus considered more typical of African Americans, while murder was believed to be a "robust" crime of whites. Disfranchising for bigamy instead of murder was a way of targeting African American voters.

Some members of the convention expressed dissatisfaction with the disfranchising offenses proposed by the franchise committee and tried to amend them. On September 22, McLaurin tried again to get his wife-beating provision included in the suffrage clause. Another delegate, L. P. Reynolds, took this one step further, suggesting an amendment to McLaurin's plan that added "or who beats his mother or mother-in-law, or the wife of any other man." The assembled group tabled these amendments and voted to approve the franchise committee's original proposal.[20]

The new Mississippi constitution eliminated the punishment of disfranchisement for the most serious criminal offenses. Mississippi no longer disfranchised for murder or any kind of assault, including rape or sexual assault.[21] Instead, the Mississippi constitution targeted lesser offenses. And, according to the account in *Ratliff*, these lesser offenses were those delegates thought African Americans were more likely to commit.

This revision furthered the agenda of the constitutional convention's majority in two ways. The delegates at the Mississippi convention sought to persuade white voters that the new constitution disfranchised as many African American voters as possible while protecting the white vote. And delegates sought to convince white voters, particularly lower-class voters, that the convention had done its best to protect their access to the franchise, as they had promised to do. The provisions disfranchising for crime fit the bill perfectly by highlighting the group's commitment to targeting African American voters while protecting white voters. Like the "understanding clause," another brainchild of the Mississippi convention, the efficacy of these laws in actually discriminating between black and white voters was as important as the perception they fostered.[22]

Mississippi's 1890 constitution offered other states in the region, in effect, a list of suggestions. The next state to hold a constitutional convention was South Carolina. Delegates to the 1895 meeting held in Columbia gained inspiration and adopted tactics from their colleagues in Mississippi.[23] Mississippi's impact on South Carolina's constitution was reflected both in the general disfranchisement provisions as well as the specific provisions disfranchising for criminal conviction. South Carolina's 1868 constitution had disfranchised for treason, murder, robbery, and dueling.[24] In 1882, with Reconstruction over and African American voters in their sights, the

South Carolina legislature expanded the disfranchising offenses to include burglary, larceny, perjury, forgery, or any infamous crime.[25] In 1895 they considered the Mississippi constitution's model in order to refine this list even more.

The various agendas of the South Carolina convention members paralleled their proposals for disfranchising for crime. Some of the most conservative and avowedly racist delegates proposed the most draconian approaches to disfranchising for crime. S. W. Gamble sought disfranchisement "for any conviction" and would have required all individuals who registered to vote to present a certification from the Clerk of the Court in their county certifying they had never been convicted of a crime. Gamble also would have required each voter to present certification from the "Township Board" that he was "not known to be guilty of adultery, fornication, willfully neglecting his wife and children, or maltreating either of them."[26] Another proposal gave the legislature free rein to "impose disqualification to vote as a punishment for crime," echoing the broad language of the Fourteenth Amendment ratified nearly thirty years earlier.[27] Delegates known for their hostility to the black vote presented lists of disfranchising offenses that bore a similarity to Mississippi's. For example, W. B. Wilson proposed disfranchising for bribery, burglary, arson, larceny, false pretenses, perjury, forgery, embezzlement, or bigamy—a list nearly identical to Mississippi's except for the substitution of larceny for theft.[28]

In contrast, delegates who opposed the wholesale disfranchisement of African Americans offered proposals that disfranchised only for major crimes. The best example of this is the suffrage proposal of Robert Smalls, one of just six African American delegates to the convention.[29] Smalls proposed disfranchising only for a handful of serious crimes—treason, murder, robbery or dueling. His proposal also would have prohibited the legislature from adding to the crimes on the list, as South Carolina had done in 1882 with the intent of targeting African American voters, as explained in the previous chapter. Finally he specified that disfranchised individuals must have been "duly tried and convicted"—language that echoed the Readmission Acts and stood in sharp contrast to proposals like Gamble's that sought to disfranchise for even allegations of criminality.[30] It is clear that Smalls hoped to limit the denial of suffrage to those properly convicted of the most serious and/or violent crimes, and his proposal reflects an intimate knowledge of the history told in the preceding chapters of this book.

After hearing all these proposals, the suffrage committee, chaired by Governor Ben Tillman, met to draft its recommendation. These delegates endorsed a proposal disfranchising for burglary, theft, arson, false pretenses, perjury, forgery, robbery, bribery, adultery, embezzlement, bigamy, and violations of election laws. In addition, any individual "confined in a public prison" could not vote.[31] The only substantive difference between this proposal and the new Mississippi constitution was the addition of adultery, election-related crimes, and the disfranchisement of individuals in prison.[32]

It was not until late in the convention that a series of amendments expanded the racial agenda of this part of the disfranchisement provision. On the thirty-ninth day of the convention, G. Duncan Bellinger proposed the addition of a raft of sex-related crimes plus some enumerated kinds of theft to the suffrage article. The group agreed, adding housebreaking, receiving stolen goods, breach of trust with a fraudulent intention, fornication, sodomy, assault with intent to ravish, miscegenation, incest, and larceny.[33] The convention, upon Bellinger's suggestion, also voted to eliminate theft and embezzlement from the list of disfranchising offenses. Following this vote, O. M. Doyle successfully proposed the addition of wife-beating to the list of disfranchising crimes.[34]

The South Carolina convention took its framework for disfranchisement for crime from the Mississippi constitution and extended it, fine-tuning Mississippi's racial strategy. Delegates took the responsibility of protecting white votes while disfranchising African Americans even more seriously than the Mississippi convention had, and the provisions disfranchising for criminal convictions reflected this.[35] The convention added to the list of sex-related crimes, crimes that African Americans might, in the racist imagination, be more likely to commit. Furthermore, they proposed eliminating embezzlement, a crime presumably thought to be too sophisticated for African Americans.[36]

South Carolina's decision to include larceny and exclude theft and embezzlement contrasted with Mississippi's decision to exclude larceny and include theft. The enumeration of specific property offenses has long been a confusing legal issue. State codes defined illegal taking of property in different ways. The exclusion of embezzlement and theft indicates that the convention was attempting to be very specific about which property crimes disfranchised. Mississippi had opted to disfranchise for any and all property crimes, including those that involved violence. South Carolina's assembly was even more specific than Mississippi in its efforts to avoid disfranchising white criminals. Theft was a broad term that encompassed larceny but also other kinds of illegal taking, such as using violence to take property; this put theft in the "white" crime category. Embezzlement was thought to be a more sophisticated crime and thus a "white" crime as well. By excluding these other kinds of illegal taking and focusing instead

on larceny—a crime that had successfully been used to target black voters in the South since the 1870s—the convention was attempting to
limit the property crimes to those most likely to be committed by African
Americans.[37]

In both Mississippi and South Carolina, the racial implications of the
provisions disfranchising for crime paralleled the goals of the two conventions. Political leaders in both states sought to protect the white vote while
reducing, if not completely eliminating, the African American vote. Their
constitutions enumerated lists of very specific crimes that seemed to be
aimed at African Americans. They avoided more general provisions—such
as disfranchisement for felony—that some believed would have affected
more white voters. Most notably, both conventions re-enfranchised
murderers.

These constitutions in these two states seemed to follow the logic
described in *Ratliff v. Beale*. Racist stereotypes and ideas about moral and
biological inferiority held that African Americans were sneaky, furtive, and
weak. Therefore, according to the court, they would be more inclined to
bigamy and arson than murder and assault. Racist conceptions of sexuality
also held African Americans to be licentious and over-sexed. This would
explain the profusion of sex-related crimes in the disfranchisement provisions of these two constitutions.

But the explanation is actually more complicated. The Committee on the
Elective Franchise crossed out murder and inserted bigamy because bigamy was an infamous crime, while murder was not. The list of disfranchising crimes put forth by the Mississippi and South Carolina conventions
was remarkably similar to the list of disfranchising offenses itemized by
some states in the early nineteenth century. Both Tennessee and Illinois,
for example, allowed suffrage by those convicted of violent crimes such
as murder. The Illinois constitution of 1848 disfranchised for infamous
crimes, defined by statute as rape, kidnapping, perjury, arson, burglary,
robbery, sodomy, the crime against nature, incest, larceny, forgery, counterfeiting, or bigamy.[38] Tennessee's statutes and constitutions, dating back
to the 1830s, were also quite similar, denying voting rights for property
and sexual crimes but granting them to individuals convicted of violent
crimes, including murder. South Carolina's 1895 constitution added only
fornication, miscegenation, and wife beating to the Illinois list and omitted
kidnapping.[39]

Neither Illinois nor Tennessee created these laws with the intention of
disfranchising African Americans. African Americans were not permitted to vote in Illinois at that time, and Tennessee disfranchised African
Americans explicitly in the 1835 constitution.[40] Instead, these states

disfranchised white men who committed crimes considered incompatible with fitness for the full rights of citizenship. Infamous crimes supposedly evidenced a lack of morality; such immorality indicated a lack of the honor necessary for suffrage and full citizenship, which was why infamous individuals have historically been denied suffrage and related rights. Those who committed violent crimes—such as murder and assault—were not necessarily infamous; therefore these convicts should have their full citizenship rights preserved.

In Mississippi and South Carolina, white political leaders hoped to target African Americans at the ballot box by disfranchising for crimes for which blacks were more likely to be convicted. But, lacking data on race and crime beyond John Burns's accounting, how did they know which crimes were "black crimes"? They concluded that African American crimes were those that evidenced immorality and lack of fitness for citizenship. In other words, since African Americans were considered degraded, morally and legally, they were likely to commit the kind of crimes historically considered to be evidence of degradation. There are a few rhetorical flourishes—South Carolina's elimination of embezzlement, considered a "white" crime, and its lengthy inventory of sex crimes stand out in particular. But the members of these constitutional conventions were acting within a historical context. They added the layer of race to existing ideas about criminal immorality and the acts that demonstrated unfitness for citizenship. White Mississippians and South Carolinians identified and believed the logic of these lists of crimes in the new constitutions—the logic that these lists offered a special way to target African Americans—because they were rooted not simply in ideas about race but in ideas about the relative morality of criminal acts.

Of course, the framers in Mississippi and South Carolina might also have taken observable realities of southern criminal justice into consideration as well. African Americans may indeed have been more likely to be convicted of bigamy, arson, and theft than murder and assault. But an understanding of the idea of infamy helps put disproportionate conviction rates, or the perception of disproportionate conviction rates, into a historical context. Why were some crimes considered to be "black crimes"? Not because African Americans committed them more frequently but because the criminal justice system was biased toward convicting blacks of these kinds of crimes. Infamy helps us understand why such disparities in southern criminal justice might have existed—or even why white southerners may have imagined such disparities. African Americans were more likely to be arrested for, prosecuted for, convicted of, and even associated with crimes that evidenced lack of honor and fitness for citizenship, because white southerners assumed them to be unfit for citizenship.

This also guided the assignment of particular crimes to whites, which explains why murder and assault were considered to be white men's crimes and therefore not deserving of disfranchisement. These two offenses had not been infamous under English common law and had not been subsequently defined as infamous crimes in the United States either. The idea that violent crimes did not produce infamy was still commonly held in the late nineteenth century. The men at Mississippi's convention who defended the voting rights of murderers would have been in agreement with delegates at Kentucky's 1890 constitutional convention who argued that murderers should retain the vote.

Kentucky's convention, held that same year, saw an impassioned debate over whether violent crime should result in disfranchisement. John D. Carroll of Henry County passionately defended the suffrage rights of those who committed crimes in "sudden heat and passion."[41] Another convention delegate, C. J. Bronston, from the city of Lexington, joined Carroll's defense of voting rights for certain violent criminals with an example. What if a man kills another by accident while playing croquet "under the excitement of the game?" Should the over-exuberant croquet player be forced to wear the "scarlet letter" and be disfranchised? What if a man shoots a gun accidentally and kills "the dearest friend he has?" Should he lose his vote for this "unfortunate but reckless conduct?"[42] Bronston believed murder should not bring about lifelong disfranchisement. He argued that murder, which had its primary impact on a single individual, was distinct from crimes that mainly affected the whole society. According to Bronston, a person should not be disqualified from voting "solely because of some great wrong that he has done to an individual." But if he has committed a crime "of such character as to affect society itself chiefly," then disqualification should be part of the punishment.[43] Crimes with such wide-reaching social impacts were those in which individuals profited from deceit—crimes such as fraud, treason, and theft—because failing to punish such crimes would encourage others to perpetuate deceit as well, thereby degrading larger societal morals. Carroll's stance also rested on the assumption that violence might be moral when anger generated a spontaneous loss of reason. Quoting the Kentucky Supreme Court's decision in *Anderson v. Winfree*, Carroll insisted that "Only those should be excluded from suffrage who are guilty of such felonies as are inconsistent with the common principles of humanity and convict the perpetrator of depravity and moral turpitude."[44] The association of violent crime and fitness for citizenship was a question actively under debate in this period in Kentucky.

The debate at the Kentucky convention also suggested the interplay of class with understandings of honor, infamy, and citizenship. The ardent defense of suffrage by those convicted of "murder -by -croquet -mallet" indicates a belief that crimes committed by wealthy men (croquet being an upper-class, white sport) did not evidence infamy and dishonor, and that wealthy men should have their rights of suffrage protected. Should constitutions protect the voting rights of all white men or only wealthy white men? Different states saw different approaches to this issue. While Mississippi and South Carolina produced constitutions that protected the voting rights of all white men, regardless of class, conventions in other southern states were more willing to disfranchise lower-class white men. In these other states white men with criminal convictions would be swept up in laws disfranchising for a broader array of crimes, a provision that would affect lower-class white men primarily and indicated a shifting understanding of infamy and fitness for full citizenship.

Soon after Mississippi and South Carolina set the standard for precise, racially targeted lists of disfranchising crimes, and soon after the Mississippi Supreme Court sought to explain the logic of these provisions in *Ratliff v. Beale*, two southern states moved in exactly the opposite direction. In 1898 and 1900, Louisiana and North Carolina adopted constitutions with a much blunter approach to disfranchisement for crime. These two states passed suffrage articles that were broader and more far-reaching than those of Mississippi and South Carolina. Both states also eliminated disfranchisement for any kind of misdemeanors, focusing instead on felonies and/or penitentiary crimes. And unlike Mississippi and South Carolina, they included violent offenders in these sanctions.

Prior to 1898 Louisiana disfranchised for treason, embezzlement of public funds, malfeasance in office, larceny, bribery, illegal voting, perjury, forgery, or "other crime punishable by hard labor or imprisonment in the penitentiary."[45] Although the journal of the 1898 constitutional convention does not indicate that any debates took place over the provisions disfranchising for crime, the new constitution made the standard for disfranchisement higher and more general. After 1898 any individual "convicted of any crime punishable by imprisonment in the penitentiary" lost the right to vote. Individuals convicted of misdemeanor election offenses, such as illegal voting, could now vote, as could people convicted of misdemeanor larceny.[46]

At about the same time, North Carolina moved from disfranchising for felonies or infamous crimes to disfranchising for felonies and crimes "for which the punishment may be imprisonment in the penitentiary."[47] Since "infamous crimes" could include some misdemeanors, such as petty larceny, the effect was similar to that of Louisiana. In other words, North Carolina raised the standard for disfranchisement, ending the possibility that individuals with certain misdemeanor convictions would lose their voting rights and establishing a standard that denied the vote to anyone convicted of serious, felony-grade offenses. (The constitutional language disfranchising for felonies and penitentiary crimes was redundant, as felonies were crimes punishable by imprisonment.)

The method of disfranchising for crime in North Carolina and Louisiana was different from Mississippi and South Carolina because of the divergent political contexts in which the conventions operated and the disparate political goals of disfranchisement. In North Carolina and Louisiana, the Populist Party had gathered a coalition of lower-class white farmers and African Americans, posing a serious threat to the political power of white Democrats in the state. Democratic leaders in these two states, therefore, sought to disfranchise both African Americans and lower-class whites. This was in contrast to Mississippi and South Carolina, where participation by lower-class white farmers in the movement for the constitutional convention and a desire to unify the white vote behind the Democratic Party had required that the white elite protect the voting rights of white men across class lines.[48]

The conventions in North Carolina and Louisiana had the political mandate to disfranchise with a broader brush—one that included lower-class whites and African Americans. In his opening speech to the Louisiana convention, the Democratic state chairman, Ernest Kruttschnitt, explained that, while his party sought to "sacrifice the fewest number of whites," some whites should "have the patriotism to give up their citizenship" to secure Democratic rule.[49] Although Kruttschnitt did not specify that those giving up their votes would be those most economically disadvantaged, that was his intention. Louisiana passed registration and secret ballot laws by statute, then a modified grandfather clause and poll tax at the 1898 constitutional convention.[50] North Carolina avoided implementing a property qualification, unlike Louisiana, and focused instead on literacy tests and poll taxes. North Carolina's leaders pushed for a suffrage plan that was, as one of its authors, George Rountree, described it, "simple and free from complications."[51] The statute disfranchising for crime in North Carolina was, similarly, straightforward—all who were convicted of felony offenses would lose the right to vote.[52]

Political leaders in North Carolina and Louisiana fully expected poor southern whites, along with African Americans, to be affected disproportionately by laws disfranchising for felony convictions.[53] This fit the political agenda of disfranchising blacks along with lower-class whites. Lack of money meant an inability to hire adequate legal counsel. Inferior class status meant lack of political connections that could be called on to help when in trouble. The southern justice system was designed to ensure that upper-class whites would be protected and spared. Laws disfranchising for all serious convictions would help erode the lower-class white vote—certainly it would do nothing to bolster their electoral participation—although no one expected these laws to carry the main burden of guaranteeing political control by elite whites. Poll taxes and literacy tests would do most of the work of restricting the electorate, but laws disfranchising for crime would help as well.

Alabama was the next southern state to revise its constitution. Quite a lot has been written about that state's 1901 constitution and its provisions disfranchising for crime. That document, which included a range of revisions to the suffrage requirements aimed at eliminating the African American vote, specified a long list of disfranchising crimes. Malcolm Cook McMillan, and others citing his work, has credited white planter and magistrate John Fielding Burns with constructing this list, explaining that Burns believed these crimes to be the ones African Americans were most likely to commit.[54] In fact, the transcribed proceedings of the convention suggest that Burns played only a minor role in crafting the list of disfranchising offenses and that much of his agenda actually met with dissent and opposition on the floor of the convention.

Furthermore, there is a logical problem with identifying Burns as an important instigator of the southern movement to construct lists of "black crimes" for insertion into the suffrage articles in order to disfranchise African Americans.[55] By the time Alabama's 1901 convention was called, four other states, Mississippi, South Carolina, Louisiana, and North Carolina, had already held conventions. Mississippi and South Carolina had pioneered the project of tailoring lists of disfranchising offenses to achieve racial ends. In other words, Alabama was not the first state to try to erode the black vote with a racially tailored list of crimes.

The disfranchisement provisions enacted in Alabama in 1901 offered only a few variations on the approaches tried in Mississippi and South Carolina. The *Montgomery Advertiser* chided the convention by describing the document as "an artistic compilation of what has been done by other states."[56] The newspaper was referring to the disfranchisement provisions as a whole, not just the criminal disfranchisement section, but the description is apt. The 1901 document did not represent an ingenious and path-breaking approach to eroding suffrage through laws disfranchising for crime. Alabama's 1901 constitution was a hybrid, reflecting both the precision of Mississippi and South Carolina in targeting those who committed certain minor crimes thought to be common among African Americans and the more general disfranchisement of all felons implemented in North Carolina and Louisiana.

In the opening days of the Alabama convention, delegates introduced over fifty ordinances and resolutions dealing with suffrage. Twenty-three of them were complete proposals for the article on the elective franchise, while others would amend just part of the existing article. With regard to disfranchisement for crime, some of these plans would have simply maintained the list of disfranchising offenses established in the 1875 constitution; a list that had included treason, embezzlement of public funds, malfeasance in office, larceny, bribery, or other crimes punishable by imprisonment in the penitentiary.[57]

But some individuals proposed radical revisions of the criminal disfranchisement provision. Several men would have disfranchised for offenses that were committed but for which the perpetrator had not been indicted or convicted, therefore disfranchising for a status, not for a crime. In other words, they would have disfranchised for some offenses even if the individual had *not* been "duly convicted." For example, William Oates proposed the addition of an expanded list of election crimes and suggested denying the franchise to anyone who was "of notoriously bad character, a tramp, professional gambler, or pauper."[58] Robert Kyle added to this list the "habitual drunkard or a vagrant."[59] Frank White wanted to disfranchise individuals convicted of felonies or offenses involving moral turpitude, and also drunkards, vagrants, gamblers, vote buyers and sellers.[60]

One of the key splits amongst the members of the constitutional convention was over whether to try to completely eliminate the African American vote or to continue to allow some amount of African American suffrage in the Black Belt. In counties with significant African American majorities, votes were manipulated ("counted in") to bring huge majorities to the Democratic Party and statewide influence to these counties. Oates and White took divergent positions on African American voting. Oates sought to protect some black voters—specifically, the "manipulable" vote of the wealthier class of African Americans in his congressional district in the Black Belt. White, in a district with few African American voters, hoped to disfranchise as many black voters statewide as possible. But these two men agreed that suffrage restrictions should affect the lower classes, black and white. According to Michael Perman, "In effect, they qualified the strictly racial intent of the [suffrage] proposal with a nonracial class-based proviso."[61] The proposals these two men made to disqualify vagrants, tramps, paupers, and the like were in accordance with their larger views endorsing the disfranchisement of the lower classes. Their plans would have affected all lower-class voters, regardless of race. Looking to protect the "better class" of African American voters, Oates assumed that such provisions would not affect them.

Most of the plans put forth for suffrage in the early days of the Alabama convention agreed that individuals who had committed felonies or served in the penitentiary should still lose the right to vote. In other words, they accepted the broad disfranchisement for all felonies under the existing law, following the approach of the North Carolina and Louisiana constitutions. But several delegates proposed adding enumerated crimes to the 1875 list. For example, William Knight of Greensboro hoped to further disfranchise for "assault and battery on the wife"—a proposal likely inspired by the Mississippi and South Carolina constitutions. Others sought to add crimes of moral turpitude—a standard akin to infamy.[62]

Burns's initial suffrage proposal enumerated a longer list of crimes and did not involve a general disfranchisement of all felons. It was different from the existing constitution and most of the other proposals being floated on the floor of the convention because it did not disfranchise for all major offenses. Missing from Burns's list were various assaults, but murder did bring disfranchisement. His enumeration of criminal convictions punishable with disfranchisement following conviction was very similar to South Carolina's 1895 list but with the addition of murder.[63]

Echoing the proposals of some of his fellow delegates—and diverging from the blueprint offered by the South Carolina constitution—Burns proposed disfranchising for a number of actions or conditions without requiring a conviction. He would deny the vote to bastards, loafers, and individuals with any "loathsome or contagious disease." But he did not list tramps, vagrants, gamblers, or drunkards, as some of his colleagues had. He also would strip the vote from mixed-race individuals, "those who shall have married any woman having a living husband, from whom she has not been legally divorced [and] those who shall have married another woman before they have obtained a legal divorce." He would disfranchise any individual "against whom a decree of divorce has been rendered by some court"; who had been divorced; who "lived in open, continuous adultery or fornication"; or who had "committed an assault and battery upon his wife, or step-daughter, or paramour." Finally citizens who committed various election offenses—casting an illegal ballot, buying or selling votes, or trying to vote without paying a poll tax—would be disfranchised by Burns as well.[64]

Many of these provisions closely resembled bills of attainder—a criminal status rendered without a criminal trial—and were therefore unconstitutional. It is possible that Burns hoped to push the courts to rule with more clarity on whether such provisions might be constitutionally permitted. He may have held out some hope for an affirmation of such statutes because in

1884 in *Washington v. State* the Alabama Supreme Court had eroded protections for suffrage by declaring that disfranchising for offenses committed before the disfranchising provision was enacted was not *ex post facto* law. In that case the court allowed states to regulate the franchise in any way as long as they did not violate the Fifteenth Amendment.[65] But Burns's provisions disfranchising for offenses with no conviction appeared to go against the language in *Washington*, because the court specified that felony disfranchisement laws were not bills of attainder because they required "a conviction in the due course of judicial proceedings before disfranchisement is made to attach." Since Burns's proposal would have disfranchised vast classes of people absent a conviction it is hard to believe that he really thought that this would have held up in court even in this period. If Burns had thought these provisions could win in court, other members of the convention had shied away from provoking a court fight due to concern that other suffrage provisions (including the "grandfather clause") would be ruled unconstitutional. Disfranchising for actions or status without a criminal conviction had little support in the convention and did not pass.[66]

The proposal that came out of the Committee on Suffrage and Election included a long list of convictions but omitted recommendations by Burns and others that would have disfranchised people without a criminal conviction. The committee's list was broad and repetitive. It required that individuals convicted of felonies, infamous crimes, or crimes involving moral turpitude lose their vote; many crimes would have fallen into at least two of those categories. Furthermore, the plan unnecessarily listed sexual offenses (bigamy, living in adultery, sodomy, incest, rape, miscegenation, crime against nature), which also fell into the "moral turpitude" category. Other crimes on the long list were felonies and thus already covered. For example the document disfranchised for all felonies and then enumerated disfranchisement for murder, which was a felony. It iterated treason, arson, larceny, and an array of property crimes that would have been either felonies or infamous crimes or both. The committee proposal also included a long list of election offenses that brought disfranchisement as well.[67]

After the Committee on Suffrage and Election made its report, debate on the recommendation commenced. Henry Reese, who like Burns was from Dallas County (Selma) in the Black Belt, proposed an amendment similar to the one that Burns had proposed weeks earlier. Reese, too, wanted to disfranchise for status and acts without convictions. In particular, Reese endorsed the position that "bastards," except those who had had "their disability of legitimacy...removed by the Legislature," should not vote. Reese expressed concern that in his district many African American voters would be able to pass the literacy test and vote. "Educational facilities there for the colored people have been unusually good; in many respects, Mr. President, better than for the white people. The Northern people have done much for the negro about Selma."[68]

According to Reese, the provision disfranchising bastards would protect white supremacy by eliminating many "objectionable elements" in the Black Belt. "In the town of Selma, along the outskirts, in the lanes and alleys, are the hatching places of the class I would have eliminated—yellow bucks around every town." This new and growing population represented a particular threat. "I would far rather trust the affairs of the State in the hands of the old slaves that we had before the war than to the element that we have around the bar rooms and crap dens of our towns."[69]

Reese was untroubled by punishing an individual for an act committed by his parents. He pointed out, "In England and in every country from which we trace our civilization it is the law, and in the Ten Commandments [as well,] that the sins of the father shall be visited upon their children to the third and fourth generation."[70] Roland Hood of Gadsden challenged Reese saying, "Wouldn't that amendment have disfranchised Alexander Hamilton and Abraham Lincoln?"—to which an unidentified delegate responded by shouting "They are all dead."[71] Ezra Coleman rejected Reese's interpretation of scripture, pointing out that "the Lord declared against the proverb and said, 'When the son hath done that which is right, he shall surely live; and that the son shall not bear the iniquity of the father.'"[72] Coleman further observed that some leading citizens of Alabama might get caught in the provision disfranchising bastards. He moved to table the motion, and the convention agreed. The Reese amendment went down in defeat.[73]

Undeterred, Burns tried again on the sixty-ninth day of the convention. He introduced another resolution recommending the disfranchisement of bastards. He pointed out that this provision would disqualify at least 48,000 men who should not be allowed to vote, while only about 300 would be unnecessarily barred by the "insertion of one word" in the article on suffrage and elections. "Competent" bastards who were "worthy to vote" could have this disability removed.[74]

Burns and his allies failed to convince the convention to extend disfranchisement to statuses and acts without a criminal conviction. The assembly refused to disfranchise bastards or individuals living in adultery, though they were willing to disfranchise individuals *convicted* of living in adultery. The committee on the franchise agreed to recommend disfranchisement for individuals convicted of being a vagrant or a tramp, but rejected disfranchising individuals on the basis of their status absent conviction. Proposals to disfranchise tramps and vagrants without conviction produced long debates over whether disfranchising these various classes of poor and/or unemployed individuals would deny the vote to college students, retired individuals, individuals between jobs, strikers, and even poor men married to wealthy women.[75]

Most of the elements of Burns's proposals that were unique were voted down at the convention, and there is no evidence that Burns carried the level of influence that has been suggested in the historical literature on felon disfranchisement.[76] The journal of the convention does not substantiate the view that Burns was some kind of mastermind behind a finely crafted list of disfranchising offenses. Burns was out of step with the majority of the convention, which saw electoral reform as an important goal. Tired of corruption, vote-buying and electoral manipulation, many delegates sought to clean up elections. While they sought disfranchisement, they wanted it to have legal sanction.[77]

Ultimately, the list of disfranchising crimes proposed by the suffrage committee was adopted by the full Alabama convention. While this part of the suffrage plan bore some resemblance to the plan adopted in South Carolina with its enumeration of property crimes and sex crimes, the two plans were quite different. Alabama's disfranchisement provision was much more far-reaching than those in South Carolina and Mississippi because it disfranchised for all felonies, as well as infamous crimes and crimes of moral turpitude.[78] It did not exclude "robust" crimes as Mississippi had; most notably, murderers lost the right to vote in Alabama. The enumerated list of misdemeanor "black" crimes made Alabama's disfranchisement provision appear similar to its predecessors in South Carolina and Mississippi. While this represented an effort to disfranchise a large number of African Americans for minor offenses, the inclusion of all felons in the disfranchisement provisions meant that "white" crimes were also punished with disfranchisement.[79]

The broader brush of disfranchisement for crime in Alabama fits with the larger analysis of this state's constitutional disfranchisement put forth by Michael Perman. The suffrage plan reduced electoral corruption and solidified Democratic dominance. Protecting white supremacy and Democratic rule was paramount in Alabama. Disfranchising African American voters was of utmost importance, but if some whites fell by the wayside, particularly those that had been convicted of crimes, this did not cause much concern.[80]

Virginia's provisions for disfranchising for crime underwent only minor revision at the 1901 constitutional convention. Virginia's 1868 constitutional convention had eliminated the "infamy" standard for disfranchisement, replacing it with disfranchisement for felony conviction; the 1868 assembly had also added embezzlement of public funds and treason to its list of disfranchising offenses.[81] Constitutional amendments approved by voters in 1876 added petit larceny.[82] The 1901 revision modified this list by disfranchising for bribery and embezzlement more generally (not just in the context of elections), obtaining money or property under false pretences, perjury, and forgery. As under the previous constitution, all felons were disfranchised for life. Finally, the 1901 constitution disfranchised anyone who had participated in any way in dueling.[83] In short, these were minor changes that did little to expand or contract the number of individuals impacted by these provisions.

Like the conventions in North Carolina and Louisiana, Virginia's framers sought to restrict the electorate as much as possible; the Virginia constitution would be remembered as ushering in one of the most significant contractions of the electorate in the South.[84] The majority of African Americans would be disfranchised and so would a large segment of the white population. As Perman writes, "not only were they eager to exclude blacks, but most of the reformers were not particularly upset about disfranchising a number of whites as well."[85] Virginia's new suffrage laws certainly accomplished these ends, and the broad felony disfranchisement standard contributed to this goal.

Texas and Georgia did not hold constitutional conventions in this period—both took the amendment route. Texas achieved disfranchisement through a poll tax amendment and a series of election laws. The provisions for disfranchising for criminal conviction in Texas did not undergo revision at this point.[86] In Georgia, a suffrage amendment ratified in 1908 did not alter the section of the constitution specifying disfranchising crimes.[87]

The timeline of constitutional disfranchisement in Florida was also different, and the history of provisions disfranchising for crime in this state during the late 1880s and 1890s is unlike others in the region. Florida's 1885 constitutional convention had the primary goal of returning power to the counties by curtailing the power of the state government. The convention also laid the groundwork for the expansion of African American disfranchisement by giving the legislature the power to pass a poll tax— though the legislature did not actually enact such a measure until 1889.[88] With regard to disfranchisement for crime, the 1885 convention offered a rare glimpse of progressivism. Black Floridians had protested the expansion of laws disfranchising for crime and in particular disfranchisement for petit larceny. As noted in the previous chapter, in 1884 the Conference of the Leading Colored Men in Florida had spoken out against disfranchisement for petit larceny.[89] Thomas Gibbs, one of seven African American representatives to Florida's 1885 constitutional convention, rejected the expansion of disfranchisement to these petty crimes, arguing "The

Justice-of-the-Peace Court system has been a wholesale disfranchising machine to disqualify blacks.... About 3,0000 voters for trivial offences or on trumped up charges have been disfranchised." Gibbs supported a proposed change in the constitution that would allow only courts of record—a higher, more formal judicial body that produced a written record of proceedings—to disfranchise individuals.[90] The measure was adopted at the 1885 constitution convention, so that after 1885 only individuals convicted in a court of record could be disfranchised in Florida.[91] This represented a small but significant erosion of the reach of laws disfranchising for crime in Florida.

Only two southern states, Mississippi and South Carolina, revised their suffrage articles in the 1890s to target African American criminals while trying to minimize the impact of this punishment on white convicts. When it came to disfranchisement for crime, the Second Mississippi Plan was followed only by South Carolina. More common were states that implemented or maintained more general provisions that disfranchised for all felonies. Disfranchising for crimes committed by both races supported the agenda of white, elite Democrats who sought to disfranchise the lower-class white population to avert future Populist-style uprisings. From this partisan perspective, disfranchising white convicts was just as politically palatable as disfranchising black convicts. In short, the suggestion that southern states acted in a coordinated, regional way to target black voters specifically with provisions disfranchising for crime in the 1890s is incorrect. The agenda of white, elite political leaders in states that disfranchised broadly— Louisiana, North Carolina, Alabama, and Virginia—was reflected in constitutions that disfranchised those convicted of a broad range of crimes. Southern constitutional conventions crafted provisions disfranchising for criminal convictions that fit their distinct political ends.

The two different approaches to criminal disfranchisement exhibited in southern state constitutions in this period reflect different political agendas and divergent perspectives on the rights of convicted individuals to the full rights of citizenship. Members of the constitutional conventions in Mississippi and South Carolina believed that the morality of the crime and the kind of judgment the court made on a convict were derived from the crime's infamy, not from its seriousness. This led them to determine that convicts who committed certain infamous misdemeanor offenses were undeserving of suffrage while those who committed some non-infamous felonies (most notably murder) should retain their rights. This logic was appealing because it fit with their ideas about race, morality, and citizenship, as well as with their electoral agenda. They argued that African Americans committed the kinds of crimes generally considered immoral and which were indicators of unfitness for citizenship—"furtive" crimes—because they believed that African Americans were, as a race, undeserving of citizenship.

In North Carolina, Louisiana, Alabama, and Virginia, broader disfranchisement provisions passed after 1890 reflected the growing view that all who committed felonies, not just infamous crimes, were degraded and unworthy of suffrage, a perspective that aided the political agenda of limiting suffrage for lower-class whites. The goal of lower-class white disfranchisement and the revision of infamy to include all who had served time in the penitentiary were mutually reinforcing ideologies. Limiting the electorate in a way that furthered the class agenda of elite whites helped produce ideas about race, crime, morality; at the same time ideas about infamy helped justify limiting access to the ballot by lower-class whites. The basis by which certain criminals were judged unworthy of citizenship shifted so that all individuals who had been incarcerated for serious offenses were now considered degraded. Felonies and incarceration in the penitentiary were evidence of degradation. Since lower-class individuals were more likely to receive criminal penalties and incarceration, this helped justify disfranchising this portion of the white population.

Political and legal changes beyond the region contributed to a growing agreement in the late nineteenth and early twentieth centuries that those serving or who had served time in prison for felonies should be denied the right to vote. Three national developments can be pinpointed. First, there was a legal redefinition of "infamous" to include all felonies. Second, there was a gradual abandonment of the ideal of rehabilitation and a baseline of harsh treatment and forced labor of prisoners. Third, the growing reach of the criminal justice system increasingly affected those on the margins of political power: racial minorities and lower-class individuals from all races.

In the last decades of the nineteenth century, states across the country began to define infamy as synonymous with felony. This ended the legal distinction between moral and immoral crimes and put more of a defining emphasis on length and location of incarceration. For example, Mississippi's legal code equated infamy with felony and incarceration in the penitentiary as early as 1871: "The terms 'felony,' or 'infamous crime,' when used in this code, shall be construed to mean offences punished with death, or confinement in the penitentiary."[92] While some in Mississippi would continue to try to differentiate between kinds of crime for political purposes at the 1890 constitutional convention, this distinction was, as we have seen, anachronistic compared to the rest of the region. Legislation in states across the nation eroded the legal distinction between felonies and infamous crimes. An Illinois statute, for example, added murder to the list of infamous offenses in that state in 1873.[93] The notion that only "*cri-men falsi*"—crimes traditionally believed to be infamous—were evidence of moral degeneration was gradually abandoned; conversely the idea that morally sound individuals might commit certain violent crimes was legally discarded. All those who committed serious crimes were seen as morally compromised, and all those who served time in the penitentiary were infamous. With this generalization of infamy to all serious crimes came the extension of disfranchisement to all convicted of such crimes.[94]

In the 1880s federal courts reinforced changes that state legislatures had made to statutes, establishing a national standard for infamy. Individuals convicted of all felonies, defined as crimes punishable by imprisonment in the penitentiary, were infamous. This stemmed from a series of Supreme Court decisions revolving around the Fifth Amendment requirement of indictment before a grand jury for anyone held under a "capital or infamous crime." In 1885, in *Ex Parte Wilson*, the Court ruled, "a crime punishable by imprisonment for a term of years at hard labor is an infamous crime."[95] The following year, in *Mackin v. United States*, the Court found that any crime "punishable by imprisonment in a state prison or penitentiary, with or without hard labor, is an infamous crime."[96] The result was a new definition of infamy derived from the level of punishment rather than moral or social distinctions between crimes.

Ideas about the moral status of crime and convicts were connected to developments in attitudes toward incarcerated individuals. Across the nation, courts exhibited a growing conviction in this period that incarceration produced degradation. A federal district court in West Tennessee articulated it best in an 1880 case stating, "this notion of moral degradation by confinement in the penitentiary has grown into a general understanding that it constitutes any offence a felony." According to the court, since imprisonment was morally degrading, all penitentiary offenses (that is, all felonies) were infamous.[97]

Including all felonies, even assault and murder, into the category of "infamous" meant an abandonment of the idea that violent crime might at times be acceptable, even if it was perpetuated by white men. This challenged the tradition of excusing male violence, particularly crimes committed in defense of honor. The idea that all felons were degraded by their incarceration undermined the idea that some violent criminals, even white men, were somehow more pure than others.

This ideological shift was evident at Kentucky's 1890 constitutional convention. While some argued the old perspective, discussed above, that violent crimes such as murder might be committed by honorable individuals, others defended the new and more expansive view of infamy—and disfranchisement—that included all felons. As a result, Kentucky law moved from a narrow construction of infamy, holding that it came from being convicted of an infamous crime, to the view that all felons were infamous, due in part to their incarceration. Convention delegate Frank Straus, of Bullitt and Spencer Counties, was among those arguing that individuals who committed manslaughter were, like all infamous criminals, "enemies of society" and should not have the right to vote. Straus rejected notions of noble violence, labeling the notion that violence might be excusable, even honorable, an "old Kentucky idea." He maintained that a man who "cannot control his temper" and kills his neighbor was not a good citizen.[98]

But, perhaps more significantly, Straus and his ideological allies believed that incarceration degraded individuals. Even if the crime itself was not evidence of an individual's depravity, the fact of incarceration made citizens unfit to vote. He explained that if society regards a man as "enemy enough to put him in the penitentiary, enemy enough to put stripes on him, enemy enough to degrade him" then he should not vote. Prison, in his view, caused degradation, and thus made men unfit for suffrage. Allowing prisoners to vote would have grave social impacts: "The spectacle of a squad of prisoners, escorted by a jailer or Sheriff, from behind the bars, or from the rock-pile, to the polls [would] degrade rather than elevate the right of suffrage, in the sight of the worthy."[99] Another delegate, John McDermott, offered a similar opinion as to why those who had been imprisoned should not vote: "I say we are not eager to give votes to persons who have served a term in the penitentiary. After they have been so degraded I do not think we should give them the right to vote if we want to elevate suffrage."[100]

These ideas echoed the position of the North Carolina Supreme Court in 1915 in State v. Earnhardt, quoted in the first chapter of this book. The idea that felons incarcerated in the penitentiary suffered a specific level of degradation due to having to wear "stripes" differentiated them from misdemeanants.[101] This kind of degradation made one unfit for suffrage.

As the votes and electoral power of lower-class southern whites became suspect, even dangerous in the Populist era, expanding infamy to include all those who had been incarcerated fit the political agenda of elite white southern Democrats. Those who could not pay fines or court fees faced longer sentences and additional time performing forced labor. In contrast, individuals who could afford legal representation were more likely to avoid conviction, secure shorter sentences, and have the wealth and political connections to pay fines and secure pardons, paroles, and acquittals more readily. Lower-class white convicts were more likely to experience conditions of incarceration that degraded their status, particularly through their exposure to the convict labor system. Convict labor affected lower-class whites more often than whites with wealth—precisely that segment of the population whose political power southern Democrats feared most.

Those who worked on unsegregated chain gangs seemed no better than the African American men they labored alongside.[102] They had lost every privilege of whiteness and were equal with African Americans.[103] Lower-class prisoners of all races became slaves of the convict lease system, as was explicitly sanctioned under the Thirteenth Amendment. Disfranchising poor white men as well as black men due to their incarceration had, by the end of the nineteenth century, become increasingly easy to accept.[104]

Developments in the law, politics, and criminal justice meant that by the late nineteenth and early twentieth centuries, infamy was defined less by race and more by class status and incarceration. But elite white men might also find themselves incarcerated and lose their suffrage rights, a situation that would challenge the hierarchies of race, class, and citizenship. What of the errant croquet player who bludgeoned his friend to death during the excitement of the game and was subsequently convicted of murder? Those white men whose class or social position elevated them beyond the degraded mass of convicts would turn to the expanding system of pardons to regain their status as citizens.

CHAPTER 5

ᴄⱴᴐ

Making New Men: Pardons and Restorations of Citizenship Rights

As growing numbers of individuals faced lifelong disfranchisement and other civil penalties for criminal convictions in the decades after 1865, some sought pardons to restore their rights. In response, southern legislatures, attorneys general, courts, and constitutional conventions established and clarified procedures for restoring civil rights. Designing and implementing processes for restoring suffrage and full citizenship rights was a direct result of the expanding impact of these laws on individual citizens. This chapter will first survey changes in procedures restoring suffrage and citizenship rights in southern states in the decades after the end of the Civil War when laws were changing rapidly and the numbers affected by them were increasing. The second part of this chapter explores the effects and operation of these laws by examining petitions for restoration of citizenship rights. Though the pardon process varied from state to state, the restoration of rights was in the hands of those with political power—governors, legislators, or judges. Petitioners often sought endorsement of their requests for pardons from local authorities and/or prominent citizens. In this way the pardon process reaffirmed hierarchies of race and class, offering a path to restoration for those who received the approval from elite gatekeepers of citizenship.

Restoring civil rights became an important issue throughout the South immediately after the war as some former Confederates lost their right to vote and hold office under Section Three of the Fourteenth Amendment and the Reconstruction Act. Individuals who had received presidential pardons sought to determine the extent to which these pardons erased their crimes.

Courts in the early nineteenth century had been reluctant to allow pardons to restore civil rights, following English common law and the precedent set in Virginia in 1830 in the case of *Commonwealth v. Fugate*.[1] But in 1866 the U.S. Supreme Court articulated an expanded view of the impact of pardons on citizenship rights in *Ex Parte Garland*. Augustus H. Garland had represented Arkansas in the Confederate Senate. For this he was disbarred for treason. He sought a pardon to resume his career as an attorney. The Court ruled that the pardon erased the crime, restoring all civil rights that Garland had lost. Addressing the issue of pardons and civil disabilities in straightforward language, the Court wrote: "If granted before conviction, [a pardon] prevents any of the penalties and disabilities consequent upon conviction from attaching; if granted after conviction, it removes the penalties and disabilities, and restores him to all his civil rights; it makes him, as it were, a new man, and gives him a new credit and capacity."[2] *Garland* reaffirmed the English common law tradition that a pardon could erase infamy, restore honor, and fully and completely restore the rights of citizenship.

Two years after the *Garland* decision southern states began to revise their constitutions as a requirement for readmission to the Union. But some states remained vague on procedures for restoring citizenship rights to those who lost them for a criminal conviction. Florida's 1868 constitution stipulated that a body consisting of the governor, attorney general, and supreme court justices had pardoning power, but did not specify whether such pardons included the removal of civil disabilities. Another constitutional provision allowed those who had been "restored to civil rights" to vote, but did not indicate how this restoration might happen.[3] Mississippi similarly empowered the governor to grant "reprieves and pardons" but did not stipulate whether or not these acts restored civil rights.[4]

Laws in other states were clearer. Alabama's political leaders refused to allow the removal of civil disabilities by any method; the 1868 constitution specified that gubernatorial pardons did not remove citizenship disabilities and did not offer any other means by which such disabilities could be removed.[5] South Carolina's 1868 constitution gave the governor an open-ended power to grant pardons and reprieves of all sorts "in such a manner, on such terms, and under such restrictions, as he shall think proper." The 1868 South Carolina constitutional convention also gave itself the power to restore rights of citizenship, as discussed in chapter 2, and the assembly heard and granted such petitions, primarily for individuals convicted of treason but also for a man convicted of killing his brother.[6]

In subsequent years, as state courts interpreted the work of these constitutional conventions, many cited *Garland* to argue that gubernatorial pardon powers included the authority to restore the rights of citizenship.

Nonetheless, differences among state constitutions left open a number of procedural questions. Louisiana courts in 1874 debated whether pardons granted after a sentence was served could restore citizenship rights. Initially, the state supreme court ruled that an individual who was pardoned after his sentence was completed was not relieved of civil disabilities. But the court reheard the case and concluded that the first decision had been wrong. Echoing the language of *Garland*, the court wrote in *State v. Baptiste*, "The doctrine, now well recognized upon this subject, we believe, is that a pardon gives to the person in whose favor it is granted a new character and makes of him a new man. When extended to him in prison, it relieves him and removes his disabilities; when given to him after his term of imprisonment has expired, it removes all that is left of the consequences of conviction—his disabilities."[7]

Virginia's courts also interpreted the state constitution, taking *Garland* into consideration, but required the governor to follow a distinct set of procedures in order to restore citizenship rights. The 1870 constitution first gave the governor the ability to "remove political disabilities consequent upon conviction for offenses committed prior or subsequent to the adoption" of the constitution.[8] Unclear though was exactly the form that the act removing disabilities would take. Did all pardons restore citizenship rights? The Virginia Supreme Court in 1883 explained in *Edwards v. The Commonwealth* that a special act, separate from a pardon, was needed to remove political disabilities. The bottom line, however, was that the state constitution empowered the governor to restore the rights of citizenship.[9] Despite the *Edwards* ruling separating the two gubernatorial acts, the published lists of pardons issued by Virginia governors between 1870 and 1908 made no distinction between pardons and removing political disabilities. It is likely that when governors issued what they termed "absolute pardons" these functioned to restore political rights. But it is not clear why the issuing of separate orders to remove political disabilities, as instructed by the Supreme Court in *Edwards,* did not begin until 1906.[10]

More confusion in Virginia came from the connection between the removal of political disabilities and the right to testify in court. An 1848 law had barred individuals convicted of a felony from serving as a witness in court "unless he has been pardoned or punished."[11] Governor William Hodges Mann (who served from 1910 to 1914) restored political rights to three men so that they could testify in court, but neither his predecessor nor successor indicated that a need for testimony justified the removal of political disabilities. The three individuals whose rights to testify were restored by Mann had completed their prison sentences, yet Mann seemed to believe that they required a pardon to testify in court. Mann pardoned

Ernest Hudson in May 1911 so Hudson could "testify in an important case." Dock Hines was similarly fortunate. Convicted of murder in 1909, Hines received a conditional pardon in 1914 and an absolute pardon in 1915. On the same day governor Mann issued a third, separate order removing Hines's political disabilities, saying this was "absolutely necessary for the ends of justice in the trial of accused persons."[12] The question of whether pardons restored the right to testify would soon be resolved by the revised Code of 1919, which eliminated the disqualification from testimony for such individuals. After 1919, the fact of conviction could affect the credibility of testimony, but Virginia no longer barred convicted individuals from testifying altogether.[13]

Gubernatorial pardons could not restore the voting rights of those disfranchised for all illegal acts in Virginia, only those acts for which an individual was convicted. This distinction became important due to a long-standing provision that barred anyone who had participated in a duel from holding public office. The 1870 constitution disfranchised such individuals as well.[14] But, the constitution did not require a conviction to disfranchise for dueling, stating simply that anyone who participated in such activities could not vote. Since there was no conviction for which the governor could issue a pardon, how might duelers have their voting rights restored? In 1877 the assembly passed a special legislative act restoring citizenship rights to several men who had dueled.[15] About two months later, the legislature passed an act allowing it to restore, with a two-thirds vote, the voting rights of any individuals disfranchised for dueling.[16]

The Florida Supreme Court also took guidance from the U.S. Supreme Court's *Garland* decision. In 1872 Florida's Republican governor, Harrison Reed, asked for a formal ruling from the state supreme court on whether pardons also restored citizenship rights: "I wish to obtain the opinion of the Judges of the Supreme Court upon the question whether the pardon of an individual, after conviction, restores the rights forfeited by the conviction. An immediate answer is necessary for my official guidance, and the information of the inspectors of the election now approaching." The state court replied with an extensive quotation from *Ex Parte Garland*, explaining that pardons did restore all rights lost due to a conviction in Florida. The only limitation was that a pardon did not restore offices forfeited or "property or interests vested in others in consequence of the conviction and judgment."[17]

Although the Florida governor and state supreme court considered the matter settled, some still rejected the power of pardons to restore rights. In 1876 Congress investigated accusations of voter intimidation in Florida's most recent election, including an accusation that a convicted but pardoned individual had been wrongly allowed to vote. The congressional report weighed in on the question, citing the state supreme court's 1872 communication with Governor Reed and quoting *Ex Parte Garland*, concluding that the man in question should have been permitted to vote.[18] But the minority report of the committee continued to dispute the ability of governors to restore voting rights through a pardon. Supporting this position was a memo from Florida Attorney General William Archer Cocke, who argued that since the state constitution did not specify that a pardon could relieve civil disabilities, there was no reason to believe it did. However, most of the cases Cocke cited predated *Garland*, including *Commonwealth v. Fugate* as well as an 1860 Illinois case, *Foreman v. Baldwin*.[19]

Many southern constitutional conventions created mechanisms or clarified processes for restoring civil rights in the three decades after the war. Alabama's 1875 constitutional convention debated whether a gubernatorial pardon should relieve civil sanctions. One proposal would have allowed the General Assembly to restore any civil rights that could not be restored by a pardon. The body rejected this plan.[20] Ultimately, the convention decided to allow the governor to restore civil and political rights through a pardon, but only if such a restoration was specifically expressed in the pardon. In other words, a pardon would not automatically restore such rights; rather the governor had to state his endorsement of restoration in the pardon.[21]

Some governors interpreted state laws differently than others. South Carolina's governor, Duncan Heyward (1903-1907), did not believe he could, or should, remove disabilities for convicted individuals unless they documented a wrongful conviction. When K. S. Villipigue asked for a pardon to restore his rights of citizenship, Heyward asked Villipigue's attorney for "proof, if possible, that the party asking the pardon was not guilty of the offense charged."[22] Governor Heyward also refused to grant a similar request to a man named J. M. Cortez.[23] The next governor, Martin F. Ansel, dropped the stipulation that pardons would be issued only to individuals wrongly convicted. He granted eleven such requests, including those of Cortez and Villipigue.[24]

Georgia's 1877 constitutional convention created a process to restore rights of citizenship by specifying that those disfranchised for criminal convictions could have their rights restored by gubernatorial pardon.[25] While courts agreed that a full pardon could relieve a person of his prison sentence and restore his rights of citizenship, Georgia governors still at times expressed uncertainty about the impact of other acts of mercy on citizenship rights. In 1916 Governor Nathan Harris wrote to Georgia Attorney General Clifford Walker, asking whether commutations also restored rights of citizenship. Walker responded that a commutation only remitted part of the penalty—the penalty of the remaining prison sentence. He explained that only a full pardon freed a person and restored his civil rights; a separate act simply removing disabilities could restore full citizenship to individuals no longer under a prison sentence.[26]

In Tennessee and North Carolina the situation was somewhat unusual because individuals lost their civil rights following a conviction for an infamous crime. Unlike other states where disfranchisement was a consequence of conviction, disfranchisement in these states was a judgment of the court. In other words, infamy was a status associated with being convicted of certain crimes, not a punishment for such crimes.[27] While governors could relieve individuals of punishment, an infamy judgment—a product of a court—could only be lifted by a court. Both states had long-established procedures outlining how courts could restore rights. In 1840 the Tennessee legislature established a process by which infamous individuals could petition the circuit court to have their civil rights restored.[28] North Carolina also had a provision dating back to 1840 that gave courts the power to restore citizenship rights following an infamy judgment.[29]

In Tennessee some still wondered whether, in the aftermath of the *Garland* decision, a pardon might also restore citizenship rights even if the courts customarily performed this function. The Tennessee Supreme Court answered in the negative in *Evans v. State* in 1872, ruling that a pardon for an infamous crime did not restore the right to testify or vote. Wiley Evans had been on trial for murder in Maury County when the prosecution presented a witness, Nelson Sheppard, who had recently been convicted of petit larceny. Evans's attorney objected to Sheppard's testimony, but the judge allowed Sheppard to testify because he had received a gubernatorial pardon. The state supreme court found that the judge committed an error in permitting Sheppard's testimony because a pardon did not reverse the penalty of infamy. Only a circuit court judge could remove infamy judgments and restore the rights of citizenship.[30]

Other states, too, considered which branch of government should hold the power to restore the rights of citizenship. The 1875 constitutional convention in Texas debated whether citizenship rights should be restored by a gubernatorial or a legislative act; the assembly decided to give this power to the governor.[31] While Texas opted to retain this power in the governorship, in 1890 Mississippi moved to transfer the authority to restore citizenship rights from the governor to the legislature. Mississippi's 1868 constitution had a standard provision allowing the governor to grant pardons.[32] The 1890 constitution established a special procedure that allowed the legislature to restore the right of suffrage to convicted individuals. The convention stipulated that the vote "shall be by yeas and nays" and the reason for the restoration "shall be spread upon the journals."[33]

Kentucky's 1890 constitutional convention also refined the process of restoring citizenship rights following a conviction. Some in the assembly questioned whether the power to restore rights was already implicit in the pardoning power of the governor or if the new constitution should specify this. James F. Montgomery from Adair County was among those concerned that the governor could not restore citizenship rights under the existing constitution, and so he proposed an amendment allowing the governor to restore civil rights five years after conviction.[34] Edward J. McDermott, citing *Ex Parte Garland*, argued that the governor already had full pardoning power, including the power to restore citizenship rights, and that Montgomery's plan would actually limit gubernatorial authority by imposing a waiting period.[35] Ultimately, the convention decided to leave this portion of the constitution unchanged.[36]

Louisiana's legislature gave statutory force to the 1874 decision in *State v. Baptiste*. Not only did state law clarify that pardons restore to an individual "all of the civil and political rights privileges and immunities which he may have lost by having been convicted and sentenced," it also specified punishments for those who failed to respect this:

> If any public officer or any other person shall deprive any such person of any civil or political right privilege or immunity on the pretense that such person has been convicted of any crime or offense and when such person who may have been so convicted shall have been pardoned such officer or person so depriving such person so pardoned of his civil or political rights shall be deemed to be guilty of a misdemeanor and on conviction shall be fined a sum not exceeding one hundred dollars and may be imprisoned at the discretion of the court or both and shall furthermore be liable to an action for damages in favor of such pardoned person.[37]

The history of restoring the rights of citizenship in this period follows in many ways the more general story of pardons and clemency. In the late nineteenth and early twentieth centuries, many states worked out constitutional and bureaucratic procedures by which convicted individuals might be relieved of punishment and sanctions. Growing adherence to legal formalism and the more rigorous use of constitutions to articulate the extent of government power—what historian William Novak has called a "cult of constitutionalism" that emerged after the Civil War—as well as the push toward standardization and bureaucratization in the Progressive Era, led states to establish formal constitutional and legal processes for restoring rights.[38]

Citizens across the South moved to take advantage of these newly clarified processes for restoring voting and citizenship rights and in doing so forced governments to work out the logistics and details of disfranchisement and suffrage restoration. I have obtained records of restorations of citizenship rights in eight states: Virginia, Tennessee, Alabama, Georgia, Florida, North Carolina, South Carolina, and Mississippi.[39] All three mechanisms for restoring rights are represented in this survey: executive, judicial, and legislative.

Regardless of the mechanism by which states restored citizenship rights, most involved some kind of petition and letter of request that usually followed the same form as petitions for other kinds of pardons. The petition gave basic information about the conviction, explained why the individual should have his rights restored, and displayed the signatures of supportive parties. In Virginia, Georgia, South Carolina, and Alabama (before 1901), individuals petitioned the governor. In Tennessee they petitioned the circuit court. In North Carolina, they petitioned the superior court. In Alabama (after 1901) and Florida they petitioned the pardon board, which then made recommendations to the governor.[40] In Mississippi the legislature passed special acts restoring citizenship rights; like any other legislation such acts were proposed by a legislator and approved by the whole assembly. In all of these states, individuals seeking the restoration of citizenship rights usually sent a letter accompanying the petition, written by themselves or by their attorney. At times, others acquainted with the case sent separate letters of recommendation or, in some instances, letters opposing restoration of citizenship rights.[41]

Petitioning for restoration often cost the petitioner money. In Tennessee petitioning the court required the payment of court fees. Two petitions from Giles County, dated 1888 and 1894, are accompanied by receipts for payment of court costs totaling $2.70 and another $2.95.[42] In North Carolina, court costs seem to have varied significantly from county to county. In 1887, Jefferson Ratliff of Anson County paid the court an astounding $14 to have his citizenship rights restored, ten years after his conviction for larceny (including three years' incarceration) for stealing a hog.[43] The same year, Alfred Exum paid $6.10 for the restoration of his rights in Wayne County. Exum, an illiterate tenant farmer, had been convicted of stealing five pounds of cotton in 1880.[44] Nearly two decades later, in Granville County, restorations were cheaper; James Weaver paid $3 to the court to file his petition.[45] For agricultural workers, who were often landless tenant farmers or sharecroppers, these costs were significant amounts, and their willingness to pay these costs indicated a commitment to make financial sacrifices in order to obtain citizenship rights.

Some petitioners hired lawyers to help them write and file petitions, thereby adding another cost, though having a lawyer was not a requirement.[46] Attorney O. V. F. Blythe charged R. L. Green $5 to file a petition for restoration in the Polk County court in Hendersonville, North Carolina, in 1908.[47] In other cases this legal assistance was likely free to the petitioner because restoring rights was at times spearheaded, as we shall see, by politicians seeking votes and prosecutors seeking court testimony.

Assistance from a lawyer, or at least someone who could write, was critical for illiterate individuals seeking the restoration of their rights. I have located several petitions that were filed by individuals who could not even sign their names. For example, in Giles County Tennessee, Alex Smith, an African American man, signed his petition, filed in 1900, with an "X". His petition was typed and signed by an attorney, suggesting that Smith hired the attorney to help generate and file the paperwork.[48] In other cases, illiterate petitioners found friends who could help them compose their application. In Georgia, Lewis Price explained to Governor William Y. Atkinson in 1895, "I am a poor ignorant negro and I have no money to pay to the lawyers to work for me. So I have to depend on my friends to do all of my writing."[49]

Despite these financial and logistical hurdles, individuals sought the restoration of citizenship for a variety of reasons. The ability to vote was obviously a concern, but convicted individuals lost, and therefore sought restoration of, other civil rights as well. Some requests for restoration were motivated by the need to testify in court, a right that convicted individuals lost after a felony conviction in a number of states. Being able to testify in court had obvious advantages. Some sought this right so they might testify in their own civil cases.[50] Such was the case of Samuel A. Pickens. In 1888 he had been convicted in Georgia of stealing a "medium size dun colored cow with horns about 4 years old, of the value of $20." In 1906 Pickens was living in South Carolina and involved in a civil suit over some land. Unable to testify in South Carolina due to his conviction in Georgia, he petitioned Georgia's governor, Joseph Terrell, seeking restoration of his citizenship.[51]

Sometimes prosecutors or defense attorneys sought restorations for witnesses barred from court testimony. In these cases, individuals petitioning for restoration had assistance—presumably both legal and financial—in filing from those who sought their testimony. In Wise County, Virginia, C. G. Lundy had his rights of citizenship restored with the help of the commonwealth's attorney who needed his testimony at a trial.[52] The published lists of restorations of citizenship in Virginia contain many that specified court testimony as the motivation. In Alabama, L. Adkins Baker's application for restoration was accompanied by a letter to the governor explaining, "Mr. Baker is an important witness in a capital case which is to be tried in our county at the next circuit court."[53] In South Carolina, Governor Martin Ansel pardoned Kirby Lark in 1908 so that he could testify as a witness for the prosecution in a murder case.[54]

Another reason for seeking restoration of citizenship rights, in addition to voting and court testimony, was to run for public office. James J. Worsham, a white man, petitioned the Maury County court in Tennessee in 1876 for the restoration of rights that he lost following conviction for "drunkenness while in office." He told the court he had been pardoned by the governor and since his conviction had "abstained from the use of all intoxicating drink." The court restored all of his citizenship rights "particularly the right to hold office."[55] H. T. Turner's 1907 appeal to the Knox County court was similar. Turner had been convicted of murder in 1872 in Carter County, subsequently pardoned, and now sought his rights of citizenship and the "removal of any disqualification he may be under to hold public office."[56]

Denial of various kinds of professional licenses represented another civil consequence of criminal convictions. Fred L. Stephenson of Georgia wished to become a notary public for a local cotton dealer but could not because of his prior conviction. He wrote to the head of the state prison commission on the company's letterhead explaining the situation and asking the secretary to recommend his restoration.[57] Thomas Cobb petitioned Georgia's governor, Joseph M. Terrell, for the restoration of his civil rights so he could obtain an engineering license. An accompanying letter from his employer described Cobb as an "expert white mechanic."[58]

Petitions and the accompanying correspondence made the case for rights in a variety of ways. They followed strategies common to those requesting pardons to release them from incarceration, seeking either to document the reform of their character since the crime or to demonstrate their innocence.[59] Whatever the reason for the pardon, the act removed infamy and produced a "new man."

Some petitioners argued that they were now worthy citizens because they were rehabilitated from their criminal ways. In Virginia, W. J. Creery wrote to Governor Andrew Jackson Montague on the letterhead of his own company, Kritzer and Creery Tinning, Plumbing, and Gas Fitting. He told the governor: "I got in trouble from using morphine which I used three years before I got in trouble. The doctor testified that I was irresponsible for my actions. Before my arrest I wandered about day and night not knowing where I was. I was arrested for stealing morphine. I am now working hard every day to earn an honest living, and it is my wish to be restored to full citizenship. As I shall ever in the future try to do right and respect the laws."[60]

Petitioners testified to employment and marriage as evidence of reform and good citizenship. In Tennessee W. E. Terrell, a white man, petitioned the Maury County court for restoration of citizenship in 1947. Terrell pointed out that he was married, had a family, was a landowner, and was employed as a salesman for a St. Louis-based company. He also told the court he was a disabled World War I veteran.[61] In Mississippi, Robert Speck explained that since his conviction he "has married and is now teaching in the public school, and is a highly respected citizen."[62] Governor William H. Mann of Virginia observed that petitioner William Earley was "living in another State, has a fine position, and is doing well."[63] James Weaver told the Granville County North Carolina Superior Court that he had "been con verted and joined the church."[64]

In Tennessee the statute governing restoration of citizenship specified that individuals should have "sustained the character of a person of honesty, respectability, and veracity."[65] Judges in the state sometimes noted that they had received evidence of this, often repeating the text of the statute verbatim. But in some hearings judges put their own twist on the statutory requirement in ways that further illuminate the characteristics they desired of citizens. In Knox County in 1910, the court found Charles Lyle was a person of "good character, honesty, sobriety and veracity."[66] The same court found that Robert Vick was a "reputable and industrious citizen" and that Sam McMickens was a "hard working man."[67] Clear at the other end of the state in Crockett County a court hearing for Francis Marion Henderson's petition for restoration found that he was a "law abiding citizen, a good neighbor, a Christian gentleman, respected by his neighbors and friends, and that he has lived consistent with his prayer of his petition."[68]

Other petitions minimized or excused previous crimes. This was the strategy adopted by several African American petitioners. The 1891 petition of Henry Colvin, an African American man from Tallapoosa County, Alabama, who had been convicted of murder, explained that there was significant doubt about his guilt. According to Colvin's white neighbors who signed the petition, "testimony against him, which was given only by witnesses of his own color, was instigated by political difference."[69] In 1897 T. L. Galloway, the U.S. attorney in northern Georgia, wrote to Governor Atkinson about an African American man named Jack Goldsmith, who had been convicted of rioting. Galloway told the governor that when Goldsmith was convicted "the excitement at Decatur over the riot was very high, and it is extremely doubtful whether this man was really guilty."[70] In North Carolina Jefferson Ratliff told the Anson County court that the only witness against him had been a "colored girl, then about thirteen years of age" who had since admitted to being paid to testify against Ratliff.[71]

White petitioners also tried to explain their criminal action or defend the morality of their acts. In Georgia, Simon J. O'Neal and another man had been convicted of manslaughter in the mid-1890s. His attorney wrote, "There was no moral turpitude in their offense. In a fit of passion, they probably did wrong; they have atoned for it."[72] J. W. Baisey's attorney told Governor Montague of Virginia that, "With the exception of the offence of which he was convicted (shooting a negro who gave him some impudence) he has always been a law abiding man, and a good citizen."[73] In Mississippi, legislators discussing a bill requesting the restoration of three Benton County men pointed out that "the offenses charged against these parties were trivial and committed while the offenders were youths . . . parties have thoroughly reformed and become good citizens and have the respect of the people."[74]

Testimony by others to a petitioner's respectability and worth as a citizen formed a key part of most applications for restoration. Particularly valuable was testimony by individuals who worked in the criminal justice system: judges, court clerks, law enforcement officials, and more. In every state surveyed, a majority of petitioners sought and received endorsement from these court officials on their petitions. Such backing indicated the court's support for the restoration—usually the same court in which the conviction occurred. Such a recommendation obviously carried a lot of weight, demonstrating that the judicial authorities who had punished the individual by taking away his civil rights now felt the punishment should be lifted. In Virginia, Hiram Bartley's application was supported by the "judge, clerk, sheriff, treasurer" as well as other local citizens.[75] Tommie Burns's 1906 petition to the governor of Georgia was accompanied by a letter from the deputy warden of the prison where he had been incarcerated.[76] In Tennessee, where restoration of citizenship was done in a court hearing, petitioners could bring witnesses, including witnesses connected to the court, along with them to the hearing—though I have found evidence of this practice only in Knox County. In 1922, D. B. Vess of Knox County brought three men, including a county judge, to court to testify to his good character and right to have his citizenship restored.[77] Cornelius Curtis, whose case is discussed at length in chapter 6, also brought witnesses to court in 1914.[78]

Even if a petitioner's supporters did not work for the court system, they nonetheless might note their occupation to add weight to their support for the restoration of rights. Social class and profession served as evidence of one's value as a citizen. Since individuals seeking restoration were claiming that they were worthy of citizenship, supporters with respectable occupations buttressed their case. In other words, good citizens—as measured by social class and occupation—were best equipped to recommend others as good citizens.

Employers sometimes wrote letters recommending pardons for their own employees who might need their disabilities removed in order to perform their jobs. James W. English of the Lookout Mountain Coal and Coke Company wrote to Georgia's governor, Joseph M. Terrell, in 1904 asking that one of his employees, Thomas Cobb, be restored to citizenship so he could obtain an engineering license.[79] One means by which letter writers indicated their prominence and status as an employer was by writing on company letterhead. In 1895 the president of the Chattahoochee Brick Company wrote a letter on company letterhead to Georgia governor Atkinson, recommending that C. E. Hill be restored to citizenship. Both the Chattahoochee Brick Company and the Lookout Mountain Coal and Coke Company employed convict labor. It is likely that these men had worked there as convicts and had succeeded in securing employment there after being released.[80]

Governors sometimes remarked on the prominence of the petition's signatories in their recommendations. In Virginia, Governor Montague restored the rights of Isham Bridgeforth "upon the recommendation of the judge, Commonwealth's Attorney, and a number of prominent citizens."[81] When Georgia Governor Allen D. Candler restored Judd Murray's rights in 1899 he wrote, "The defendant, for fifteen years since his conviction, has lived an upright, honest life and has made a useful citizen. These facts are testified by some of the best citizens of Morgan County, including county officials, who ask that this removal of disabilities be granted him."[82] Governors also observed when petitions were supported by "leading citizens," and "reliable citizens," and "substantial citizens."[83]

Those petitioning for the restoration of their voting rights asserted that they were worthy and decent individuals wrongly affected by laws aimed at immoral and degraded convicts. Middle- and upper-class white men objected to their exclusion from the body politic to which their race, class, and gender would have ordinarily granted them access. African American petitioners often made similar arguments about their honor and moral fitness, but in states where black voting was limited or nearly eradicated, such petitioners sometimes took different approaches to securing their rights.

In Georgia, Alabama, South Carolina, and Tennessee, African American men succeeded, at least in some instances, in having their voting rights

restored in the late nineteenth and early twentieth centuries. This is notable because African Americans faced disfranchisement and the denial of
citizenship rights in southern states throughout this era. In these states
African American men who sought the restoration of their voting rights
followed some of the same strategies as their white counterparts—getting
support for their petitions from politicians, employers, and prominent
white members of their community. From this survey of pardon records,
it appears that African American men had the most success in having their
voting rights restored in Tennessee.

African American men in Tennessee, on at least a few occasions, petitioned for the restoration of their citizenship in groups. In 1875 three
African American men, Toney Long, Frank Lawrence, and Eli Bowen were
all indicted for larceny offenses in the Maury County Criminal Court in
Columbia, Tennessee, and were convicted a few days later. Each had faced
accusations from white businessmen, probably their employers. Long was
found guilty of stealing cash, Lawrence of stealing tools, and Bowen of
stealing wheat. Eleven years later, on May 25, 1886, Long and Lawrence
were together in court again, now petitioning for the restoration of their
citizenship rights. A few years later, in 1892, Bowen, too, petitioned for
the restoration of his rights. Long, Lawrence, and Bowen likely knew each
other; if they were not already acquainted, they would have met in court or
perhaps while serving in the state penitentiary. Perhaps Long and Lawrence
told Bowen of their success in getting their rights restored and explained
the process to him, prompting Bowen to follow suit a few years later.[84]

When white men recommended African Americans for citizenship they
were sometimes careful to point out that such men were political allies,
demonstrating that political considerations shaped the decision to restore
voting rights. In 1880 A. G. Gordon wrote to Alabama Governor Rufus
Cobb recommending J. H. Culver for the restoration of citizenship, explaining that Culver "is a colored man but votes the Democratic ticket all the
time." Gordon further bolstered his case by pointing out that Culver had
been convicted of stealing a pocket knife, a theft that Culver had claimed
was accidental. "He is a young man and it seems a hard case to keep him
from voting for only a $1.50 pocket knife."[85] In Georgia in 1894, the mayor
of Milner, Georgia, wrote to Governor Atkinson asking for a pardon for
Berry Burt, an African American man, so he could vote in the next election: "Enclosed I send petition from Berry Burt...could get more signatures to petition by having more time but our election for county offices is
next Wednesday and we have not got time to wait."[86] In Georgia the 1897
petition of another African American man, Jack Goldsmith, stated that
"the restoration of this colored man to citizenship will meet with the hearty

approval of the citizens of Dekalb County." This suggested perhaps that support for the governor or his allies from local black citizens might follow the approval of his request.[87] African American men also might get their citizenship restored when they were needed to testify in court. Such was the experience of Townsend Lide in Darlington County, South Carolina. He was sentenced to a year in prison for "theft of cotton." Governor Robert Cooper restored his citizenship rights at the request of a county prosecutor who needed him to testify in court against "another negro."[88]

Others supporting petitions for citizenship by individuals of all races offered more explicit explanations of the political advantage associated with the restoration of an individual's rights. Elected officials and party leaders played a frequent role in recommending individuals for restoration. This was especially true in Mississippi, where restorations required legislative approval; each pardon had to be introduced by a legislator who thereby indicated his support for restoring that individual's rights. While recommending such requests might have been simply part of their constituent services, it is clear from evidence in other states that partisan agendas and the desire to enfranchise supporters sometimes motivated these actions.

W. J. Dozier wrote to Georgia Governor Nathan E. Harris in 1916 to request a pardon for Will Giles. Dozier told Harris, "We need his vote in our upcoming primary."[89] The absence of support from elected officials could sometimes be explained away by partisanship as well. Martin Tipton wrote to Virginia Governor Mann in 1910, "You will observe that the petition is not signed by any of the County officials, I did not present it to them as they are strong Republican and would not likely sign the petition as they know it means a vote for Judge Saunders."[90] Finally, individuals making a case for their own restoration also pointed out their partisan loyalties. R. E. McLemore wrote to Governor Mann requesting his rights be restored. He told Mann that he had "always been a strong Democrat and voted for you, and enjoyed your speech at East Radford and waived [sic] my hat high."[91]

White men might also use their race to get their citizenship restored. William Gaskin had been convicted of larceny of livestock in Kershaw County, South Carolina, in 1901. A year later, after he served his year-long sentence, he sought restoration of his citizenship rights because, as the governor noted, "he is a white man and wishes to preserve his citizenship."[92] In the racially charged environment in South Carolina in 1901, suffrage and citizenship was a privilege of whiteness and therefore worth noting in such a request.

In 1917 a Virginia man wrote to the Democratic governor, Henry Carter Stuart, attempting to explain why he supported the re-enfranchisement of a Republican, named Noah L. Vanover. "We are not asking this for political reasons, as Vanover has always been a Republican, but of the liberal type that votes for a man on the opposite side when convinced that it is for the best interests of his country, and, Governor, you know that brand of Republicans are scarce out our way." So, why should Vanover be allowed to vote? According to the letter, he "shrinks from his children growing into manhood and womanhood knowing that their father is a citizen in name only. He is a poor, hard-working man and the recent loss of two of his children has chastened and greatly changed him."[93]

This letter demonstrates that at times personal agendas trumped partisan ones. But it also indicates that being able to vote and exercise the rights of citizenship held a significant symbolic place. Vanover was not alone in this sentiment. In 1905, C. G. Pate petitioned Georgia Governor Terrell for the removal of his political disabilities. Pate was an illiterate man, unable to even sign his name, whose race is unclear from the historical documents. He had been convicted of larceny earlier that year and ordered to pay a $50 fine or spend six months on the chain gang. Now free (friends had raised money to pay part of his fine so he could be released early), he asked Governor Terrell to restore his political disabilities. Why was Pate so anxious to have his rights restored? He explained that "the said conviction casts a reflection not only upon your petitioner but on his children and grandchildren." The petition of Abe Brown, an African American man, asked Georgia Governor William Atkinson to "pardon him so that he may have restored to him the rights of citizenship of which his conviction has deprived him, and that he and his family may have the disgrace, which has attached to him and thereby reason of said conviction in some measure, removed."[94]

Citizenship was more than the right to vote, testify, run for office or obtain professional licenses. Possessing civil rights was a component of manhood and important to individuals and their families. Voting was a public act, and attendance and participation at the polls was a public affirmation of one's manhood and membership in the body politic. More generally, the language used to describe the importance of full citizenship and suffrage in some of these letters illustrates the social burden imposed on those who were denied citizenship. This perspective on the value of citizenship and the shame of disfranchisement was echoed by John D. Carroll, a delegate at Kentucky's 1890 constitutional convention. Carroll explained: "I do not know of any more degrading or humiliating punishment that can be inflicted on a citizen than depriving of him the right to vote and hold office because of some crime he has committed, if he is otherwise entitled to vote and hold office. It is a punishment that is continually recurring; that is present with him at every election; that humiliates and degrades him in the sight of his neighbor every time an election is held."[95]

Being restored to citizenship relieved petitioners from the civil and social consequences of infamy. The echoes of the historic tradition of infamy are striking. Under English common law, individuals who were infamous were "tainted"—denied certain citizenship rights—a status that could be transmitted to future generations. Though, of course, the United States Constitution banned the inheritance of such a status, it is clear that the disgrace of being denied the rights of citizenship echoed this past tradition. Being restored to citizenship might reestablish honor and reputation not just to individuals, but in the eyes of some, to their whole family.

Regaining rights did not merely remove a persistent penalty. Restoring an individual to civil equality restored him to social equality. The petition of Fred Stephenson in Georgia illustrates this sense of connection between civil rights and social status. Stephenson asked that his disabilities be removed so that he could become a notary public, but he also told the governor, "I am very anxious myself to be once more on equal footing with my fellow man."[96] Also evident is the sense of humiliation faced by those who lost their political rights, and the value that they placed on getting them restored. Virginian Lewis Hill quietly expressed the personal pain that he felt at the possibility of a lifetime without voting rights when he told Governor Mann in 1910: "I am a young man and I believe that after I am 'reinstated' I can go forth in this world with a more cheerful heart."[97]

Having access to citizenship was not only evidence of redemption, but might in some cases offer hope for rehabilitation. In 1902 Henry Manning's attorney wrote to Georgia's governor, Joseph M. Terrell, asking for a restoration of Manning's citizenship rights. He asked for a pardon and restoration for Manning (who had been convicted of manslaughter) "so that he will feel that it is his imperative duty to return home and life the life of a law abiding citizen."[98] In Alabama, when Governor Thomas M. Seay pardoned J. F. Jarman in 1887, he wrote, "the restoration of political rights in this case would be just and would probably tend to encourage the prisoner to good citizenship."[99] When Governor Claude Swanson of Virginia restored the citizenship of Peter Manger, he wrote that "he should be...given full privilege and a chance to redeem himself."[100] Having the rights of citizenship might even be therapeutic. A Virginia judge who recommended that Howard L. Adams be restored to citizenship told the governor that removing his disabilities "will enable him to gain the lost confidence."[101]

The disfranchisement of veterans with criminal convictions was, to some, wholly unjustified, and many petitions emphasized the plaintiff's veteran status. Throughout U.S. history, individuals with military service have been regarded as particularly deserving of civil rights and the privileges of citizenship.[102] At times, even third parties unrelated to the petitioner took it upon themselves to request pardons for veterans they felt were unfairly disfranchised. One letter to Virginia's governor, Andrew J. Montague, stated that, "There is in this neighborhood an old Confederate soldier and was a good one he only has one eye [sic]. The other one he lost at Cold Harbor in our Civil War. About 97 or 98 he shot a negro in this county and was tride [sic] and sent to the penitentiary for 12 months. He served out the 12 months and I write this to ask you to give him a pardon so he will be able to vote this fall."[103] The idea that servicemen and veterans, even if convicted, could be denied the right to vote troubled J. L. Lypps of Jonesville, Virginia, as well. In January 1918 he wrote to Governor Stuart asking him to restore the voting rights of four young men he knew. He told Stuart, "I don't think it rite for them to have to go and fite for the country and not be allowed to vote for the roolers of our country like other men... I think it rite that they should be allowed the same privileges as other men [sic]."[104]

Individuals also highlighted their own military service in requests for pardons. R. E. McLemore of Pulaski County, Virginia, told Governor Mann that he had been in the Second Virginia Volunteers in the Spanish American War.[105] Roy Smith, of Houston County, Alabama, hoped that his plans for military service would speed along his application in 1917. He told the Board of Pardons that he had just applied to work as a mechanic in the U.S. Army Air Corps.[106]

In Mississippi support for restoring voting rights for convicted veterans produced legislation restoring all who served in the First and Second World Wars. In February 1948 the Mississippi House passed a bill titled, "Restoration of Right of Suffrage to World War Veterans." The state senate approved it on March 2, the same day that a group of veterans gathered in Jackson to lobby for expanded veterans benefits, particularly in the area of housing.[107] Under this law, any individual who had lost the right to vote because of conviction of a crime and who served honorably in the armed forces during World War I or World War II (and received an honorable discharge) could have his or her suffrage restored. To get their voting rights back, veterans were to bring their discharge or release paper to the chancery clerk of their county. In passing this bill, the legislature relied on Section 253 of the Mississippi constitution, which allowed the legislature to restore the voting rights of convicted individuals, provided the vote was by a two-thirds majority and the reasons "spread upon the journals." The assembly must have decided that if individual restorations could proceed that way, restorations for veterans could be approved *en masse*.[108]

A number of factors made petitions by women for restoration of citizenship rare before 1920. Women could not vote in southern states for most of the period under study, so they were less likely to feel the impact of civil penalties for criminal conviction. Nevertheless, in states that also disqualified former convicts from court testimony, women would have faced that penalty. Petitions from women were also less common because women have historically been less likely to face criminal conviction. All the same, a loss of the rights of citizenship for a woman could bring both inconvenience and disgrace.

After women achieved the right to vote, increasing numbers petitioned for the restoration of their rights. The first petition from a woman in a southern state that I have been able to locate is the petition of Mollie Mullins of Tarpon, Virginia. In 1923 Mullins's husband, G. W. Mullins, wrote to Governor E. Lee Trinkle to request her rights be restored. He told the governor that she had been "convicted of a frivolous charge when a child." (She had been convicted of petit larceny and fined $5 in 1906.) The couple sent a petition signed by nine men, including the local sheriff and county court clerk. Smith, the commonwealth attorney, wrote to Trinkle describing Mullins as "a lady worthy of the favor to have her disabilities removed that she may exercise the rights of suffrage."[109]

In Florida, several of the earliest petitions from women were filed along with their male spouses. In 1928 four members of the Harvey family—two men and two women—were convicted of perjury in Baker County, Florida. They all served prison time. Three years later, as a family, they applied for unconditional pardons explicitly for the purpose of restoring their citizenship rights.[110] In another Florida case, marital ties connected two convicts: Mr. and Mrs. J. A. Conner were convicted, together, of murder in Gilchrist County Florida in 1928. The governor granted them conditional pardons, releasing them from prison, about a year later. Then they both applied for, and received, full pardons, restoring them to citizenship in 1931.[111]

In Tennessee only four female petitioners appear in the counties surveyed during this period, and all four came in the 1940s. The sole female petitioner in Maury County was Mrs. Hay Long Wall, a white woman, who was convicted of arson in 1930. The daughter of the former mayor of Mt. Pleasant, Tennessee, Wall owned the town's movie theater. When the theater burned down, also damaging a number of neighboring buildings, the district attorney charged her with deliberately setting the fire to collect insurance money. Wall hired a prominent local attorney who arranged for her to plead guilty with a jail sentence of one day. As a consequence of the conviction, the court rendered her infamous. She and a lawyer returned to court to make a successful plea for restoration fifteen years later.[112]

In Knox County three women filed for restoration between 1941 and 1948. The first was Louise Douglas, whose infamy judgment stemmed from a series of crimes she and a male accomplice committed in late 1931. The two of them forged checks to steal furniture and were convicted of acting under false pretenses. She received a sentence of one year in the state penitentiary; the judge sentenced her accomplice to six months in the county workhouse. Both were rendered infamous upon conviction, although this judgment appears to have been misapplied, since false pretenses was not an infamous offense Tennessee.[113] In 1941 Douglas, now married and known as Louise Glass, returned, accompanied by an attorney, to the Knox County Circuit Court to ask for a restoration of her citizenship rights. In approving her petition, the court clerk recorded an unusually lengthy statement from the judge: "[D]uring her incarceration in the penitentiary [Glass] made a model prisoner, and that since her release she has been a respectable citizen, and that she is a person who is believed on oath by her associates in life, and held in high esteem by her neighbors and friends, and that she in the opinion of the court has regained her respectability and veracity in the neighborhood and county and State in which she lives."[114]

In all of these cases it appears that the severity of the crime was rarely if ever a factor in whether petitions for restoration were approved or rejected. Individuals with a range of crimes succeeded in getting their voting rights restored. Electoral violations, long considered to be an offense particularly deserving of disfranchisement, were frequently pardoned. While restorations of citizenship following larceny and burglary convictions were the most common, since these offenses were particularly widespread, individuals received restoration of their rights for murder, manslaughter, incest, bigamy, election violations, forgery, violating prohibition laws, embezzlement, various grades of assault, and rape.

While the vast majority of petitions for re-enfranchisement that I have examined were successful, some were denied, though the reason for denial is not often clear. The records of Alabama's pardon board between 1915 and 1917 indicate that of the thirty-eight individuals who sought restoration of their rights, twelve were denied. In only two instances was any reason given. Will Kennedy Clark (convicted of vagrancy) was denied when some local citizens petitioned against his restoration, but no further information is given.[115] Daniel Conwill sought unsuccessfully to have his rights restored in 1915, several years after his conviction for manslaughter. The pardon board responded, "The offense is not a felony and therefore does not deprive of political rights."[116] Conwill's case was not unique; in Tennessee several petitions for restoration were not granted because the individual was not actually disfranchised. The complexity of Tennessee's infamy laws meant that many individuals misunderstood their status. Such was the case of L. C. Lovett, who sought to have his rights restored in Knoxville in 1926. Lovett had been convicted a year and a half earlier of violating the age of consent law. Upon hearing his petition, the judge observed that violating the age of consent law was not an infamous offense. Since Lovett had not lost his rights, the court could not restore them. The petition was dismissed.[117] In other cases, technical issues, not negative judgments about the petitioner, meant pardons were rejected. In Virginia some petitions for restoration were rejected by governors who refused to restore an individual's rights until they had been out of jail for a year.[118]

Individuals who were believed to be unreformed or unworthy of citizenship also met with opposition. Governor Swanson of Virginia received two letters opposing the restoration of rights to a man named Newt Clemmons. Wise County attorney W. G. Dobson told Swanson, "He is a very unstable man and one in my judgment who has no political convictions of his own, and such a character as I believe ought not to be entitled to vote." Wise County Clerk H. A. W. Skeen also wrote to the governor about Clemmons: "Newton has not reformed. I have not heard of him stealing but he lives a dissipated [sic] life. He does nothing but gamble." Swanson did not restore Clemmons's rights.[119]

Gambling was seen as evidence of immorality and bad citizenship and was therefore useful in derailing requests for restoration. In 1918 the postmaster of Ben Hur, Virginia, J. R. Schneller, wrote to Governor Westmoreland Davis, seeking to dissuade him from restoring the rights of Frank Garrett. Schneller attacked Garrett's character and political leanings. "We don't want him reinstated because he is a gambler and has been caught gambling on Sundays and other days." Garrett's political views were the biggest problem. "[H]e will vote the republican [sic] ticket....I am begging you not make republicans for we need all the Democrats we can get."[120]

Governor Mann also rejected a pardon based on information he received about the applicant, Hugh Arrington. Arrington had been convicted of illegally marking ballots. Mann wrote to Arrington's attorney, "I cannot commit myself in advance in reference to the Arrington matter. From what I have learned about them they are not good citizens, either crazy or criminals, and a strong petition would be required." Governor Mann did not restore Arrington's rights.[121]

African Americans were more likely to have their petitions for restoration denied in Virginia, possibly the most difficult state for black former convicts to receive a restoration of voting rights. Virginia also stands out because citizens there seem to have been more willing to contact the governor to oppose restorations of citizenship, which they did in blatantly partisan and racial terms.[122] Convicted African American men in Virginia appeared to be aware of the obstacles they faced, and they used a variety of tactics to try to secure a pardon. In 1904 an African American man named Doc Edwards petitioned Governor Montague to have his rights restored. Edwards told the governor that he worked as a butcher. He explained that he had bought a quantity of calfskins and had been accused by a rival butcher of taking three skins that did not belong to him. He was convicted of petit larceny. His petition pointed out that he was a property owner and had never been in legal trouble before. When after a year Governor Montague had failed to act on his case, he wrote Montague again. "A few days ago I received a letter from you in which you asked me to support you in the Senatorial Fight [*sic*], and would gladly do so if I were in a position to vote for either."[123] Edwards's letter is particularly interesting as he seemed to think, or wanted the governor to think, that once his rights were restored he would be able to vote. If this were true, he would have been one of a very small number of African American men in Virginia who voted in this period. There is no evidence that the governor ever restored Edwards's rights.

Only one bill restoring citizenship in Mississippi failed to pass the legislature, but this unsuccessful effort offers some evidence of partisanship in the restoration process in that state. In 1896 Representative Rufus K. Prewitt of Choctaw County introduced a bill to restore the citizenship rights of J. L. McIntyre, one of Prewitt's constituents. The *Mississippi House Journal* identified Prewitt as a member of the "Populite" party, and he would run for governor of the state under the Populist Party banner in 1899.[124] The Mississippi House rejected Prewitt's request to restore McIntyre to citizenship. Given the fact that this was the only bill for restoration to fail in a twenty-four-year period, partisan factors—i.e., Democratic reluctance to give voting rights to supporters of the Populist Party—are a reasonable explanation for its rejection. Over the years, a handful of efforts at legislative restoration of citizenship received a few "no" votes, but nearly all were unanimously approved.[125]

In Virginia, white Democrats sought to block African American voting for explicitly partisan and racially biased reasons. In 1903, about a year after the ratification of the 1902 disfranchising constitution, T. A. Lynch wrote to Governor Montague's secretary:

> I have just learned that an effort will be made to the Governor to remove the disabilities of one D.W. Robinson (Col.) of Pocohontas, Va, convicted of petit larceny by confession on May 4th last. This is a negro that registered at that place last year, and is now exiled from the polls by his own acts and we want him to so remain. This is one of the aristocratic negro voters so termed by the debarred

colored citizens.... No doubt his petitioners will make the usual roseate plea for his restoration of citizenship. We want him to remain where he is.[126]

Lynch wrote to Governor Swanson three years later about a similar case, Samuel Young, another African American man convicted of petit larceny. Since his conviction, Lynch wrote, "Samuel has been running with the dehorned crowd, but anxious to be a voter... The Democrats here are anxious for him to remain as he is.... If the case comes to you I trust you will not interfere." [127]

Occasionally, white men in Virginia did support African American men who sought to have their citizenship rights restored. Doc Edwards had sent the governor a petition signed by local businessmen—presumably white—including another local butcher and a "fish and oyster dealer." Remarkably, even African Americans who were committed Republicans could get some support for re-enfranchisement from white Democratic officeholders. Such was the case of Henry Gaines of Botetourt County, disfranchised for a felony conviction sometime around 1900. F. G. Woodson, who served as the county clerk, wrote to Governor Swanson about Gaines in 1907. He described Gaines as a "very worthy colored man" who "has heartily repented his sin." Woodson said that he had been approached on numerous occasions by Gaines's pastor, asking for help getting Gaines's citizenship restored. As the county clerk, his support for Gaines's effort was critical. The pastor had told Woodson, "they want his disability removed because they want him to hold an office in the church." Woodson explained to the pastor that this was unnecessary; "he could hold an office in the church as it is." But Gaines and the pastor insisted that citizenship restoration was a prerequisite for church office. Woodson told the governor that he was ambivalent about the request but tepidly supported it. "Gaines is a Republican and will vote the Republican ticket if he is allowed to register, and I do not know whether or not this is the motive he has in trying to have his disability removed, though I think not."[128]

Woodson's letter challenges the idea of absolute and bitter racial and partisan divides in Virginia politics in this most partisan and racist decade. A white Democratic officeholder was willing to do a favor for a local African American Republican and write to the governor on his behalf. Perhaps Gaines's involvement in the church had won his respect. It is clear that Gaines's pastor was a respected acquaintance of Woodson's. Gaines drew on ties within and beyond the African American community to recover his rights.

It is also possible that the story about holding office in the church was all a ruse. Gaines and his pastor may have sought to persuade Woodson to help restore Gaines's voting rights by reassuring Woodson that Gaines had no plans to vote. The two may have been playing on stereotypes of ignorance and irrationality that whites held of African Americans, seeking to convince Woodson that they either misunderstood the law or foolishly insisted on a restoration of citizenship before holding church office.

It is possible that registering to vote or having full rights of citizenship was indeed a prerequisite for holding office in Gaines's church. African American civic and benevolent organization did, at times, use such techniques to encourage political participation by their members. For example, the *Baltimore Afro American* reported in 1920 that in Florida "churches and fraternal organizations including the Masons and Elks required all members to pay their poll taxes and register to vote before they became members in good standing. Despite fears and threats of arrest and violence, organizations insisted that their members go to the polls and make an effort to vote."[129]

Whether he was dissembling or telling the truth, what is most significant about this story is that Gaines made a successful case to Woodson to support the restoration of his political rights. Even with a gubernatorial pardon in hand, however, Gaines may not have been able to vote, and this fact may have made Woodson willing to support his petition. The newly passed constitution of 1902 would have given local officials a variety of tools to deny Gaines the vote, even if the governor had restored his political rights.[130]

Pardons complicated the already difficult problem of managing information about voter eligibility. Individuals pardoned by the governor or legislature had to communicate that information to local election officials. The simplest way to do this was just to carry the pardon along to the registration or election, and many did this.[131] But what exactly a pardon should look like was not always clear. In Florida in 1876, a man named Gilbert Wood brought some kind of official document along with him to the precinct, asserting that it was a pardon that granted him voting rights. Witnesses later testified differently as to what the document actually was. One witness said it was a pardon, but due to an oversight it lacked the official state seal. Another said that it was a certificate of discharge from the penitentiary, not a pardon, and therefore did not make Wood eligible to vote.[132]

On other occasions, convicted individuals who did not produce written pardons at the voting booth succeeded in convincing election officials of their eligibility to vote nonetheless. An example of this comes from an election held in Virginia's Eastern Shore in 1884. Several months before the election, a number of individuals had been arrested and tried for unlawfully catching oysters in the Chesapeake Bay. The law required that oysters be caught using tongs—long-handled devices that allowed oystermen to grab their catch from the shallow oyster beds. Some oystermen, however, used an illegal device known as a dredge. Dragged along the oyster bed, this device caught more oysters in less time, but it also significantly damaged the oyster beds. Governor William Cameron's attempts to put a halt to this practice became a chapter in Virginia's "oyster wars."[133]

Five of the men arrested for dredging in the Chesapeake on February 17, 1882, sought to vote in the election that fall in Accomack County. But when they appeared at the polls, several of the Democratic poll watchers recalled their arrest and incarceration and sought to stop them from voting. Poll watchers from the Readjuster party claimed the men had been pardoned and were eligible to vote. Though none of the five had copies of their pardons with them, they asserted that, since they were free from jail before their year-long sentences had expired, they must have been pardoned. Somewhat confused by the situation, officials allowed the five to vote but noted "Dredgers" next to their names in the poll book.[134]

On the other hand, applying for a gubernatorial pardon could settle once and for all whether someone actually had ever lost his voting rights. Some individuals applied for restorations of citizenship rights, only to find their rights had never been removed. As mentioned, Daniel Conwill of Perry County, Alabama, wrote to the state Board of Pardons in 1915 asking to have his voting rights restored, as he had lost them due to a manslaughter conviction. The board responded to his request by explaining that, since manslaughter was not a felony, under state law he had not lost his voting rights.[135]

Individuals who sought restoration of their rights rejected their designation as infamous and refused to accept the idea that their prior convictions and/or their incarceration marked them as dishonorable for the remainder of their lives. In this way, petitions restoring citizenship offered a critique of the justice system from those who personally endured its penalties. Convicted criminals seldom appear as actors in histories of American politics. Today, many believe that former convicts are not interested in politics and unlikely to vote. These petitions undermine these assumptions, demonstrating that former convicts were willing to make sacrifices of time and money and to draw on their personal connections in order to regain access to the vote.

Furthermore, these demands for citizenship restoration by individuals with former convictions changed the historical trajectory of disfranchisement. Their efforts helped produce an accumulation of knowledge by the state about citizenship restoration and a regularization of processes over time. Governors learned how to evaluate and act on such requests, seeking advice from attorneys general when unique or complicated questions of law arose. Pardon boards established systems for processing such requests. All this came about because people were making such requests. When a former convict named Thomas Owens petitioned the Georgia constitutional convention in 1868 asking to be restored to citizenship alongside former Confederates (discussed in chapter 2), the convention had no idea how to respond. Ultimately, they evaluated his petition on the grounds of his service to Reconstruction, essentially treating him like others who had lost their vote for rebellion. Owens and other former convicts laid the groundwork for an expansion of restorations of citizenship, insisting that states respond to their claims. As a result, by the end of the century restorations of citizenship for former convicts were regular occurrences in every state examined.

But it is important to recognize that embedded in the critiques and challenges represented by these efforts was its opposite—the validation and entrenchment of a system in which certain rights are denied for a lifetime following criminal convictions. Allowing those who the state penalized with disfranchisement to have their rights restored put a kind of safety valve in the system. Rights could be denied to a broad range of convicts, but the deserving few who could demonstrate their distinctiveness could claim exemption from these penalties. This made wide-reaching laws such as the disfranchisement of all convicted felons more palatable, even though these laws would occasionally affect those with wealth and political power. Since access to restoration of citizenship often hinged on political connections rather than actual evidence of superior morality, it meant that upper-class whites in particular could escape lifelong sanctions. Such individuals had greater access to the judges, prosecutors, sheriffs, and prominent businessmen needed to sign petitions and endorse requests for pardons. In the states described in the last chapter, where constitutional conventions sought to protect the vote of upper-class white men, pardons allowed such men to avoid lifelong disfranchisement. The pardon process allowed for a kind of fine-tuning of these laws so that all white men would not be caught in their nets.

While some individuals who lacked privileges of race and class could use personal and professional connections to obtain the restoration of their citizenship rights, many who faced lifelong disfranchisement lacked not only those connections, but also the financial or social resources to petition for restoration. This situation sustained the perceived connection between class and morality and existing bifurcations of civil rights. Infamy created the denial of civil rights but the denial of civil rights also *generated* infamy. While race, class, or social connections might free some from infamy, those who failed to regain suffrage—African Americans and lower-class white men—were further marked as infamous and degraded.

For all convicts, regardless of their race or class status, the process of suffrage restoration confirmed their place as dishonorable outcasts. While removing infamy from an individual, pardons secured the place of this status in law and society. "Worthy" citizens signed petitions for restoration, attesting to the fitness of applicants. Then, state officials—governors, legislators, or judges—evaluated these claims and passed a final judgment on the application. This hierarchical classification of citizen and non-citizen established a system of gatekeepers who prevented undeserving intruders from gaining the full rights of citizenship. Gathering signatures from neighbors to prove one's value as a citizen added a local layer to civil degradation and the quest for restoration of suffrage. Restoration of voting rights not only involved supplication to distant political authorities such as the governor or a judge, but to members of one's own community as well. James Q. Whitman has written that, "Mercy is akin to degradation: when we show a person mercy, we confirm his inferior status—more gently, but just as surely, as when we degrade him. A society with a strong tradition of acknowledging and enforcing status differences will thus often be a society with a tradition of mercy."[136] The process of applying for restoration of suffrage, and the mechanisms by which such restorations were granted, thus reinforced the degradation of convicts by stigmatizing them as outsiders in the local community and excluding them from the polity of the state.

CHAPTER 6

✧

Courts, Voting Rights, and Black Protest in the Early Twentieth Century

Although civil rights organizations paid scant attention to laws disfranchising for crime in the early twentieth century, individual black citizens did challenge their operation in some cases when they felt unfairly excluded from suffrage. This chapter considers court cases initiated by three African American men between 1914 and 1916. None of these plaintiffs claimed discrimination based on race. Neither national nor local civil rights groups were involved in these cases. Nonetheless, these cases represent some of the first court challenges by African Americans— or indeed any individuals disfranchised for crime—to the enforcement of laws disfranchising for crime. The obstacles faced by these plaintiffs and the limitations of their legal strategies underscore the significance of the collective legal efforts that the NAACP would offer in other key cases. Despite these impediments, two of these three plaintiffs scored legal victories affirming their voting rights in an era in which legal triumphs for African Americans were rare. These cases also forecast Election Day scenarios and legal issues that remain present to this day.

This chapter begins with the story of Cornelius "Canary" Curtis, disfranchised in Knoxville Tennessee for a 1907 larceny conviction. In 1914, Curtis petitioned for the restoration of his rights of citizenship and was denied twice by the local courts. He brought his case to the Tennessee Court of Civil Appeals, which ruled in his favor. The Tennessee Supreme Court affirmed the appeal court's judgment in 1915. The second incident in this chapter involves the 1916 election in St. Louis, Missouri. Democratic Party operatives in the city coordinated efforts to target African American voters, many of whom had recently migrated to Missouri from southern states, with stepped-up enforcement of laws disfranchising for crime. After the election two men, Henry Lucas and John Sullivan, who were among those wrongfully disfranchised by false accusations of prior criminal convictions, initiated civil suits against Democratic Party leaders. These court cases are some of the earliest legal actions by African Americans challenging the enforcement of laws disfranchising for crime.

For nearly half a century, laws disfranchising for crime had been crafted and enforced in the South with the intent of eroding African American electoral participation. These cases in Knoxville and St. Louis were in borders states, in places where African Americans were not entirely excluded from citizenship and electoral participation. But the relatively peaceful racial climate in both locales was under threat in these years. In St. Louis, white Democrats feared that African American migrants from the South were "colonizing" the city on behalf of the Republican Party.[1] Republicans, in turn, accused Democrats of "southernizing" elections—manipulating election practices, including laws disfranchising for crime, to target African American voters.[2] Knoxville, in East Tennessee, was historically known for more peaceful race relations than Tennessee cities to the west, particularly Memphis. But racial tensions were escalating there, too, and a race riot and a near-lynching would erupt in 1919.[3] In both these cities the degrading racial climate and challenges to African American citizenship are reflected in general assaults on African American civil rights as well as these specific incidents involving disfranchisement for criminal convictions. And in both cities, African Americans turned to the courts when their right to vote came under attack.

These events occurred not only in pivotal locations but also at a critical time in the context of the black freedom movement nationally. What historian Rayford Logan called the "nadir" of African American history had come to an end, though this was not clear at the time.[4] The string of defeats—twelve in a row—for African American voting rights that occurred in federal courts between 1890 and 1908 was coming to a close; beginning in 1915 the NAACP would eke out a slow pattern of victories in the courts that would escalate over the next several decades.[5] When Curtis filed his appeal, the landmark case challenging Oklahoma's "grandfather clause," *Guinn v. United States*, had been argued before the U.S. Supreme Court but had not been decided.[6] The two St. Louis cases were filed just a year after the remarkable success in *Guinn*. While there is no evidence that the NAACP or any other activist groups had any connection to these cases or that the national movement inspired these actions, it is striking that these three African American men were moved at this precise moment to go to court and challenge those who sought to disfranchise them.

In December 1907 a Knox County court convicted Cornelius Curtis of larceny for stealing some money that had been left in an office on Prince Street in downtown Knoxville where he worked as a janitor. The judge sentenced twenty-three-year-old Curtis to five years in prison and judged him infamous. After serving about three and a half years he was pardoned for good behavior in March 1911. Following his release from prison, Curtis resumed working as janitor for various Knoxville businesses.[7]

As a result of the infamy judgment, Curtis became disfranchised and disqualified from testifying in court (except in his own criminal case) because Tennessee law defined larceny as an infamous offense. Curtis's loss of citizenship rights for an infamous conviction was the result of a number of constitutional and legislative developments that dated back to the early days of the state. In 1829 the legislature established a legal definition of infamy, categorizing a number of criminal offenses "infamous" and barring infamous individuals from testifying in court.[8] Tennessee's disqualification of infamous individuals from court testimony was similar to that of many other U.S. states in this period, as was a clause in Tennessee's 1835 constitution authorizing the legislature to exclude from suffrage individuals convicted of infamous crimes.[9] In 1851, the legislature established a process by which infamous individuals might have their civil rights restored, by petitioning the circuit court.[10]

When Cornelius Curtis first petitioned the Knox County Circuit Court for the restoration of his citizenship rights in 1914 he had good reason to believe that his request would be granted. Petitions for restoration of citizenship rights were fairly common in Tennessee in the late nineteenth and early twentieth century. The Knox County court had restored citizenship rights to twenty-nine individuals in the previous two decades.[11] Nor should Curtis have been particularly concerned that his race would be a barrier to the restoration of his citizenship. Two men, Alfred Easley and Zack Hale, who successfully applied for restoration of citizenship in 1901 and 1902 respectively, are identified in the court records as African American. But Easley and Hale may have been the last African American men whose petitions were approved by the county court for some time. In the two decades after Curtis's case I have found no more petitions from African American citizens, successful or unsuccessful, in the Knox County records. This absence suggests that African American residents of Knoxville understood the local court to be inimical to their petitions based on Curtis's experience there.[12]

Successful applications for the restoration of citizenship rights were relatively common for blacks and whites alike across Tennessee in these decades. In Giles County, a mid-state county with a relatively large African American population, twenty-nine men, sixteen of whom were African

American, sought the removal of infamy judgments at the circuit court in Pulaski between 1885 and 1920. All but one of these African American petitioners was successful. Court records in Maury, Crockett, and Haywood Counties likewise contain successful petitions from African Americans.

In other southern states African American men met with mixed success in getting citizenship rights restored after convictions in this period, as discussed in the previous chapter. African American voters in Tennessee, however, seemed to face the fewest obstacles to restoration of citizenship of all the states surveyed here—at least until the Curtis case. This is partly due to the fact that Tennessee did not have the same historic commitment to black disfranchisement that other southern states did. Political machines dominated Tennessee in this period, and rival factions sometimes sought African American votes to tip close races in their favor. In Knoxville, where the Republican Party controlled local politics, opposing candidates sought the support of African American voters. The city's relatively small African American population meant that black voting would never threaten white political dominance but it could be important in close races. Though African American electoral participation dropped in the 1890s following the enactment of voter registration, secret ballot laws, and a poll tax, it recovered somewhat in subsequent decades.[13]

The process for restoration of citizenship rights in Tennessee varied little from county to county, and Curtis's application followed the standard procedure. Individuals had to demonstrate to the circuit court that they had "sustained the character of a person of honesty, respectability, and veracity."[14] The most common way to demonstrate such character was to present petitions attesting to it. These petitions generally stated the date of the infamy judgment and the crime that provoked it, verified the petitioner's residence in the county, and attested to the petitioner's good character. Signatories usually included neighbors, employers, local businessmen, and sometimes individuals connected to the criminal justice system, such as the judge, prosecutor, or court clerk.

Most individuals seeking restoration of citizenship waited one to three years to petition the court, as this would support their claim of "sustained" good character. However, some successful petitions were submitted within months of the petitioner's release from prison.[15] Applying for the restoration of his citizenship rights about three and a half years after his release from prison put Curtis well within the average bounds of such petitions. The obstacles he faced do not appear to be due to his failure to follow standard procedure.

In November 1914, Curtis filed a petition in the Knox County Circuit Court to be restored to his rights of citizenship. The court notified the district attorney of Curtis's filing ten days before the hearing, as prescribed by Tennessee law, and he declined to challenge it. Four witnesses accompanied Curtis to court and testified to his good character. They were present and former employers, some of whom had known Curtis for many years, even before his conviction and sentence to prison. And all were among the white elites of Knox county—two prominent lawyers, a deputy sheriff and secretary of the Knoxville Board of Commerce, and a court reporter. These men testified that Curtis had been a "trusted, faithful servant." They "had trusted him in their houses and were willing to trust him again." Curtis, they assured the court, was an "honest and faithful colored man."[16]

Like many of the African American men who petitioned for the restoration of their citizenship in the state, Curtis was not a wealthy man. Successful petitions from illiterate individuals and landless tenant farmers can also be found in Tennessee court records, despite the financial and logistical challenges such individuals faced in seeking the restoration of citizenship.[17] But Curtis had connections among the city's white business elite, likely stemming from his employment downtown, that would soon prove useful. Among his duties was cleaning the Women's Building on Main Street, and one story holds that Curtis had identified the cause of the 1906 fire that had destroyed the building on Christmas Eve. Following the fire, Curtis had found the remains of a firecracker in the alley behind the building. Curtis was clearly a well-known figure in downtown Knoxville.[18]

Curtis's case was unusual only in that witnesses presented their testimony directly in court. Signatures on the petition ordinarily sufficed as evidence, but the actual appearances of these witnesses at the court that day suggest that Curtis may have anticipated opposition to his petition. Given the prominence of these men in the local community, he must have assumed their presence would have been particularly helpful should the judge be inclined to question his application.

While the image of white southern men supporting their African American employees' efforts to regain the rights of citizenship might seem anomalous, this was not uncommon.[19] For example, in 1897 John W. Arnow Jr. wrote to Georgia governor William Atkinson to recommend his two farmhands for restoration of citizenship rights. Arnow explained, "Allonzo Jones and Robert Cowan lived with me for the last 5 years and have been good faithful servants and had no trouble and I think they deserve a pardon." Jones and Cowan signed the document with "X" indicating they were illiterate.[20]

A similar example occurred in Alabama in 1886. Two African American men, Daniel Butler and Elias Peavy, petitioned Governor Edward O'Neal for citizenship rights they had lost following conviction for grand larceny. In addition to a petition recommending both men for citizenship, signed by twelve people, each man sent a letter from his employer. Peavy's employer, William Gaddis, told the governor that the two had a long history of business transactions. Peavy had bought land from him after renting the property for several years. Gaddis wrote, "He has made an uncommonly good citizen for a colored man, and the petition he will offer will show you in what estimation he is held by his white neighbors." Butler in turn offered a letter written on his behalf from the man he had been convicted of stealing cotton from twelve years earlier. Edmund Williams wrote that Butler had "resided on my place" much of the time since his release from prison, and that "his conduct has been entirely exemplary and honorable."[21]

The letters from Arnow, Gaddis, and Williams indicate the complex intersection of social structures and personal relationships that marked southern life in the late nineteenth and early twentieth century. White men of property were on occasion willing to use their social status to assist efforts by African American employees and acquaintances to gain certain rights. White men were the gatekeepers of citizenship, but in some circumstances they clearly were willing to open those gates to African American men who they knew and respected. Such respect might even transcend prior animosity; Williams was willing to advocate for an African American man whom he had accused of criminal conduct in the past.[22]

On the other hand, such assistance by white men reaffirmed their status as guardians of citizenship. Benevolence can function as a means of articulating and even strengthening social hierarchies. By extending assistance to poor African American men, Gaddis and Williams, as well as the other white signatories, were confirming their own standing in the social and political hierarchy of their community. Similarly, while the assistance Curtis received from his white employers may have had a basis in genuine friendship and affection, Curtis's relationship to them was nonetheless grounded in hierarchies—the occupational hierarchy of employer and employee and the social hierarchy of race. Helping their African American janitor with a legal problem was a way to highlight the benevolence of paternalism, thereby obfuscating the unequal power relations and violence also endemic to such a system.

For Curtis, electoral politics may have been an additional factor in drawing the support of prominent Knoxville men for his petition, and they may explain the opposition his claim faced. In Knoxville, 1915 was an election year, and voters would soon elect a new Mayor, Democrat John E. McMillan. McMillan had spoken out against the Ku Klux Klan and had solicited votes from the city's black population, even dispatching operatives to African American neighborhoods to distribute blank poll tax receipts.

Though there is no direct evidence connecting Curtis to McMillan's campaign, African American votes were valuable in Knoxville in 1915. [23] Curtis may have sought to use this situation to get his citizenship rights restored; his advocates may have been hoping to gain votes for McMillan from Curtis and others in the African American community. In refusing the petition, Judge Von A. Huffaker may have been seeking to obstruct the franchise of a potential supporter of McMillan.

Following the testimony by the witnesses, Curtis himself took the stand. The judge questioned Curtis, who described his former offense and told of his release for good behavior. Curtis said he had never had any legal trouble since leaving prison, but did mention that he had been accused of stealing keys from "Mr. Turner." More questioning of Curtis and the witnesses clarified that no one believed that Curtis had been involved in the theft of Turner's keys. In fact, a cook in the Turner household admitted to misplacing the keys and located the keys a few hours after they had been lost.[24]

Despite the testimony of prominent witnesses in Curtis's favor, Judge Huffaker refused to grant Curtis restoration. Huffaker dismissed Curtis's petition and charged him a court fee. Curtis was not willing to abandon his quest for restoration of citizenship rights and applied for a rehearing the following January. Again the judge heard the petition, again the district attorney failed to appear in court to contest the petition, and again the judge dismissed the case after charging Curtis another fee.[25]

Curtis, still undaunted, decided to file an appeal. At some point in the process he secured legal representation from a prominent Knoxville attorney, Malcolm McDermott. McDermott was dean of the University of Tennessee law school and would soon become president of the Tennessee Bar Association.[26] One must assume that McDermott's involvement came through Curtis's professional connections.

Curtis needed money to pursue an appeal because the court required an appeal bond. This was basically a prepayment of the court costs, guaranteeing that the appellant could pay the court costs, should the court find against him. Such bonds could be either in cash or property. Curtis offered neither cash nor property but instead filed a "pauper's oath." This provided a mechanism by which he could avoid paying the appeal bond. Filing an appeal and applying for a pauper's bond would all have required an extensive knowledge of the workings of the criminal justice system, another area where legal advice or assistance would have been valuable.

The Tennessee Court of Civil Appeals granted the appeal and heard the case. At the court hearing, the counsel for the attorney general contested Curtis's claim on several counts. First he contested the Appeals Court's jurisdiction on the matter, claiming that such petitions could only be heard in circuit court. Second the attorney general asserted that Curtis had lost his citizenship when he was rendered infamous and therefore was not eligible to file as a pauper. According to this argument, Curtis's infamy made him incompetent to testify in court and therefore incompetent to take the pauper oath.

The court sided with Curtis in all of these matters. First, it asserted its right to overturn a circuit court's judgment, claiming appellate jurisdiction on all judgments of the circuit court, including petitions for restoration of citizenship. It also upheld Curtis's right to apply for a pauper's oath. The court found that since infamous individuals could testify on their own behalf in criminal cases, they should also be able to make an affidavit on their own behalf in order to appeal judgments against them. Though the court recognized that infamous individuals had limitations on their citizenship, they were nonetheless residents and therefore entitled to make such an affidavit. Finally, the court ruled to restore Curtis's rights to vote and testify in court. The controversy over the missing keys, the court found, did not amount to a reason to deny Curtis's petition. "This record satisfies us that the petitioner had nothing to do with the loss of those keys, and the Circuit Court should have . . . granted him the relief sought in his petition." Curtis was granted the restoration of his citizenship rights and charged for the cost of the court proceedings. A few months later the Tennessee Supreme Court affirmed the judgment.[27]

Curtis was able to use his personal and professional connections to successfully navigate the legal process, scoring a victory in the Tennessee Court of Civil Appeals. The historical record does not indicate why his original petition was denied in the circuit court. Presumably the missing key story was not the real issue, as that appears to have been resolved quite easily, but it is not clear why the circuit court twice refused to grant his petition. Race or political inclinations may have been an issue, or it may have been something else entirely. Whatever the reasons for the initial refusal at the circuit court level, the appeals court found the local court's reasoning inadequate and agreed that Canary Curtis should have full citizenship rights.

A year after Curtis's victory in Tennessee, a dispute over the enforcement of laws disfranchising for crime brought two African American men to court in Missouri as well. Missouri's 1875 constitution disfranchised individuals convicted of felonies or infamous crimes.[28] The question that had been raised in other states as to whether petit larceny was a disfranchising crime had been answered in the affirmative in Missouri through both legislative and judicial action. State law dating back to 1845 disfranchised for a variety of criminal offenses including larceny "in any degree."[29] Then in 1912 the state supreme court affirmed that the civil disabilities incurred for felony grand larceny should also be assigned to those convicted of misdemeanor petit larceny.[30] The court's decision helped set the stage for the controversy that would unfold in the 1916 election in St. Louis.

The 1916 election was also important because it occurred during a shift in the balance of political power in the city. St. Louis was an important destination in the Great Migration. As African Americans migrated from the South into the city in the early twentieth century, they enhanced the political power of the Republican Party. In 1910 St. Louis had 43,960 African American residents, and this number climbed to 69,854 by 1920, a 58 percent increase. In comparison the white population of the city only increased 9.4 percent in this period.[31] Voting by the new migrants helped put the GOP in control of city politics until the 1930s.[32] Democrats, in this period of social and political transition, sought to limit the electoral impact of the new southern migrants in various ways.

Legal challenges to the voting rights of the new southern migrants to St. Louis began in 1910 during a hotly contested election for State Superintendent of Public Schools. Democrat Howard A. Gass filed a court challenge to the victory of Republican William P. Evans, claiming that 1,100 African American votes had been illegally cast for the Republican candidate. These illegal votes, Gass argued, had come from recent African American migrants who had improperly registered. Many had listed their residence as lodging or boarding houses in African American neighborhoods, and sometimes many individuals claimed to live at the same address. Gass suggested that those who listed temporary addresses did not really live there and were engaged in election fraud. Furthermore, Gass pointed out, individuals who did live in such "disreputable" residences should not be able to vote. He argued that these votes should be stripped from Evans's total, which would give Gass the victory.[33]

The court responded to these arguments by defending black voters and taking issue with suggestions of African American immorality and criminality. First, the court explained why African Americans tended to live in temporary residences in segregated neighborhoods: "prevailing social conditions irresistibly drive negroes to herd together." So, contrary to the claim by the appellant, the court did not believe it to be irregular or suspicious for large numbers of African American voters to be registered to vote in the same or adjacent residences was. The court also pointed out that these new migrants moved frequently, so the fact that many voters could not be located weeks and months after they voted was no surprise and did not prove electoral corruption.[34]

As for the claim that African American voters, by virtue of their residence in disreputable locations, should be disfranchised, the court responded this way: "Exconvicts [*sic*], unpardoned, may be disfranchised; but up to this time technical or actual sexual morality is not made a statutory test of a voter by the Missouri lawmaker. When that day comes, if ever, there will be fine grinding in the mill—but no matter about that. As the law now stands, we do not understand it would avail contestant aught to show that all or any of those negroes were ethically incorrect."[35]

The tactics used by Democrats to dispute African American votes failed in 1910, but with partisan and racial tensions escalating in 1916 some party leaders tried again. In March St. Louis had held a special election to consider a residential segregation ordinance, which passed by a large majority. Despite the new law's title, "An Ordinance to Prevent Ill Feeling, Conflict and Collisions Between the White and Colored Races, and to Preserve the Public Peace," its passage indicated an escalation in racial tensions.[36] That fall's presidential election was hotly contested, and many correctly predicted that Missouri would be a key battleground. Democrats hoped the state would go to Woodrow Wilson, while Republicans hoped to put the state's electoral votes in Republican Charles Evans Hughes's column. The result in densely populated St. Louis was critical to both sides.

In the weeks before Election Day a group of Missouri Democrats came up with a plan. In charge of the effort was Breckenridge Long, a local attorney and Democratic Party operative, who would later serve as Woodrow Wilson's assistant secretary of the navy and Franklin Roosevelt's ambassador to Italy. Long is also remembered as a key player in the Roosevelt administration's decision not to relax immigration laws to allow Jewish refugees from the Holocaust to enter the United States.[37] First, Long dispatched about twenty young attorneys to comb the criminal court records and compile lists of African American voters who had been convicted of crimes.[38] This research produced a list of approximately three thousand names, about 25 percent of the registered African American voters in the city.[39] Later, accounts of this controversy in the press emphasized that Democrats collected names only of African Americans. Democrats would use these lists to challenge African American voters at the polls. Long later testified that the plan had been hatched by Edward A. Glenn, a long-time Democratic Party activist.[40]

Then, Long and his allies used their influence over the Police Board, which was dominated by Democrats, to undermine the authority of the Election Commission, where Republicans held a majority. The Election Commission had ordered that police officers be "shifted"—moved around town to different neighborhoods—on Election Day, arguing that officers who worked in particular neighborhoods had built connections with local citizens and thus might be more liable to corruption. Thus on Election Day, the police department was supposed to transfer officers to new districts for the day, with the hope they would enforce the laws more fairly. Long, however, asked his allies on the Police Board to refuse to comply with this plan.[41]

The day before the election, the *St. Louis Republic* published a statement by Long warning African American voters: "Democratic challengers in every affected precinct in the sixteen wards have been given a precinct list of the negroes who have registered illegally. AS RAPIDLY AS THEY ARRIVE AT THE POLLS THEY WILL BE CHALLENGED. IF THEY INSIST ON CASTING THEIR BALLOTS AND START TO SWEAR IN THEIR VOTE, THEY WILL BE ARRESTED AT ONCE, CHARGED WITH PERJURY."[42] The police geared up to help. Chief of Police William Young instructed his officers that election laws should be "rigidly enforced.[43] Republicans responded by publishing a notice in the local African American newspaper, the *St. Louis Argus*, reassuring their supporters. Voters who were properly registered "need not fear any man," and free legal counsel would be available for those that needed it.[44]

Motivating the Democrats was the specter of "negro colonization." Democrats claimed that Republicans intentionally brought African Americans in from the South and registered them to vote in attempt to boost Republican ballots. The *Republic* asserted that Republicans had "colonized" three thousand illegal voters in St. Louis. Fred English, a former Democratic candidate for Congress, claimed to have personally witnessed this importation of voters: "On October 19 I went to Union Station to take a train to Maysville, KY.... I saw a Mobile & Ohio train come into Union Station with fifteen coaches full of negroes. There were so many negroes on the train that they blocked up the midway of Union Station. I questioned about twenty of the negroes as to their reason for coming and they said that they had come from Mississippi on a $3 excursion, but nearly all of them stated that they intended to stay in this part of the country for a few weeks. This sort of thing went on in several of the States bordering Missouri in an attempt to swing the election, and the committee finding this out began the investigation which resulted in the uncovering of about 3,000 illegally registered negroes in this city."[45] St. Louis Police Chief William Young did his part to heighten tension and animosity, claiming, "Thousands of negroes in the south were...invading St. Louis, East St. Louis and other northern cities in an effort to carry close states for the Republican Party."[46]

Highlighting "colonization" and tying migration to political corruption would offer an excuse to disfranchise black voters while energizing the Democratic base. A similar set of circumstances was simultaneously unfolding across the river in East St. Louis, Illinois. There, allegations of crime and electoral manipulation by recent black migrants led to escalated racial tensions and rumors of a "colonization conspiracy," culminating in the East St. Louis race riot in July 1917.[47]

While Democrats had claimed that black southerners were entering the city to aid Republicans, Republicans suggested that voter suppression tactics from the South had come to the city instead. The *St. Louis Argus* wrote, "This effort on the part of St. Louis Democracy is an effort to Southernize the ballot."[48] Indeed, the events that would unfold on Election Day in St. Louis closely resembled the 1888 election in Richmond, Virginia.[49]

On Election Day in St. Louis, Democrats dispatched workers to precincts in African American neighborhoods. These "challengers" had lists of African Americans in each precinct identified by Long's men as having prior, disfranchising convictions. When African American men tried to vote, challengers would consult the list they held of convicted individuals, to determine if that voter was on the list. [50] Newspaper accounts are at variance as to exactly what information the challengers possessed. One challenger claimed that his list included full names and addresses of targeted voters.[51] However, in a statement released ten days after the election, the city's election commissioner, a Democrat, said that challengers confronted any black voter whose last name matched one on their lists regardless of the address.[52] In fact, the techniques of challengers may have differed from precinct to precinct. Court records did not list addresses, so it is not clear how address data, if it existed, was gathered.[53]

When men whose names appeared on the lists attempted to vote, the challengers would step forward and dispute their right to vote. At this point, apparently, some voters gave up and left without voting. However, other voters contested the challenge. According to protocol, when this happened, the "precinct judges" would have to decide how to proceed. Each precinct had four judges charged with assessing the qualifications of each voter, two Democrats and two Republicans. In the event of a challenge, the judges would ask the voter to swear that he had never been arrested or convicted and the challenger to swear to the challenge. Then the four had to decide between these two conflicting stories. Generally, they voted along party lines, two to admit the challenged vote and two to reject it. This split decision resulted in the voter being allowed to vote, but the ballot placed in a separate envelope for "rejected ballots." The legitimacy of the vote would be assessed later.

A variety of scenarios unfolded across the city. At each of the city's five hundred polling places, police officers were stationed inside. In some precincts police officers arrested African American voters immediately after they were challenged. In other instances, they waited until the judges had allowed the individual to vote and then arrested him. Police escorted others out of the polling place without arrest but prevented them from voting. The *St. Louis Argus*, the city's African American paper, reported that some individuals simply left without voting, "refus[ing] to be humiliated."[54] By noon eighty-nine African American men had been arrested at polling places.[55] The final count held that police arrested ninety-six African Americans and two whites upon allegations of trying to vote with prior, disfranchising convictions.[56]

As word of the proceedings spread, Republican leaders sought to halt these tactics. By 9:30 a.m. a group, including Republican City Committee chair John Schmoll and Republican mayor Henry Kiel, came to city hall seeking intervention. They met with the Board of Police Commissioners who agreed to tell officers to cease arresting voters based solely on the accusations of challengers; three of the four precinct judges now had to request the arrest for the police to act. The Board of Election Commissioners issued an order that challengers should have personal knowledge of people they challenged. They could not simply read names from a list.

At midday Circuit Court Judge Karl Kimmel, a Republican, issued an injunction to restrain police from intimidating voters.[57] This slowed the arrests, but Democrats continued to use other tactics to suppress Republican votes throughout the rest of the day. Democratic operatives continued to challenge African American voters with allegations of former convictions.[58] About one thousand voters cast ballots that judges marked as rejected.[59]

The Seventeenth Ward saw the largest number of challenged voters.[60] For example, when Matthew Bell, a forty-one-year-old black fireman, tried to vote in the Seventeenth Ward, he was confronted by Democratic challenger John McFadden. Bell was allowed to vote but judges placed his ballot in the provisional ballot envelope. When Joseph P. Crofts, a thirty-six-year-old porter, tried to vote in another Seventeenth Ward precinct, Democrat Michael Weisman challenged him. The judges allowed Crofts to vote but then police arrested him. Events like this took place in African American neighborhoods in other parts of the city as well.[61]

On Election Day the Republican Party did its best to protect African American voters, using the parts of city government under the party's control. Republicans held the majority of the seats on the Election Commission, and Mayor Henry Kiel was a Republican as well.[62] Bondsmen hired by the party waited at the police stations to free arrested men as soon as possible. Judge Kimmel and another Republican circuit court judge, Calvin Miller, signed bonds so that individuals who were arrested were immediately released. Then, Republican Party workers drove them back to the precincts to try to vote again. Their efforts were still, sometimes, unsuccessful. For example, when William Baker tried to vote that morning in the Fourth Ward, he and two other men were arrested. When he was released on bond later in the day, he returned to the polling place but the election officers there still refused to let him vote.[63]

Democrats used their power over the police department to try to block the participation of African American voters while Republican leaders tried, in kind, to protect these voters. African American Democrats, though, were not so lucky. Police mistakenly arrested a Democrat named Frank Edge along with a number of other African American men. Edge's vocal insistence that his arrest was a mistake led Republicans to realize that he was a Democrat. They refused to bail him out with the others. While all the Republicans were freed, Edge remained in jail the rest of the day.[64]

An important side effect of all this controversy was significant delays for voters, particularly at precincts in African American neighborhoods.[65] A Republican Party official told the press that he knew of precincts where the wait stretched to two hours while challengers and judges interrogated the voters.[66] In a precinct on Laclede Avenue, according to another Republican leader, sixty voters waited two hours to vote, but only eight were successful.

Like Canary Curtis in Knoxville, several voters used their professional connections to protect them or aid their efforts to vote. When James Cole tried to vote, a challenger claimed that he had served a term in the county workhouse in 1905. Cole, though, was exceptionally well-known and respected locally. He had, according to the *Argus,* "served in some of the fashionable and well-known families in St. Louis for nearly fifty years at various functions." He was also personally acquainted with all of the judges, who therefore allowed him to vote.[67] Police also arrested two men who worked as janitors in the Municipal Court Building, as well as the porter of the former mayor and the chauffeur of an Election Board member. Their arrests were among those highlighted in reports to the press.[68] Julius S. Walsh Jr., the industrial commissioner of the Wabash Railroad, protested when his stableman, James Siler, and his butler, George Miller, met with threats and intimidation when they tried to vote. Siler insisted that these men had led crime-free lives and had valid registrations.[69] A subsequent newspaper article confirmed that "businessmen and others, whose employees had been arrested without cause, protested against this action."[70]

The day after the election, the *St. Louis Daily Globe Democrat* published a list of arrested voters in an article titled "GOP Voters Arrested in Police Intimidation." The article chronicled the experiences of forty-nine individuals arrested on Election Day. All but two of these men were African American, and most had tried to vote in the Seventeenth or Sixth Wards. Averaging just over forty years of age, these men worked in a variety of professions, including as porters, laborers, waiters, firemen, barbers, teamsters, cooks, and drivers.[71]

Three days after the election Republican Circuit Court Judge Calvin Miller discharged all of the men arrested at the polls that day.[72] The police continued to insist they had done nothing wrong in arresting them. In an angry rebuttal, Chief Young told his officers to assist fully with the prosecution of "all negro criminals who voted or attempted to vote last Tuesday."

Republican leaders also sought to prevent Democrats from using such tactics again. The Election Board met and voted to revise the challenger statutes.[73] The *St. Louis Argus* supported this plan, editorializing that the law gave "judges of election booths arbitrary power to reject ballots of challenged voters."[74] A grand jury investigated, calling members of the election board to testify and indicting several election officials working in the Sixth and Seventeenth Wards for feloniously hindering the election. However, it is doubtful that these cases actually went to trial.[75] A group of individuals formed the "Citizens' Nonpartisan Committee," aimed at prosecuting all election frauds, but it is unlikely to have had much impact.[76]

The most dramatic outcome of the events on Election Day, however, were two lawsuits filed in the weeks after the election by African American men who had been refused the right to vote. The first to file was Henry Lucas, a thirty-two-year-old teamster and Missouri native. Lucas had been arrested in the fifth precinct of the Eighth Ward following an accusation from a Democratic challenger, Theodore Sandman, that he had a prior grand larceny conviction and had spent time in prison for it in 1906.[77]

The arresting officer, James. E. Sullivan, later testified that Sandman requested the arrest. Sullivan explained, "I said to Lucas: 'This man accuses you of illegal voting and orders you arrested.' Lucas said 'I am not guilty. I was never arrested before in my life.' We stood there awhile, and then Sandman said: 'Let's go up to the station with him.'"[78] When the three arrived at the Soulard Street station, Captain George T. McNamee asked why Lucas was arrested. Sandman said Lucas was guilty of fraudulent voting. Sandman claimed to have a "slip of paper" with Lucas's name on it. Later Sandman said that a man named "Briney" Kennedy had given him the paper. The police kept Lucas in jail for two and a half hours until Republican Party workers bailed him out.[79]

Lucas sued Sandman, Breckenridge Long, and John J. Kennedy, the Democratic city committeeman in the Eighth Ward. He asked $5,000 in actual damages, $5,000 in punitive damages, and court costs.[80] Lucas had support from the local Republican establishment and was represented in court by a prominent St. Louis law firm, Ferris and Rosskopf, which had close connections to the Republican Party.[81] Not only was support obviously useful in providing him with counsel, he likely also had help paying the court costs. Records from the trial indicate that the court costs amounted to $251.85, and Lucas had been required to give bond or deposit security in advance to cover these costs. He had opted to deposit cash.[82]

A few weeks into the trial Lucas chose to drop the suit against Long and focus on Sandman and Kennedy.[83] Then the judge upheld a motion for an "involuntary non suit" against Kennedy, effectively dismissing that case and leaving Sandman the sole defendant.[84] Lucas and his attorneys took depositions from police officers, precinct workers, and Democratic Party officials.[85] Lucas's suit explained that Sandman caused him to be wrongfully arrested and detained in an attempt to intimidate him, "disgrace" him, and "deprive him of his liberty."[86] Sandman replied that he had the right under law to challenge voters. Sandman maintained that the decision by the police to arrest Lucas was not his fault; he did not have the power or authority to arrest anyone.[87]

The suit dragged out until 1920 when the jury ultimately found in favor of Lucas, awarding actual damages of $250 and $50 in punitive damages. Lucas received full payment of the judgment.[88] Sandman moved for a new trial but the judge refused his request.[89] Lucas had won.

Another disfranchised African American voter, John L. Sullivan, filed suit shortly after Lucas. Sullivan claimed that when he tried to vote, a Democratic challenger asserted that he had been convicted of petit larceny in 1896 and had served a forty-one day sentence in the workhouse. Sullivan denied all of this. He said he had never been in the workhouse nor convicted nor arrested anywhere. He was not even living in St. Louis in 1896, having moved there in 1910.[90] He was freed on bond after about two hours and returned to the polling place to again try to cast his ballot. The Democratic precinct judge again refused him the vote, saying he had already voted. As Sullivan continued to argue, the judge finally gave him a ballot but warned him it would be put in the "rejected" envelope.[91]

His $11,000 claim—$1,000 in actual damages and $10,000 in punitive damages—charged a large group of individuals with intimidating him on Election Day. Sullivan, who was represented by attorney Taylor R. Young, identified a total of twenty people in his suit: Long, four members of the Police Board, Police Chief William Young, George Warner (who he identified as "president of the Democratic machine" of the Sixth Ward), the two Democratic precinct judges, members of the Democratic Central

Committee, the local police captain, and the two police officers who arrested him. Finally he named Horace Rumsey, identified as "a Democrat and anxious and willing to assist in the perpetration of the fraud herein mentioned."[92] Sullivan's agenda was more ambitious than Lucas's. Lucas had simply sued those who had tried to block him from voting. Sullivan hoped to reach further into the police department and larger Democratic establishment, essentially claiming a conspiracy. He sued not just on his own behalf but also on behalf of the black community, asserting that the twenty defendants conspired together to "concoct a scheme to prevent the plaintiff and thousands of other people of his color" from voting. He also claimed that the defendants "employed a number of young lawyers" to search criminal records and compile a list of disfranchised voters. Then these lists were used to target the plaintiff and "voters of his color."[93]

Sullivan had a much harder time than Lucas paying the court costs, due in part to the large number of defendants. About fifty people were subpoenaed and deposed in preparation for the trial, for a total cost (according to a defense motion) of about $700.[94] Court documents indicate multiple requests for dismissal by the defense due to failure to pay the costs. On February 17, Sullivan deposited $50 with the clerk with the agreement that he would pay another $50 in thirty days.[95] A March 1918 motion to dismiss was set aside when Sullivan paid another $50 on March 30, 1918.[96] However, the records of the case cease at that point, and it appears that the case was never heard in court.[97]

Lucas and Sullivan undertook their efforts independently of the small but growing effort to secure civil rights through legal challenges in this period. The NAACP was active in St. Louis but does not seem to have responded to the events on Election Day or supported these two lawsuits. The articulated strategy of the group was to take cases "which show actual discrimination because of color" and those that "test broad principles."[98] The cases of Sullivan and Lucas did not fit the bill. They were not incidents of *clear* racial discrimination by the standard of the day—certainly not as clear as the racially restrictive residential segregation ordinance or grandfather clause case, for example.

The cases of Lucas and Sullivan illustrate the shortcomings of a lack of coordination in legal strategy—a coordination that the NAACP would bring to civil rights cases in years to come. While it is possible that there was an agreement that Lucas would pursue a narrow claim and Sullivan a broader one, this is unlikely, and there is no evidence of it. There remains no other reasonable explanation for why they would pursue separate claims. Their duplication of efforts was costly and inefficient, and it must have reduced the impact of their assertions. In particular, Sullivan's claim that Long et al.

conspired to disfranchise a wide swath of the black population certainly would have been bolstered by more plaintiffs.

The difficulties that all three of these plaintiffs—Canary Curtis in Knoxville, and Henry Lucas and John Sullivan in St. Louis—faced in financing their lawsuits underscore the significance of the NAACP's subsequent contribution to the black freedom movement. Lack of financial resources proved a challenge to Curtis and an insurmountable obstacle to Sullivan because filing civil suits costs money. With assistance from the dean of the University of Tennessee law school, Curtis solved the problem of covering court costs by filing a pauper's oath. Lucas, too, received assistance from white allies, in this case allies with an explicitly partisan agenda. Sullivan may have also had help from Republican allies, but not enough to pursue his case to the finish.

White attorneys stood up for these black plaintiffs in the courts, but African American ancestors and community members also made their victories possible. Curtis was following in the footsteps of other African Americans who had succeeded in getting voting rights in Knox County and Tennessee more generally. His sense of entitlement to those rights clearly motivated his claim and stemmed at least in part from the fact that other black men had won their voting rights in Tennessee courts. Reaching back even further into history demonstrates that both of these victories were due to the fact that African Americans had obtained the right to equal standing in court in the Reconstruction years. In the American constitutional system, the right to standing in court is a critical element of citizenship and a right that is essential to the defense of other rights.[99]

While Lucas and Sullivan were the only men to take St. Louis officials and local Democratic operatives to court, a collective outrage in the black community about the events that day must have encouraged them to pursue their cases. Many of those who faced obstacles on Election Day confronted their accusers, challenged their assertions, and demanded the right to vote. Many who were arrested returned to the polls to try again. Dozens told their tales to the newspapers.[100] When Sullivan and Lucas went to court they spoke for all these disfranchised voters in the city.

In Re: Curtis set two important precedents for convicted individuals in Tennessee. First, this case determined that individuals whose civil rights had been denied due to prior convictions could still file a pauper's oath in Tennessee. Furthermore, the court held that Curtis had the right to the restoration of his citizenship since he demonstrated that he was a respected citizen. The court rejected the idea that restoration was a kind of favor handed out when judges felt benevolent. Rather, the court saw restoration as a right: a convicted individual who behaved well and had several "unimpeachable" citizens who can testify on his or her behalf was "entitled to be restored to his rights as a citizen."[101] Curtis proved that former convicts could and would demand their legal rights.

Curtis's triumph was not followed by successful petitions for citizenship by other African American men in Knoxville. Records indicate that he was possibly the last African American man to be restored to citizenship in that city for at least several decades.[102] Perhaps sensing the degenerating racial environment in the city or concerned about negative responses to his legal victory, Curtis and his family moved away at some point in the next five years. In the 1920 Census he is listed as living in Belmont, Ohio, and working as a laborer in a steel mill; ten years later the family had settled in Cleveland, where Curtis was employed as a janitor at a florist.[103]

The 1916 election in St. Louis offered images that foreshadowed recent elections in the United States, most famously the 2000 election in Florida in which African American voters were disproportionately affected by false accusations of prior, disfranchising convictions. But for now the "southernization" of elections in St. Louis stopped. A growing tide of Republican power in St. Louis meant that the party would strive to protect the political rights of its voters in the coming decade. Black southern migrants to St. Louis would find a new political landscape, in which their votes counted, unlike the one they left behind.

While the victories of Lucas and Curtis were limited, they were nonetheless victories that were achieved by mobilizing personal resources, forming alliances, and doggedly pursuing legal action in times and places where the odds were stacked against African American plaintiffs and in which a national consensus on African American voting rights had yet to be reached. Despite the fact that all three of these men acted independently of the NAACP and despite the fact that none claimed to have been victims of racial discrimination, their insistence on their right to vote at this critical moment in history was part of the larger struggle by African Americans for the rights of citizenship. Beyond the key court battles fought by the NAACP, and beyond the organized civil rights movement, were unorganized acts of protest that also fanned the flames of resistance. African Americans challenged laws and practices that denied them access to the ballot box in diverse settings.

Conclusion

I started researching this book by looking at changes to suffrage provisions in state constitutions. The first I examined was the Tennessee constitution of 1835. Article IV disfranchised African Americans, mulattos, Indians, and individuals convicted of certain crimes. Surveying early statutes governing suffrage, I found a 1748 Virginia law that barred these same groups from testifying in court.[1] At the time, I did not think these early laws were important. I was looking for evidence that laws denying rights of citizenship to felons were aimed at African Americans. How could the disfranchisement of felons have anything to do with race in an era when African Americans could not vote? What I finally figured out, and what has become the central argument of this book, was that the connection between denying the vote to convicts and denying the vote to African Americans predates the Civil War by at least half a century. Felon disfranchisement is about race but not exactly in the ways that those familiar with these laws today have imagined.

The doctrine of infamy is essential to understanding the connection between disfranchising convicts and African Americans. The rights to suffrage and the full privileges of citizenship for these two populations have been conceived of in relation to each other since the earliest days of this nation. Both slaves and convicts had limitations put on their civil rights due to their bondage and captivity. Americans, following European legal traditions, believed that the degraded social status produced by this bondage produced the degraded civil and legal status of infamy. The rights of degraded individuals stood in contrast to freemen, those "not infamous nor subject to another man's will," who enjoyed suffrage and the full privileges of citizenship. It is not a coincidence that slaves and convicts appear together in the Thirteenth Amendment, with its allowance of slavery as a punishment for crime, and in the Fourteenth Amendment's simultaneous

affirmation of the civil rights of African Americans and refusal to protect the suffrage rights of convicts. These amendments sought to remove
African Americans from their degraded social and civil status by distinguishing their civil rights from those of convicts.

If the dichotomy between infamy and citizenship seems at times a moving target, that is because it was. The law could produce infamy through
conviction for an infamous crime, and infamy could be reflected in a person's status before the law. One could be infamous for breaking a law—a
law, for example, that made larceny (which was an infamous crime) a felony.
Or one could be degraded by one's incarceration, wearing a prison uniform,
and working on a chain gang. These two interpretations of infamy each
served to define and reinforce the other. Infamy was also something of a
self-fulfilling prophecy. Being treated as someone infamous made one infamous. If white men were denied suffrage due to failure to pay taxes, they
were "degraded from the rank of one of the sovereigns."[2] If you were subject
to extra-legal violence, as many free African Americans were, it proved that
you were not worthy of civil or social equality with white men. Convicts
who "wore stripes" were infamous and undeserving of suffrage in a way
that misdemeanants, who did not wear that uniform, were not because
"stripes" were evidence of degradation.[3] This ambiguity in the definition
of infamy did not serve as an obstacle, but rather an opportunity for those
with political power and control of the criminal justice system. It enabled
white elites in the South to target individual African Americans with disfranchisement for criminal convictions while simultaneously justifying the
disfranchisement of the whole race.

The relationship between infamy and felon disfranchisement offers a
snapshot of how legal hierarchies both reflect and produce social hierarchies and cultural beliefs. Convicting African American men of infamous
crimes fostered the belief that the entire race was undeserving of suffrage.
This history also underscores the importance of considering language and
the law together. Referring to African Americans as "degraded," as was so
common in the early nineteenth century, was not just a figure of speech.
It was a reference to a legal and civil status, and its use helped maintain
African Americans in an inferior social status. Calling convicts "degraded"
connected their status to that of slaves, justifying the attenuation of their
civil rights.

The fact that the civil restrictions placed on African Americans (slave
and free) and convicts were being worked out in law and practice simultaneously helps explain why the lifelong denial of suffrage rights to those
convicted of crimes took hold more persistently in the South. While many
states across the country restricted the voting rights of those with criminal

convictions in the first half of the nineteenth century, only constitutional conventions in northern states debated, limited, and in some cases rejected these provisions. In the North, the dominant penal ideology allowed for the possibility that criminals might reform, while at the same time abolitionists and anti-slavery activists succeeded in convincing some in that region that African Americans could be elevated and redeemed as well. In the South one's civil and social status—generated by race or by criminal conviction—was fixed, and infamy and degradation lasted a lifetime.

Infamy also helps explain why laws disfranchising for crime were one of the first techniques used to disfranchise African Americans in the South after 1865. In the aftermath of the Civil War many white southerners believed that African Americans were undeserving of suffrage because (individually and collectively) the race was infamed by slavery. The whipping of scores of former slaves in North Carolina in 1866, treating them as convicts so they could be disfranchised for infamy, is perhaps the most revealing window into this ideology. In other states, though, white southerners found alternative ways to treat the former slaves as criminals and deprive them of suffrage in advance of the 1867 elections. The open language of the Fourteenth Amendment, allowing for disfranchisement for any crime, offered an opportunity that white southerners seized. But the impact of this effort went beyond individual voters. Associating African Americans with criminality, degrading them through legal and extra-legal violence, and denying them the dignity traditionally associated with those deserving of suffrage perpetuated the infamy of the entire African American race.

Those who supported black suffrage saw that these laws were being used for racial and partisan ends and fought back—giving more proof of the racial agenda of felon disfranchisement in the 1860s and 1870s as well as evidence of opposition to this practice. At the federal level, Radical Republicans tried to close the loophole in the second section of the Fourteenth Amendment by tightening the language in the Reconstruction Act that allowed southern states only to disfranchise for "felony at common law." They went further in the Readmission Acts, allowing disfranchisement only for felonies for which the offender had been "duly convicted, under laws equally applicable to all the inhabitants of said State." But their efforts faced a variety of opponents in Congress, and a move to constitutionally limit disfranchisement for crime in the Fifteenth Amendment failed. At constitutional conventions in southern states in 1868, defenders of African American suffrage tried, with limited success, to restrict or in some cases even eliminate penalties disfranchising for crime. This failure to constitutionally restrict disfranchisement for crime at the state level, along with waning federal authority over southern governments, set the stage for a campaign by the Democratic "redeemers," who retook control of southern state governments in the 1870s, to target black voters with disfranchisement for minor larcenies.

The nineteenth-century South kept alive and even developed the concept of infamy through law and practice. The ideas that degrading punishment could produce infamy and infamous individuals should face lifelong disfranchisement not only persisted but thrived in the region. The complicated mutually defining relationship between slavery and infamy, between convicts and African Americans, among those in a degraded race, those degraded by punishment, and those whose crime evidenced degradation was incubated in the region so that it became part of the legal and intellectual tradition of modern America.

Just as being treated with the same degraded civil status as convicts contributed to the denial of full civil rights for African Americans during slavery and Reconstruction, so did regarding convicts as civilly equal to African Americans give felon disfranchisement validation and permanence in the late nineteenth and twentieth centuries. Forced labor by convicts, particularly forced *public* labor in chain gangs and convict road crews, coupled with inhumane treatment for those incarcerated in prisons, underscored that convicts occupied a degraded status. While infamy still had a racial component, class was central too, as poor whites found themselves victimized by this system and working in labor gangs alongside African Americans. This conveniently aided the political agenda of elite southern whites, who found lower-class white votes increasingly threatening in the Populist era. At the national level, "infamous crimes" came to include all felonies, and this more general accounting of criminality mean that distinctions between honorable and dishonorable crime diminished. All who were incarcerated in prison were felons, degraded, humiliated, and ineligible to vote.

The South has played a significant role in shaping American criminal justice practices and policy in general and laws disfranchising for crime in particular. Recent historical scholarship has begun to explore the role of the South in shaping the agenda for criminal justice across the nation, specifically this region's influence in creating a system of mass incarceration, a nationwide acceptance of racial disparities in incarceration, and a criminal justice system that prioritizes retribution over rehabilitation.[4] Those men in Connecticut, Vermont, Maine, Pennsylvania, and Maryland who opposed, or at least sought to limit, lifelong disfranchisement for criminal convictions did not persuade the nation to adopt their position. They lost the argument, and their counterparts in the South won.

But courts and legislatures beyond the South contributed as well. Certainly, Congress failed to limit the ability of states to disfranchise for minor crimes, even after it was clear that the Fourteenth Amendment would allow this. Legal changes at the federal level that ended the distinction between "felony" and "infamous crime" coupled with changes in the ideology of corrections that privileged harsh treatment over rehabilitation lay the groundwork for national acceptance of the idea that all who were incarcerated in prison were degraded and undeserving of suffrage. Lifelong denial of suffrage for criminal convictions expanded across the nation in the late nineteenth and twentieth centuries. All of the new states added to the union between 1889 and 1912, except Utah, disfranchised felons or individuals convicted of infamous crimes in their first constitutions.[5] Pennsylvania, which had rejected efforts to disfranchise convicts on several occasions in the nineteenth century, denied the vote to incarcerated individuals in the mid-twentieth century through a series of court decisions and modifications of election laws.[6] When Alaska and Hawaii became states in 1959 (and disfranchised felons in their new constitutions), they joined 42 other states in laws denying the vote to certain convicted individuals.[7] Furthermore, over the course of the entire twentieth century, the number of people affected by laws disfranchising for crime increased exponentially as the number of felony convictions increased and levels of incarceration skyrocketed. By 2010 an estimated 5.85 million Americans could not vote due to a criminal conviction.[8]

The regional cross-fertilization of ideologies of morality, punishment, and citizenship was accompanied by a more literal exchange of statutory restrictions on suffrage. Laws disfranchising for crime were appealing to leaders of states outside the region, too, because they offered a model for eliminating certain groups from the franchise. Together this resulted in a nationalization of the southern idea that incarcerated individuals were a degraded "other" undeserving of suffrage rights.[9]

One of the first examples of southern suffrage laws, including laws disfranchising for crime, inspiring legislation outside the South, can be found in the Republic of Hawaii. In 1887 a group of wealthy American sugar planters who supported annexation of Hawaii to the United States forced King Kalākaua to sign a new constitution. Referred to by some as the "Bayonet Constitution" this document formed the Hawaiian Republic, stripping the monarchy of power. To seal their power, the new, governing planter class deprived native Hawaiian men of voting rights with literacy tests, property requirements, residency requirements, and a provision denying the vote and public-office-holding to individuals who had been convicted of any of an enumerated list of crimes.[10]

Kentucky, too, drew inspiration from the suffrage laws of its neighbors to the south—in particular laws disfranchising for poultry theft. In 1904 the Kentucky legislature passed a law mandating incarceration for one to five years for anyone convicted of stealing "chickens, turkeys, ducks or other fowls."[11] The racial intent of the new poultry theft law was immediately clear to informed observers. Chicken theft was now a felony, punishable by disfranchisement.[12] The *Louisville Times* gloated that now, "there is no longer any necessity for imposing an educational qualification to deprive the negro of the right of suffrage."[13] The *Washington Post* found irony in the fact that the first person convicted under this new law was a white man from a leading family—further demonstrating that the law had been aimed at African Americans.[14] The *Bourbon News* reported on an arrest under the new law, as well, with what was intended to be a humorous tale of two white women who caught an African American couple stealing turkeys.[15] Kentucky's 1904 legislative session was known for its overtly racist legislation; it also passed the Day Law, which segregated all schools in Kentucky.[16] Both disfranchisement for chicken theft and the Day Law had symbolic significance beyond their practical effects. They showed that the white men who dominated state government would use their political power to pass legislation that both excluded African Americans from full citizenship and insulted the black population.

In Idaho laws disfranchising for crime offered political advantage to the ruling political class of non-Mormons. Idaho's 1889 constitutional convention disfranchised anyone convicted of polygamy or bigamy—provisions targeting members of the Mormon faith. In addition, the document offered a sweeping plan to disfranchise for a range of beliefs and practices associated with Mormons, including anyone who encouraged individuals to commit bigamy or belonged to a group that supported bigamy. Even more generally it would disfranchise anyone who belonged to an organization that "teaches or advises that the laws of this state prescribing rules of civil conduct are not the supreme law of the state." The intention was clear: deny Mormons the right to vote. Convention member George Ainslie of Boise approvingly noted that not only did the provision disfranchise Mormons but the later section also denied the vote to "anarchists and communists who believe in no law whatever."[17]

Hawaii, Kentucky, and Idaho are examples of states that emulated southern disfranchisement laws. Leaders in these states selected minor crimes that they hoped would disproportionately affect racial, religious, or ethnic minorities and then disfranchised individuals convicted of these crimes. But it is important to recognize the complicity that occurred at the federal level, including the Fourteenth Amendment's provision allowing states to disfranchise for "any crime" and Congress's unwillingness to eliminate this opportunity in the Fifteenth Amendment. Individual states acted with the permission of the nation in targeting certain groups for disfranchisement due to criminal convictions.

Felon disfranchisement is only part of the history of disfranchisement in the nineteenth-century South, but it is important to the larger history of American citizenship. There is no evidence that the reach of these laws exceeded that of literacy tests, poll taxes, registration laws, or other disfranchisement techniques. However, laws disfranchising for crime played a role in southern politics and the lives of southerners. Disfranchising for minor larcenies was an early and explicit rejection of the federal standards, outlined in the Reconstruction and Readmission Acts, which limited disfranchisement to felonies. For individuals denied the vote due to these laws, as well as in a number of elections where these laws did seem to shape the electoral outcome, these laws had significant impacts. The demand for restoration of citizenship by individuals disfranchised for a criminal conviction helped force southern state governments to construct and maintain a mechanism for this within the pardon process. Individuals who sought restoration of citizenship demonstrate the impact that disfranchisement of any kind had on peoples' lives and dignity and underscore the social value gained from voting.

Many contemporary issues in felon disfranchisement have historic antecedents and debates over these laws today often turn on historical analysis. Local and state election administrators have used felon disfranchisement laws for racial and partisan ends for decades. Not only does this history demonstrate that local election administrators have historically been the central figures implementing laws disfranchising for crime, it also shows that state and local governments have consistently failed, throughout the nation's history, to enforce these laws in a fair and uniform way. People who should have been able to vote have often been denied the vote due to false allegations of a disfranchising offense; convictions have been secured through suspect judicial processes prior to an election for partisan ends; and people who should have been disfranchised have been allowed to vote. Sometimes these appear to have been honest mistakes made by officials charged with merging complicated statutory and constitutional requirements with voter registration data and court records. In many cases though, other agendas—partisan, racial, personal—seem to have been at work. In short, felon disfranchisement laws have long been subject to abuse.

While most states today maintain laws disfranchising for crime, in the past decade many have revised laws and procedures for restoring citizenship, streamlining the restoration process or in some cases making restoration of voting rights automatic with completion of sentencing for certain classes of felons.[18] This echoes the history told here. While states historically maintained strict laws disfranchising for crime, restoration of voting rights was rarely opposed and happened with relative frequency. States today are more likely to make restoration of voting rights easier than to eliminate felon disfranchisement entirely. Felon voting laws combined with the process of seeking restoration help maintain hierarchies of citizenship.

The most significant historical debate at present involves congressional intent in the Fourteenth Amendment. This is important because if, indeed, Congress intended to endorse disfranchisement for any crime in Section Two then voting is not a fundamental right for felons and therefore is not subject to equal protection claims. Legal scholars Christopher M. Re and Richard M. Re have mined historical sources to make a case that not only did Congress intentionally authorize laws disfranchising for crime in Section Two, but also that disfranchising for crime was central to the philosophy of political rights developed in the Reconstruction era. They argue that "retributive disenfranchisement" was the necessary counterpart to "egalitarian enfranchisement"; disfranchising for immoral actions helped legitimate the elimination of "morally insignificant" barriers to voting such as race.[19]

Did the 39th Congress intend to allow states to disfranchise any and all convicts for their entire lives in the Fourteenth Amendment? It is clear that many in Congress believed that individuals who were infamous were civilly degraded and therefore could not vote. This was a long-standing legal tenet and largely beyond debate. Who exactly was infamous, though, was a contested issue, as we have seen, in the mid- to late-nineteenth century. Was infamy the product of any kind of incarceration? Incarceration only in the penitentiary? Was it limited to those who were incarcerated for infamous crimes—thereby excluding murderous croquet players and other violent offenders? This evaluation of the long history of felon disfranchisement supports the argument that lawmakers did not expect "crime" to encompass all crimes. The "crime" for which one could become infamous, degraded, and disfranchised would have been limited by the kind of punishment that could be incurred or to those who committed infamous crimes. That was how such laws were written in state codes and constitutions in this era. A man who spent one night in a local jail for drunkenness would not have been, as a result, degraded and infamous.[20]

While a majority in Congress would have believed that some (but not all) criminal offenses should produce disfranchisement, there is good evidence that disfranchising rebels was foremost on their minds when they discussed and approved Section Two. Unlike the Thirteenth Amendment, which allowed slavery as punishment for any crime for which someone had been "duly convicted," Congress failed to put any restriction on the kinds of crime excepted from the apportionment penalty in Section Two— not even the requirement of due conviction specified in the Thirteenth Amendment. The reason for this omission was that Republicans in the South hoped to disfranchise for acts committed in the context of the rebellion for which convictions had not been secured—those who "killed or otherwise abused loyalists" (in Alabama) or " wrote or published newspaper articles or preached sermons" in support of treason (in Louisiana), for example. Requiring due conviction would have been a barrier to such provisions, and Republicans in Congress did not want to limit their allies in southern states.[21] When they discovered, in the course of the 1867 election, that their open-ended language allowed for all kinds of chicanery whipping to disfranchise (North Carolina) or disfranchising individuals for crimes committed while slaves (South Carolina)—they quickly restored the felony standard in the Reconstruction Act and required due conviction and equal protection in the Readmission Act. In sum, the open-ended language of Section Two indicates a focus on disfranchising former rebels, and Congress soon realized that Section Two needed to be limited by statute in states that were using its open-ended language for racial and partisan ends.

Re and Re raise a more theoretical issue as well. They assert that the philosophy of "formal equality" not only allowed but *required* disfranchisement for crimes, in order to stand in opposition to the older vision of citizenship that had been based instead on status.[22] The historical record does not, in my view, offer the articulation of such a philosophy. The pairing of African Americans and convicts in the rhetoric of citizenship was nothing new. As we have seen, the citizenship rights of these two populations were considered in relation to each other well before 1867. Distinguishing African Americans from convicts was necessary to lift them from infamy after 1865 and separate these two connected groups. The Thirteenth Amendment did not reduce convicts to the status of slaves; it elevated African Americans from the degraded status they shared with convicts.

Suggesting that Radical Republicans were articulating a new political philosophy based on one's acts rather than status is inaccurate. Continuing to disfranchise women (gender being a status, not an act) was not an exception to the rule but an indication that something more complicated was at work. Status remained a consideration in the assignation of political rights. Disfranchisement both produced and reflected degradation, which was a status. The language of degradation is prevalent in the congressional debates in this period. Thaddeus Stevens spoke of disfranchising former

Confederates by exclaiming, "Do not they deserve humiliation? Do not they deserve degradation?"[23] Section Two of the Fourteenth Amendment sought to guarantee the degradation of former rebels by consigning them to the same status as convicts. Even if rebels were not convicted of crimes, southern states could degrade their status to that of convicts through disfranchisement; degradation did not come from their act but from their punishment. Citizenship was product and indication of one's status, not one's acts.

The goal of Republicans in Congress was not so much to define citizenship by virtue but to lift African Americans from degradation. This did not require that convicts remain disfranchised and degraded. Iowa Congressman William Loughridge, during the debates over the Fifteenth Amendment, compared the status of whites and blacks, pointing out that even white men who were "destitute of talent...ignorant, vicious, and depraved" were still "acknowledged sovereigns" because they could vote. African Americans, because they were disfranchised, were "ruthlessly and cruelly thrust down and consigned...to hopeless degradation." Loughridge was pointing out that African Americans could be lifted from degradation by guaranteeing them suffrage. The Reconstruction Amendments had sought to elevate African Americans from their degraded status by freeing them from the infamy of slavery, giving them equal treatment before the law, and enfranchising them. But in 1869 their degradation persisted, in Loughridge's view, because of obstacles to suffrage. Passing the Fifteenth Amendment would give them the dignity of sovereigns and remove from them the degradation of infamy.[24]

Courts and legal scholars today debate whether voting is a fundamental right for felons, with legal precedent answering that question in the negative. The historical record indicates that lawmakers in the nineteenth century would have framed this issue in a different way to say that disfranchisement was fundamental to the degradation of felons. This ideology stems from a larger tradition in which the rights and privileges of citizenship granted to some seem to have enhanced value when they are denied to others, and possibly a larger human tendency to define oneself by denigrating others. Race is certainly not absent in this history. To the contrary, race both rationalized and motivated laws imposing lifelong disfranchisement for certain criminal acts in the post-Civil War period. But a variety of factors have led to the persistent sense that individuals with prior criminal convictions, particularly those who have experienced incarceration, are marked with a disgrace and contamination that is incompatible with citizenship. Laws, political agendas, and ideologies have intersected over time to produce, today, a class of individuals who are excluded from suffrage, disproportionately impoverished, members of racial and ethnic minorities, and often subject to labor for below-market wages. The rights of prisoners resemble the rights of slaves in a variety of ways, and as this book has demonstrated, this is not a coincidence. It is the result of political, legal, and ideological developments in the South and in the nation.

ACKNOWLEDGMENTS

I am delighted to be able to thank the people and institutions that have supported my research for this book.

In the early stages of this project, a Soros Justice Fellowship from the Open Society Institute bought me a year off from teaching so that I could conduct research and begin writing. The OSI also put me in touch with a great network of scholars and activists, who have inspired me at every stage of this project. I would like to acknowledge, in particular, the hard work of OSI staff members Adam Culbreath and Christina Voight. I am very grateful for OSI's support.

A number of people have read and commented on this manuscript. I really appreciate their time, energy, and smarts. They include: Morgan Kousser, Jack Chin, Michael Perman, Steven Lawson, Susan Hartmann, Alec Ewald (who wrote one of the most thoughtful reader reports one could imagine), and anonymous readers. Others who commented on conference papers, book and grant proposals, and individual chapters include Susan Cahn, John Dittmer, Leigh-Anne Francis, Ashland Johnson, Danielle McGuire, Peter Wallenstein, Heather Thompson, Chris Waldrep, and anonymous readers from the *Journal of Southern History*. I was fortunate to be a participant in Southern Methodist University's Clements Center Symposium on Sunbelt Prisons and receive feedback on parts of this project from organizers Robert Chase and Norwood Andrews, in addition to other symposium participants. Virgil Statom pitched in with proofreading and indexing when I needed a helping hand.

Along the way, others have provided all kinds of support. Alfred Brophy extended thoughtful encouragement and feedback. Derek Krissoff provided early enthusiasm that was immensely helpful. Katherine Osburn was a delightful and tolerant travel companion on research trips. Other friends and colleagues have shared their kindness and wisdom with me in ways too many to list.

James Cook and the staff at Oxford University Press have been fantastic to work with. It has been a joy to combine e-mails about the publishing process with commentary on English football.

I have visited a number of archives while working on this project, and I am indebted to the archivists and staff at the following institutions: Tennessee State Library and Archives, The Library of Virginia, State Archives of North Carolina, The North Carolina Collection at the University of North Carolina, South Carolina Department of Archives and History, Georgia Archives, Alabama Department of Archives and History, Alabama Supreme Court and State Law Library, Mississippi Department of Archives and History, Missouri State Archives–St. Louis, Missouri State Archives, and the State Archives of Florida. I owe special thanks to Michael Everman at the Missouri State Archives–St. Louis for his persistence and kindness.

I want to take this opportunity to express publicly my frustration with the office of Florida Governor Rick Scott. I tried repeatedly and without success to access the Florida State Board of Pardons Application Case Files. These records, even those dating back to the 1890s, are restricted to permission of the Governor, and users are instructed in the catalog record for this collection to submit their requests for permission to the Office of Clemency. Repeated phone calls, e-mails, letters, and faxes to the Office of Clemency requesting access to certain files from the 1890s through the 1940s went unanswered. I filed an Open Records Act request, explaining the problem and getting a response from the Office of Clemency; it came back explaining that I needed to contact the Office of Clemency to request permission from the Governor's office. Eventually I gave up. This kind of mismanagement is a disgrace to Florida and the nation.

I want to acknowledge the support of my colleagues at Middle Tennessee State University. I shall be forever grateful to the late Thaddeus Smith, who brought joy and good humor to my time at MTSU. Jan Leone, Amy Sayward, and James Beeby were chairs of the history department at various stages of this project, and I am glad for their fine stewardship and support for faculty research. Finally, Kathy Slager deserves massive thanks for using her superpowers to make it possible for me to simultaneously finish this book, serve as graduate director, and keep my sense of humor.

At every moment my family has been by my side. My dad Peter Holloway is my greatest professional and personal inspiration, and I love him beyond measure. My mom passed away long before I began this project, but I still miss her. My brothers Ken and Greg Holloway are my favorite compatriots in the halls of academia. I get tons of love and joy from my other family members: Tom Lynn, Natalka Kononenko, Shu-Ling Holloway, Heather-Michelle Wilson, and Jackie Urow. Finally, as I conclude these chapters I am looking forward to a future with Amanda Kail. I am very grateful for her love.

NOTES

PREFACE

1. Virginia Constitution, art. 3, sec. 1 (1870, amended 1876); *House Reports*, 51 Cong., 1 Sess., No. 1182, Pt. 1: *Edmund Waddill vs. George D. Wise* (Serial 2810, Washington, D.C., 1890), 1–21.

2. *House Reports*, 51 Cong., 1 Sess., No. 1182, Pt. 2: *Edmund Waddill vs. George D. Wise: Views of the Minority* (Serial 2810, Washington, DC, 1890), 14–15; quote on 14.

3. The Sentencing Project, *Felony Disfranchisement Laws in the United States 2010* (Washington, DC: The Sentencing Project, 2010), 1; Christopher Uggen, Sarah Shannon, and Jeff Manza, *State-Level Estimates of Felon Disenfranchisement in the United States, 2010* (Washington, DC: The Sentencing Project, 2010), 5; Statement of Marc Mauer, Executive Director, The Sentencing Project, Prepared for the House Judiciary Committee Subcommittee on the Constitution, Civil Rights and Civil Liberties, Hearing on H.R. 3335, "The Democracy Restoration Act of 2009," March 16, 2010.

4. This analogy has been made by a number of individuals including J. Whyatt Mondesire, "Felon Disenfranchisement: the Modern Day Poll Tax," *Temple Political and Civil Rights Law Review* 10 (Spring 2001): 435–441; Erika L. Wood and Neema Trivedi, "The Modern Day Poll Tax: How Economic Sanctions Block Access to the Polls," *Clearinghouse Review: Journal of Poverty Law and Policy* 41:1 (May-June 2007): 31–45. I am indebted to Steven F. Lawson for reminding me of this comparison.

5. Jeff Manza and Christopher Uggen, *Locked Out: Felon Disenfranchisement and American Democracy* (New York: Oxford University Press, 2006), 79–80; *Felony Disfranchisement Laws in the United States*, 1; Uggen, Shannon, and Manza, 1, 11–12, 16.

6. The Sentencing Project, *Felony Disenfranchisement Rates for Women* (Washington, DC: The Sentencing Project, March 2008), 2–3.

7. Ryan S. King, *Expanding the Vote: State Felony Disenfranchisement Reform, 1997-2008* (Washington, DC: Sentencing Project, 2008); Nicole D. Porter, *Expanding the Vote: State Felony Disenfranchisement Reform, 2010* (Washington, DC: Sentencing Project, 2010); *Felony Disfranchisement Laws in the United States*, 1.

8. Florida Constitution, art. VI, sec. 4 (1968); *Fla. Stat.*, title IX, chap. 97.041(2)(b) (2000); *Fla. Stat.*, title XLVII, chap. 944.292 (2000).

9. Scott Hiaasen, Gary Kane, and Elliot Jaspin, "Felon Purge Sacrificed Innocent Voters," Palm Beach *Post*, May 27, 2001, A1; Gregory Palast, "Florida's Flawed 'Voter-Cleansing' Program," Salon.com, December 4, 2000.

10. Editorial, "How America Doesn't Vote," *New York Times*, February 15, 2004, sect. 4, p. 10; Jeffrey Toobin has disputed the impact of the purge list, noting that many counties ignored them because they were so clearly full of errors. The truth of the matter is less relevant here than the fact that the 2000 election brought an unprecedented amount of public attention to felon disfranchisement laws. Jeffrey Toobin, *Too Close to Call: The Thirty-Six-Day Battle to Decide the 2000 Election* (New York: Random House, 2002), 169.

11. Abby Goodnough, "Disenfranchised Florida Felons Struggle to Regain Their Rights," *New York Times*, March 28, 2004, p. A1; John Lantigua, "How the GOP Gamed the System in Florida," *The Nation*, April 30, 2001, 11–17.

12. Nkechi Taifa, *Re-Enfranchisement! A Guide for Individual Restoration of Voting Rights in States that Permanently Disenfranchise Former Felons* (Washington, DC: The Advancement Project, 2002).

13. *Johnson v. Bush*, 214 F. Supp. 2d 1333 (S.D. Fla. 2002).

14. King, *Expanding the Vote*, 1–3.

15. For perspectives on felon disfranchisement in the international context see Alec C. Ewald and Brandon Rottinghaus, ed. *Criminal Disenfranchisement in an International Perspective* (New York: Cambridge University Press, 2009).

16. *Richardson v. Ramirez*, 418 U.S. 24 (1974).

17. *Richardson v. Ramirez*, 418 U.S. 24 (1974). This case has been used to reject challenges based on racially disparate impacts. See for example, *Farrakhan v. Gregoire*, 623 F.3d 990 (9th Cir. 2010); *Simmons v. Galvin*, 575 F.3d 24, 32 (1st Cir. 2009); *Hayden v. Pataki*, 449 F.3d 305 (2d Cir. 2006); *Johnson v. Governor of Fla.*, 405 F.3d 1214 (11th Cir. 2005).

18. Unlike infamy, "moral turpitude" had a vague legal meaning that had to be interpreted by the courts and state attorney general in decades to come. In 1985, in *Hunter v. Underwood* the U.S. Supreme Court heard testimony on how "moral turpitude" had come to be defined in Alabama, concluding that this provision had been enacted with racially discriminatory intent and interpreted in a racially discriminatory way. *Hunter v. Underwood*, 471 U.S. 222 (1985).

19. Malcolm Cook McMillan, *Constitutional Development in Alabama, 1798-1901: A Study in Politics, the Negro, and Sectionalism* (Chapel Hill: University of North Carolina Press, 1955), 275 n76.

20. *Underwood v. Hunter*, 730 F.2d 614, 621, n. 13 (11th Cir., 1984); J. Morgan Kousser, "Disfranchisement Modernized" (book review), *Election Law Journal* 6:1 (2007), 104–112.

21. *Hunter v. Underwood*, 471 U.S. 222 (1985). The decision in *Hunter v. Underwood* followed the logic of a few earlier cases in which lower courts found laws disfranchising for crime unconstitutional due to racial bias in the construction of the list of disfranchising crimes and their enforcement. One related, earlier case was *Allen v. Ellisor*. This case did not overturn an existing statute, though, because the South Carolina legislature changed the statute after the case was remanded to the district court. *Allen v. Ellisor*, 664 F.2d 391 (4th Cir., 1981). See also *Williams v. Taylor*, 677 F.2d 510 (5th Cir., 1982); William Walton Liles, "Challenges to Felony Disenfranchisement Laws: Past, Present, and Future," *Alabama Law Review* 58 (May 2007): 615–629.

22. *McGlaughlin v. City of Canton, Mississippi*, 947 F. Supp 954 (S.D. Miss., 1995).

23. Historians have testified in a number of Voting Rights Act challenges over the years, documenting the agenda of racial exclusion and minority vote dilution behind "at-large" (rather than district) elections, redistricting plans, runoff elections, and more. J. Morgan Kousser, *Colorblind Injustice: Minority Voting rights and the Undoing of the Second Reconstruction* (Chapel Hill: University of North Carolina Press, 1999). For a discussion of the Voting Rights Act and felon disfranchisement laws, see David Zetlin-Jones, "Right to Remain Silent? What the Voting Rights Act Can and Should Say About Felony Disenfranchisement," *Boston College Law Review 47*, no. 2 (2006): 411–454.

24. The two men filed the original claim, but Cotton's case was severed and dismissed upon appeal.

25. Gabriel Chin, "Rehabilitating Unconstitutional Statutes: An Analysis of *Cotton v. Fordice*, 157 F.3d 388 (5th Cir. 1998)," *University of Cincinnati Law Review 71* (Winter 2003): 421–55.

26. *Cotton v. Fordice*, 157 F.3d 388 (5th Cir. 1998); *Johnson v. Bush*, 214 F. Supp. 2d 1333 (S.D. Fla. 2002).

27. Gabriel Chin refers to the "rehabilitating" of these statutes in his article. Chin, "Rehabilitating Unconstitutional Statutes," 421.

INTRODUCTION

1. For region-wide overviews of the enactment and implementation of such disfranchisement techniques see J. Morgan Kousser, *The Shaping of Southern Politics: Suffrage Restriction and the Establishment of the One-Party South, 1880–1910* (New Haven: Yale University Press, 1974); Michael Perman, *Struggle for Mastery: Disfranchisement in the South, 1888–1908* (Chapel Hill: University of North Carolina Press, 2001); V.O. Key, *Southern Politics in State and Nation* (New York: Alfred A. Knopf, 1949), 533–643.

2. Mississippi and South Carolina disfranchised for a narrower list of crimes, and the significance of this difference will be explored in chapter 4. Some southern states did not specifically disfranchise felons but instead defined this population to include all individuals who had been convicted of crimes punishable with penitentiary time. This was essentially the same as a felony.

3. For a comparison of Greek *atimia*, Roman *infamia*, and English attainder in the context of infamy and disfranchisement see Katherine Irene Pettus, *Felony Disenfranchisement in America: Historical Origins, Institutional Racism, and Modern Consequences* (New York: LFB Scholarly Publishing, 2005), 11–37.

4. William Eden, *Principles of Penal Law* (London: B. White, 1771), 54.

5. William Blackstone, *Commentaries on the Laws of England: A Facsimile of the First Edition of 1765–1769*, vol. 5 (Chicago: University of Chicago Press, 1979), 372.

6. John Bouvier, *Bouvier's Law Dictionary and Concise Encyclopedia* 3rd revision, 8th ed. (Kansas City: Vernon Law Book Company, 1914), II, 1553–54. *Dane's Abridgement of American Law* listed infamous punishments as "death, gallows, pillory, branding, whipping, confinement to hard labor, and cropping." Nathan Dane, *A General Abridgement and Digest of American Law, With Occasional Notes and Comments*, vol. 2 (Boston: Cummings, Hillard, and Company, 1823), 569–570.

7. *Judicial and Statutory Definitions of Words and Phrases*, vol. 4, edited and compiled by the members of the editorial staff of the National Reporter System (St. Paul: West Publishing Company, 1910), 3577.

8. James Q. Whitman, *Harsh Justice: Criminal Punishment and the Widening Divide Between America and Europe* (New York: Oxford University Press, 2003), 102–107

9. Comparing England with continental Europe (primarily France and Germany), Whitman finds that "The old low-status punishments had been in retreat for a long time in England—much more so than on the continent." Nonetheless, he finds that this retreat from low-status punishments eventually took place in continental Europe as well. Whitman, *Harsh Justice*, 101–150, 153, 165, quote on 165.

10. Colonial America of course followed the English model, but Whitman finds that "in the less status-conscious culture of the British colonies" all criminals were punished the same. America diverged from Europe in the nineteenth century— "the American nineteenth century marks the beginning of a slow, definitive decline of high status punishment." Whitman, *Harsh Justice*, 171.

11. Tennessee Acts of 1829, chap. 23, sect. 71, John Haywood and Robert L. Cobbs, *The Statute Laws of the State of Tennessee*, vol. 1 (Knoxville: F. S. Heiskell, 1831), 253; Tennessee Constitution (1835), art. IV, sect. 1. See also, Donald L. Halladay, "Infamy as Ground of Disqualification in Tennessee," *Tennessee Law Review* 22:4 (December 1951), 547; Neil P. Cohen, "Tennessee Civil Disabilities: A Systemic Approach," *Tennessee Law Review* 41:2 (1974), 253. The Tennessee legislature established a different set of standards for disqualifying individuals from office. In the 1858 code, the conditions for disqualification from holding public office followed the section that defined infamy and read, "Every person convicted of a felony and sent to prison except for manslaughter is disqualified from holding any office under this statute." Felony conviction and prison time set the standard for this penalty, not the specific list of crimes that defined infamy. Tennessee Code of 1858, chap. 15, sect. 5227, Return J. Meigs and William F. Cooper, comp., *The Code of Tennessee: Enacted by the General Assembly of 1857– '8* (Nashville: E.G. Eastman, 1858), 925.

12. Virginia Constitution (1830), art. III, sect. 14; Arkansas Constitution (1836), sect. 12.

13. Bill Cecil-Fronsman, *Common Whites: Class and Culture in Antebellum North Carolina* (Lexington: University Press of Kentucky, 1992), 161. Unlike the other states discussed here, North Carolina did not disfranchise for infamy in the constitution or statutes; it appears to have simply been a tradition. The constitution specified simply how rights might be restored following disfranchisement for infamy. North Carolina Constitution, art. I, sect. 4, part 4 (1776, amended in 1835).

14. Alabama Constitution (1819), art. IV, sect. 5; Mississippi Constitution (1817), art. IV, sect. 5.

15. Quoted in Cecil-Fronsman, *Common Whites*, 161.

16. *Commonwealth v. Fugate*, 29 Leigh 724 (Va. Gen. 1830).

17. Governor Zebulon Vance, quoted in Cecil-Fronsman, *Common Whites*, 161.

18. At issue before the court was whether larceny was a "like crime" to robbery. One might argue, the court explained, that burglary is quite different from larceny. Kentucky statute defined burglary as larceny with violence. The existence of violence might be seen as increasing the "atrocity of the crime." But the court argued, in fact, that larceny *is* like burglary because both are infamous crimes. Both larceny and burglary are evidence of depravity and moral turpitude. From this perspective, the violence of burglary is irrelevant in assessing the seriousness of the crime, or more specifically, the depravity of the offender. Violence, then, offered no particular indication of immorality.

19. *Anderson v. Winfree*, 85 Ky. 597 (Ky. App. 1887). Kentucky's 1792 constitution disfranchised for "high crimes and misdemeanors," which the court interpreted to mean infamous crimes. "Laws shall be made to exclude from office and from suffrage, those who shall thereafter be convicted of bribery, perjury, forgery or other high crimes or misdemeanors." Kentucky Constitution (1792), art. VIII, sect. 2. This provision was unchanged in the second and third constitutions, passed in 1799 and 1850. Kentucky Constitution (1799), art. VI, sect. 4; Kentucky Constitution (1850), art. VIII, sect. 4. *Anderson v. Winfree*, 85 Ky. 597 (Ky. App. 1887).

20. *Official Report of the Proceedings and Debates in the Convention Assembled at Frankfort, on the Eighth Day of September, 1890, to Adapt, Amend, Or Change the Constitution of the State of Kentucky* (Frankfort, KY: E. P. Johnson, printer to the Convention, 1890), 1835–1836. A longer explanation of these ideas is in chapter 4.

21. Bertram Wyatt-Brown, *Southern Honor: Ethics and Behavior in the Old South* (New York: Oxford University Press, 1982), quote on 369.

22. George M. Fredrickson, *The Black Image in the White Mind: The Debate on Afro-American Character and Destiny, 1817–1914* (New York: Harper and Row, 1971), 5–6, 12–15; Emil Olbrich, *The Development of Sentiment on Negro Suffrage to 1860* (Madison: The University of Wisconsin, 1912); Walter F. Willcox, "Negro Criminality" in Alfred Holt Stone, *Studies in the American Race Problem* (New York: Doubleday, Page, and Company, 1908), 443–476.

23. Laws of Virginia, 1748, quoted in D.W. Woodbridge, "The Effect in Virginia of Conviction of Crime on Competency and Credibility of Witnesses," *Virginia Law Review* 23:470 (1937), 470–471.

24. Blackstone, *Commentaries on the Laws of England*, 373–79.

25. *The Congressional Globe*, 42:3 (May 11, 1830), 964.

26. Jesse Cooper, quoted in Guion Griffis Johnson, *Ante-Bellum North Carolina: A Social History* (Chapel Hill: University of North Carolina Press, 1937), 603.

27. Quoted in Whitman, *Harsh Justice*, 31.

28. Quoted in Whitman, *Harsh Justice*, 31.

29. Gustav Radbruch, quoted in Orlando Patterson, *Slavery and Social Death: a Comparative Study* (Cambridge, Mass.: Harvard University Press, 1982), 128.

30. Rebecca McLennan has cautioned against conflating slavery with imprisonment, or more specifically with the involuntary servitude of prisoners. Rebecca M. McLennan, *The Crisis of Imprisonment: Protest, Politics, and the Making of the American Penal State, 1776–1941* (Cambridge: Cambridge University Press, 2008). My point here is not to equate these statuses but to consider connections between them, both in terms of the law and social attitudes. My research and analysis seeks to historicize changes in the construction of citizenship by considering the status of those excluded from citizenship— an exclusion that has in various ways and times included slaves and convicts. This is not to say, though, that these two statuses are static or unchanging but rather to argue that they have shaped each other.

31. Joan Dayan, "Legal Slaves and Civil Bodies," in Russ Castronovo and Dana D. Nelson, eds, *Materializaing Democracy: Toward a Revitalized Cultural Politics* (Durham, NC: Duke University Press, 2002), 53–94.

32. Rebecca McLennan seeks to account for Congress's abrogation of the rights of convicts in the Thirteenth and Fourteenth Amendments in her book on the

history of the American penal state. She finds that most northern states had an established tradition of "forced productive labor for convicts" at this time. Since "an unqualified, truly universal, proscription of slavery and involuntary servitude would have effectively rendered most Northern penal systems illegal," Congress allowed involuntary servitude as punishment for crime in the Thirteenth Amendment. Similarly, she writes, "when they came to frame the Fourteenth Amendment, legislators were careful not to interfere with another constitutive characteristic of the prevailing systems of penal involuntary servitude: state laws that stripped prisoners of voting and various civil rights." Just as Congress drafted the Thirteenth Amendment to avoid undermining penal traditions across the nation, "the Fourteenth implicitly legitimated the states' disfranchisement of ordinary convicts." McLennan, 86–87.

33. Constitution of the United States, amend. XIV, sect. 2, "Representatives shall be apportioned among the several States according to their respective numbers, counting the whole number of persons in each State, excluding Indians not taxed. But when the right to vote at any election for the choice of electors for President and Vice President of the United States, Representatives in Congress, the Executive and Judicial officers of a State, or the members of the Legislature thereof, is denied to any of the male inhabitants of such State, being twenty-one years of age, and citizens of the United States, or in any way abridged, except for participation in rebellion, or other crime, the basis of representation therein shall be reduced in the proportion which the number of such male citizens shall bear to the whole number of male citizens twenty-one years of age in such State." In 1972, the Congressional Research Service described Section Two as a "historical curiosity," a fair assessment, until the Supreme Court interpreted this clause in 1974 to justify disfranchisement for crime in *Richardson v. Ramirez*. Congressional Research Service, *The Constitution of the United States: Analysis and Interpretation* (Washington, DC: GPO, 1972), 1528–1529; *Richardson v. Ramirez*, 418 U.S. 24 (1974). Gabriel Chin has argued that the Fifteenth Amendment effectively repealed Section Two of the Fourteenth Amendment. See Gabriel J. Chin, "Reconstruction, Felon Disenfranchisement, and the Right to Vote: Did the Fifteenth Amendment Repeal Section Two of the Fourteenth Amendment?" 92 *Georgetown Law Journal* 259 (2004), 259–316.

34. *Richardson v. Ramirez*, 418 U.S. 24 (1974).

35. Jason Morgan-Foster, "Transnational Judicial Discourse and Felon Disenfranchisement: Re-examining *Richardson v. Ramirez*," *Tulsa Journal of Comparative and International Law* 13:279 (Spring 2006), 279–319; Richard W. Bourne, "*Richardson v. Ramirez*: A Motion to Reconsider," *Valparaiso University Law Review* 42:1 (Fall 2007) 1–32. For other discussions of felon disfranchisement and Section Two, see also John R. Cosgrove, "Four New Arguments Against the Constitutionality of Felony Disenfranchisement," *Thomas Jefferson Law Review* 26 (2004), 157–202; Abigail M. Hinchcliff, "The 'Other' Side of *Richardson v. Ramirez*: A Textual Challenge to Felon Disenfranchisement," *Yale Law Journal* 121 (2011), 194–236; Howard Itzkowitz and Lauren Oldak, "Restoring the Ex-Offender's Right To Vote: Background and Developments," *American Criminal Law Review* 11 (1973), 721–770.

36. Morgan-Foster, "Transnational Judicial Discourse," 289–291.

37. Morgan-Foster, "Transnational Judicial Discourse," 289–291.

38. Bourne, "*Richardson v. Ramirez*: A Motion to Reconsider," 15–16. Italics in original.

39. Katherine Irene Pettus has made a similar argument, suggesting that Congress had no idea that Section Two of the Fourteenth Amendment contained a loophole that would allow states to deny the vote to so many people for such small crimes. Citizenship and suffrage, she points out, had been elite privileges, and disfranchisement for crime had occurred only rarely in the past. Congress failed to imagine that this form of disfranchisement could be expanded so widely, certainly not to the extent it was in the late twentieth century. Pettus also argues for a broader interpretation of the implications of the Section Two, beyond the amendment's impact on voting by convicts upheld in *Richardson v. Ramirez*. She points out that Section Two severed civil rights from political rights. The first section of the amendment granted all the "privileges and immunities" of citizenship to all native-born Americans. But in the second section allowing states to deny suffrage, Congress failed to affirm that suffrage was a fundamental right of all citizens. True, states had to pay a penalty of reduced congressional representation to those excluded on the basis of race, but even this form of disfranchisement was permitted under the amendment—just discouraged by its potential impact on congressional representation. Congress did not guarantee voting rights; rather it chose to reduce the political power of states that abridged these rights in impermissible ways. This prioritization of partisan objectives over the protection of fundamental rights, she argues, is also evident in the Fifteenth Amendment, which ultimately proved, too, a weak defense of suffrage. Pettus, *Felony Disenfranchisement in America*, 89, 108–110, 120–121.

40. Bourne, "*Richardson v. Ramirez*: A Motion to Reconsider," 19.

41. Scholarship on Reconstruction has long emphasized the twin goals of the Fourteenth Amendment—the enfranchisement of African Americans and the removal of white southern Confederates from political power. William A. Russ Jr. wrote in the *Journal of Negro History* in 1934, "So clearly did these planks of the radical program interweave and supplement each other that either one without the other could not have produced the results deemed so essential by radical politicians; hence both principles were incorporated into the Fourteenth Amendment and written into the procedure of the reconstruction acts. They were, in reality, two interlocking phases of the same consummation, namely— radicalization or Republicanization of the South in the interest of the victors in the war. Two revolutions were achieved, therefore, when the formerly submerged class of blacks was catapulted into political power and when the old leaders were relegated into obscurity." William A. Russ Jr., "The Negro and White Disfranchisement During Radical Reconstruction," *The Journal of Negro History* 19:2 (April 1934), 171.

42. Richard M. Re and Christopher M. Re, "Voting and Vice: Criminal Disenfranchisement and the Reconstruction Amendments," *Yale Law Journal* 121 (2012), 1684–1670.

43. Whitman, *Harsh Justice,* 154.

44. Richard B. Morris, "The Measure of Bondage in the Slave States," *Mississippi Valley Historical Review* 41 (September 1954): 219–40. Rebecca M. McLennan explores late eighteenth and early nineteenth-century debates over forced convict labor in northern prisons and its implications for the citizenship and the rights of workers. McLennan, *The Crisis of Imprisonment*, 27–47.

45. Quote from George Washington of Campbell County, *Official Report of the Proceedings and Debates in the Convention Assembled at Frankfort, on the Eighth*

Day of September, 1890, to Adapt, Amend, Or Change the Constitution of the State of Kentucky (Frankfort, KY: E. P. Johnson, printer to the Convention, 1890), 1808.

46. Quoted in Douglas Blackmon, *Slavery by Another Name: The Re-enslavement of Black People in America from the Civil War to World War II* (New York: Doubleday, 2008), 215.

47. Perman, *Struggle for Mastery*, 138.

CHAPTER 1

1. Quoted in Emil Olbrich, *The Development of Sentiment on Negro Suffrage to 1860*, Bulletin of the University of Wisconsin No. 477 (Madison: University of Wisconsin Press, 1912), 45–46; Laws of North Carolina, 1777, chap. II, sect. XLII, in Walter Clark, ed., *The State Records of North Carolina*, vol. 24 (Goldsboro, NC: Nash Brothers, 1905), 61.

2. Quoted in Olbrich, *The Development of Sentiment on Negro Suffrage*, 46. Italics in original.

3. For an overview of debates in state constitutional conventions over disfranchisement for crime in the nineteenth and twentieth century see John Dinan, "The Adoption of Criminal Disenfranchisement Provisions in the United States: Lessons from the State Constitutional Convention Debates," *Journal of Policy History* 19:3 (Fall 2007), 282–312.

4. Keyssar also points out that in a few locations property-owning women had access to the vote prior to changes in suffrage requirements that specified voters must be men. Alexander Keyssar, *The Right to Vote: The Contested History of Democracy in the United States* (New York: Basic Books, 2000), 26–30, 53–67.

5. Jeff Manza and Christopher Uggen, *Locked Out: Felon Disenfranchisement and American Democracy* (New York: Oxford University Press 2006), 51–54, quotes on 51 and 53.

6. Tennessee Constitution (1835), art. IV, sect. 1, 2. The constitution allowed black men who presently had citizenship rights to continue to exercise them.

7. Connecticut Constitution (1818), art. VI, sect. 1, 2, 3.

8. New York Constitution (1821), art. 2, sect. 1, 2; Erika Wood and Liz Budnitz, *Jim Crow in New York* (New York: Brennan Center for Justice, 2010), 8.

9. Manza and Uggen, *Locked Out*, 49–53, 237–239.

10. In the following citations, with regard to states with constitutional provisions that were not self-executing (i.e., constitutions that authorized the legislature to pass laws disfranchising for crime), I have listed both the date of the constitutional provision and the relevant executing statute. It is likely, however, that constitutional provisions often served to disfranchise even in the absence of the required statute. Louisiana first disfranchised for "bribery, perjury, forgery or other high crimes or misdemeanors" in 1812; Louisiana Constitution (1812), art. VI, sect. 4; "An Act To Deprive Certain Persons of Their Political Rights," January 1825, *Acts Passed at the First Session of the Seventh Legislature of the State of Louisiana* (New Orleans: M. Cruzat, 1824–1825), 38. Mississippi first disfranchised for bribery, perjury, forgery, or other high crimes or misdemeanors in 1817 Mississippi Constitution (1817), art. VI, sect 5; "An Act to Regulate Elections in the State," passed March 3, 1833, *Laws of the State of Mississippi* (Jackson, MS: State of Mississippi, 1838), 418. Alabama first disfranchised bribery, perjury, forgery, or other high crimes or misdemeanors in 1819; Alabama Constitution (1819), art. 6, sect. 5; "An Act

Excluding from Suffrage, Serving as Jurors, and Holding Offices, Such Persons as May be Convicted of Bribery, Forgery, Perjury, and other High Crimes and Misdemeanors," *Acts of the General Assembly of the State of Alabama, 1819* (Huntsville: John Boardman, 1820), 67–68. This act was amended in 1827 to include those convicted of larceny, receiving stolen goods, subordination of perjury, and certain kinds of fraud. John G. Aiken, compiler, *A Digest of the Laws of the State of Alabama* (Philadelphia: Alexander Towar, 1833), 129. Missouri first disfranchised for bribery, perjury, or other infamous crime in 1820; Missouri Constitution (1820), art. III, sect. 14. Virginia disfranchised for any infamous offense in its 1830 constitution. Virginia Constitution (1830), art. III, sect. 14. Tennessee first disfranchised for infamous crimes in 1835; Tennessee Constitution (1835), art. IV, sect. 2; Tennessee Code of 1858, chap. 2, art. IV, sect. 834, *The Code of Tennessee: Enacted by the General Assembly of 1857–'8* (Nashville: E. G. Eastman, 1858), 225. Arkansas disfranchised for a bribery, perjury, or other infamous crime in 1836; Arkansas Constitution (1836), art. IV, sect. 12. Texas first disfranchised for infamous crimes in 1836; Texas Constitution (1836), general provisions, sect. 1. Florida disfranchised for bribery, perjury, or other infamous crime in its pre-statehood constitution of 1838; Florida Constitution (1838), art. VI, sect. 4; "Title Third: Of Electors, Offices, and Offices and Elections," chap. III, sect. 2, part 3, in Leslie A. Thompson, *A Manual or Digest of the Statute Law of the State of Florida* (Boston: C. C. Little and J. Brown, 1847), 72. South Carolina's 1865 constitution allowed the legislature to pass laws disfranchising for crime; South Carolina Constitution (1865), art. IV. Georgia disfranchised for treason, embezzlement of public funds, malfeasance in office, crime punishable by law with imprisonment in the penitentiary, or bribery in 1868. Georgia Constitution (1868), art. 2, sect. 6. North Carolina's provisions are complicated and unclear in this period; they describe how individuals facing civil penalties due to infamy can have their rights restored, though there is no constitutional provision disfranchising for infamy. However, it is a fair assumption that the presence of a provision for restoration of civil rights indicates the imposition of civil disabilities such as disfranchisement—though it is possible that civil penalties were limited to disqualification from office holding. I would conclude, therefore, that North Carolina was likely to have been disfranchising certain convicts by 1835. North Carolina Constitution (1776, amended 1835), art. 1, sect. 4, part 4 states, "The General Assembly shall not have power to pass any private law...to restore to the rights of citizenship any person convicted of an infamous crime." North Carolina Statutes of 1840, Chapter 36, Section 1 states, "Any person either now or hereafter convicted of any infamous crime, whereby the rights of citizenship are forfeited, may be restored to the same under the following rules and regulations...." James Iredell, *A Digested Manual of the Acts of the General Assembly of North Carolina* (Raleigh: Weston R. Gales, 1847), 21.

11. See previous footnote for specific date for each state.
12. *Proceedings and Debates of the Convention of the Commonwealth of Pennsylvania to Propose Amendments to the Constitution, Commenced and Held at Harrisburg, on the Second Day of May, 1837*, vol. II (Harrisburg: Packer, Barrett, and Parke, 1837), 496.
13. *Proceedings and Debates of the Virginia State Convention of 1829–1830* (Richmond: Samuel Shepherd and Company, 1830), 422.

14. *A Report of the Debates and Proceedings of the Convention of the State of New York; Held at the Capitol, in the City of Albany, on the 28th Day of August, 1821* (New York: J. Seymour, 1821), 101.
15. *Proceedings and Debates of the Virginia State Convention of 1829–1830*, 433.
16. Quoted in Daniel Sharfestein, *The Invisible Line: Three Families' Histories of 'Passing' from Black to White* (New York: Penguin Press, 2011), 50. Citing *State v. Cantey*, 50 S.C.L. 614 (S.C. Ct. App. 1835). While this quote might seem anomalous or unrepresentative of a larger pattern, my point is that this dichotomy between infamy, degradation, and disfranchisement on the one hand and honor, respectability, and citizenship on the other was a strong presence in the region in this period. This South Carolina court's opinion is but one piece of evidence of this connection. Similarly, Tennessee's 1835 constitution disfranchised African American men, except those who were "a competent witness in a court of justice against a white man." The competence of witnesses was established by statute, which stipulated that Negros, Indians, mulattos, or individuals "descended from negro or Indian ancestors, to the third generation inclusive" were all barred from testimony. While the constitution's framers may have simply relied on this statutory definition as a shorthand, it is notable that the statutory definition of competence could be changed over time. In other words, the constitution's suffrage provision was framed so as not to disfranchise those who were legally able to exercise the right of testimony. Those who could testify in court were not infamous, and therefore suffrage was contingent, under the constitution, on one's status as a citizen under the statute prescribing the authority to testify in court. The disabilities of race—indeed race itself—then, were defined constitutionally in relation to statutory definitions of infamy. Tennessee Constitution (1835), art. IV, sect. 1, 2; Tennessee Acts of 1794, chap. 1, sect 32, Seymour D. Thompson and Thomas M. Steger, *A Compilation of the Statute Laws of the State of Tennessee* (St. Louis: W. J. Gilbert, 1872), 1552.
17. *A Report of the Debates and Proceedings of the Convention of the State of New York . . . 1821*, 183.
18. *Debates and Proceedings in the New York State Convention for the Revision of the Constitution* (Albany: Albany Argus, 1846) 783–785, quote on 785.
19. *Jones v. Robbins*, 8 Gray 329 (1857).
20. *State v. Earnhardt*, 86 SE 960 (1915).
21. Alabama Constitution (1819), art. VI, sect. 3; Mississippi Constitution (1832), art. VII, sect. 2; Tennessee Constitution (1834), art. IX, sect. 3; Louisiana Constitution (1845), title VI, art. 130; Michigan Constitution (1850), art. VII, sect. 8. Ohio disqualified duelers from holding office in 1851. Ohio Constitution (1851), art. 15, sect. 5.
22. *The Debates and Proceedings of the Constitutional Convention of the State of Michigan*, vol. II (Lansing: John A. Kerr, 1867), 292.
23. Southern constitutional conventions in this period are documented in less detail, and therefore I have been able to examine events at northeastern constitutional conventions more closely. Southern states whose convention journals I have examined are Louisiana (1845), Virginia (1830), North Carolina (1835), and Kentucky (1849). While I have not been able to examine debates at other southern conventions, the resulting constitutions did not limit or restrict disfranchisement for crime the way some states in the northeast did.
24. Quoted in *The Public Statute Laws of Connecticut*, vol. 1 (Hartford: Hudson and Goodwin, 1808), 358.

25. *The Public Statute Laws of Connecticut,* vol. 1, title 78, chap. 1, sect. 6, 357.
26. *The Laws of Vermont of a Publick and Permanent Nature,* chap. 85, sect. 6 (Windsor, Vermont: Simeon Ide, 1824), 567.
27. Lewis Hamilton Meader, "The Council of Censors in Vermont," *Proceedings of the Vermont Historical Society* (Burlington: Free Press Association, 1898), 117.
28. Quoted in Brian J. Hancock, "The Voting Rights of Convicted Felons," *FEC Journal of Election Administration* 17:1 (1996), 36. I would like to thank Alec Ewald for calling these New England statutes and some of these sources to my attention.
29. Chap. 11, sect. 12, 13 *Laws of Vermont of 1832* (Montpelier, VT: Knapp and Jewitt, 1832).
30. *The Debates, Resolutions, and other Proceedings, of the Convention of Delegates* (Portland, Maine: A. Shirley, 1820), 94–95.
31. A number of states considered disfranchisement, disqualification from office holding, and other penalties for dueling in this period, including Virginia, Louisiana, and Kentucky, Ohio, and Michigan. Michigan's 1850 constitution disfranchised and disqualified from office holding anyone who "engaged in a duel." Michigan Constitution (1850), art. VI, sect. 8.
32. *Proceedings and Debates of the Convention of the Commonwealth of Pennsylvania, to Propose Amendments to the Constitution: Commenced and Held at Harrisburg, on the Second Day of May, 1837,* vol. 4 (Harrisburg, Penn.: Packer, Barrett, and Parke, 1838), 243–259, quotes on 249 (first two), 253 (third).
33. *Debates of the Convention to Amend the of Pennsylvania: Convened at Harrisburg, November 12, 1872* (Harrisburg, Penn.: Benjamin Singerly, State Printer, 1873), vol. II, 48–58, quotes on 50 (first quote), 53.
34. Pennsylvania Constitution (1873), art. VIII, sect. 9; art. II, sect. 6.
35. *Debates and Proceedings of the Maryland Reform Convention to Revise the State Constitution* (Annapolis: William McNeir, Printer, 1851), 87, 99–101, quotes on 87, 101; Maryland Constitution (1851), art. X, sect. 5.
36. *The Debates of the Constitutional Convention of the State of Maryland, Assembled at the City of Annapolis, Wednesday, April 27, 1864,* vol. II (Annapolis: Richard P. Bayly, 1864), 1289–1294, quotes on 1289, 1291.
37. *The Debates of the Constitutional Convention of the State of Maryland . . . 1864,* 1294.
38. *Report of the Proceedings and Debates in the Convention to Revise the Constitution of the State of Michigan, 1850* (Lansing: R. W. Ingals, 1850), 298.
39. Mark E. Kann, *Punishment, Prisons and Patriarchy: Liberty and Power in the Early American Republic* (New York: New York University Press, 2005); Robert Perkinson, *Texas Tough: The Rise of America's Prison Empire* (New York: Metropolitan Books, 2010).
40. For accounts of the South's convict labor system see Mary Ellen Curtin, *Black Prisoners and Their World, Alabama, 1865–1900* (Charlottesville: University of Virginia Press, 2000); Alex Lichtenstein, *Twice the Work of Free Labor: The Political Economy of Convict Labor in the New South* (New York: Verso, 1996); Perkinson, *Texas Tough,* 73. Rebecca M. McLennan's work questions this dichotomy of southern and northern systems, pointing out that northern prisons, too, extracted labor from inmates. Rebecca M. McLennan, *The Crisis of Imprisonment: Protest, Politics, and the Making of the American Penal State, 1776-1941* (Cambridge: Cambridge University Press, 2008). The North's ideology of reform and the faith of northern policymakers that rehabilitation was possible is the relevant issue here—not so much whether that ideology reflected a reality—because it undermined the idea

of lifelong infamy as a result of incarceration. On routine torture and violence of prisoners at Sing Sing prison in New York and the use of convict labor in this facility see Timothy Gilfoyle, *A Pickpocket's Tale: The Underworld of Nineteenth-Century New York* (New York: Norton, 2006).

41. Myra C. Glenn, *Campaigns Against Corporal Punishment: Prisoners, Sailors, Women, and Children in Antebellum America* (Albany: State University of New York Press, 1984), 12–14; Lawrence M. Friedman, *Crime and Punishment in American History* (New York: Basic Books, 1993), 74–75.

42. Ira Berlin, *Slaves Without Masters. The Free Negro in the Antebellum South* (New York: Pantheon Books, 1975), 334; Stephanie McCurry, *Confederate Reckoning: Power and Politics in the Civil War South* (Cambridge, Mass.: Harvard University Press, 2010), 43.

43. Perkinson, *Texas Tough*, 70–78, quote on 72.

44. *State v. Keyes*, 8 Vt. 57 (Vt. 1836).

45. New York (State) Commissioners of the Code, *First Report of the Commissioners of the Code*, book 1 (Albany: Weed, Parson, and Co. 1849), 49.

46. *A Report of the Debates and Proceedings of the Convention of the State of New York...1821*, 364.

47. United States Constitution, amend. XIII, "Neither slavery nor involuntary servitude, except as a punishment for crime whereof the party shall have been duly convicted, shall exist within the United States, or any place subject to their jurisdiction."

CHAPTER 2

1. Robert Avery to Jonathan C. Robinson, December 17, 1866, Letters Received, Second Military District, Records of the U.S. Army Continental Commands, RG 393, National Archives of the United States, file P-715, 1866, M619, roll 504. I found this document because it was cited in Steven F. Miller, Susan E. O'Donovan, John C. Rodrigue, and Leslie S. Rowland, "Between Emancipation and Enfranchisement: Law and the Political Mobilization of Black Southerners, 1865–1867," *Chicago-Kent Law Review* 70:3 (1995), 1059–1077.

2. "Whipping and Selling American Citizens" *Harper's Weekly*, January 12, 1867, 18. This article was also reprinted in *The Daily Miners' Register* (Central City, CO), January 24, 1867, p. 3.

3. "The True Problem," *Atlantic Monthly*, March 1867, 374.

4. Eric Foner, *Reconstruction: America's Unfinished Revolution* (New York: Harper and Row, 1988), 204–205.

5. J. R. Bomford to E. D. Townsend, August 10, 1866, Letters Received, Second Military District, Records of the U.S. Army Continental Commands, RG 393, National Archives of the United States, file P-715 1866, M619, roll 504. For discussion of the debate over whipping in the larger context of Reconstruction politics in North Carolina, see Mark L. Bradley, *Bluecoats and Tar Heels: Soldiers and Civilians in Reconstruction North Carolina* (Lexington: University Press of Kentucky, 2009).

6. Constitution of the United States, amend. XIV, sect. 2.

7. *Acts of the General Assembly of the State of South Carolina, Passed at the Sessions of 1864–1865*, (Columbia, SC: Julian Selby, 1866), 271–273.

8. South Carolina's 1790 Constitution did not disfranchise for conviction. South Carolina Constitution (1790), art. 1, sect. 4. This article was amended in 1810 but still made no mention of disfranchising convicts. South Carolina

Constitution (1790, amended 1810), art. I, sect. IV; South Carolina Constitution (1865), art. IV, sect. 1.

9. African Americans could not vote in South Carolina under the 1865 Constitution, which specified that one must be a "free white man" to vote. South Carolina Constitution (1865), art. IV, sect. 1.

10. *Proceedings of the Constitutional Convention of South Carolina, 1868* (Charleston: Denny and Perry, 1868), 840. On Robertson see Peggy Lamson, *The Glorious Failure: Black Congressman Robert Brown Elliott and the Reconstruction of South Carolina* (New York: Norton, 1973), 49.

11. Historians of the Reconstruction Acts and the Fourteenth Amendment generally discuss them in the order in which they became law. In other words, the Reconstruction Acts—enacted in 1867—are considered to have preceded the Fourteenth Amendment, which was ratified in July 1868. However, Congress passed the Fourteenth Amendment before the Reconstruction Acts, and southerners were, as I have shown, able to anticipate its provisions.

12. William Horatio Barnes, *History of the Thirty-Ninth Congress of the United States* (New York: Harper and Brothers, 1868), 504.

13. *Congressional Globe*, House of Representatives, 39th Congress, 2nd Sess., 324 (January 7, 1867).

14. Barnes, *History of the Thirty-Ninth Congress*, 504–506.

15. *Congressional Globe*, House of Representatives, 39th Congress, 2nd Sess., 815 (January 28, 1867).

16. *Congressional Globe*, House of Representatives, 39th Congress, 2nd Sess., 504 (January 16, 1867).

17. For example, Stevens reminded Rep. Eliot, "Throughout all the South they are whipping negroes under pretended convictions for crime, so as to render them, under their laws, disqualified from ever voting." Eliot replied, "I am in favor of the object the gentleman has in view; still I think it liable to the objection I have indicated." *Congressional Globe*, House of Representatives, 39th Congress, 2nd Sess., 815–816 (January 28, 1867).

18. "An Act to Provide for the More Efficient Government of the Rebel States, March 2, 1867," chap. 153, *United States Statutes at Large*, vol. 14 (Boston: Little, Brown and Company, 1868), 428–429.

19. On the disfranchisement of former Confederates under the Fourteenth Amendment and the Reconstruction Act, see Eric Foner, *Reconstruction*, 275–278.

20. "Interpretation of the Reconstruction Acts," June 18, 1867, House Exec. Doc. 34, 40th Congress, 1st Sess., 6.

21. "An Act Supplementary to an Act Entitled 'An Act to Provide for the more Efficient Government of the Rebel States,'" March 23, 1867, *United States Statutes at Large*, vol. 15 (Boston: Little, Brown, and Company, 1869), 2.

22. "General Instructions to Officers of Registration, for Their Information in Revising the Lists of Voters," Headquarters of the Second Military District, Charleston SC, August 27, 1867, in "General Orders—Reconstruction," House Exec. Doc. 342, 40th Congress, 2nd Sess., 58–60.

23. [Untitled Circular], October 31, 1867, in "General Orders—Reconstruction," House Exec. Doc. 342, 40th Congress, 2nd Sess., 69–72.

24. On commercial interactions between slaves and whites see Timothy James Lockley, *Lines in the Sand: Race and Class in Lowcountry Georgia, 1750–1860* (Athens: University of Georgia Press, 2004), 57–97.

25. McCurry, *Confederate Reckoning*, 43.
26. [Untitled Circular], October 31, 1867, 69–72.
27. [Untitled Circular], October 31, 1867, 69–72.
28. *Proceedings of the Constitutional Convention of South Carolina, 1868*, 540.
29. *Proceedings of the Constitutional Convention of South Carolina, 1868*, 861.
30. *Proceedings of the Constitutional Convention of South Carolina, 1868*, 861.
31. South Carolina Constitution (1868), art. X, sect. 12.
32. David G. Croly, *Seymour and Blair, Their Lives and Services* (New York: Richardson and Company, 1868) 282.
33. The South Carolina Constitutional Convention also considered revisions to the judicial system, debates that evidenced concern with the fairness of the system at the time. See James Lowell Underwood, "African American Founding Father: The Making of the South Carolina Constitution of 1868," in James Lowell Underwood and W. Lewis Burke Jr., ed., *At Freedom's Door: African American Founding Fathers and Lawyers in Reconstruction South Carolina* (Columbia: University of South Carolina Press, 2000), 1–35.
34. Justice of the peace courts existed as a relic of fourteenth-century English law, brought to the United States by British colonists. For descriptions of nineteenth-century magistrates' courts in the South see: Laura F. Edwards, "Status without Rights: African Americans and the Tangled History of Law and Governance in the Nineteenth Century U.S. South," *American Historical Review* 112:2 (2007), 371–373; see also S. F. Davis, "Something about Some of the Justices' Courts of Mississippi," *Case and Comment* 22 (1915), 42–45. For a history of and assessment of the value of these courts written in the 1920s see Chester H. Smith, "The Justice of the Peace System in the United States," *California Law Review* 15 (1927), 118–141.
35. "Report of the Senate Committee on Privileges and Elections with the Testimony and Documentary Evidence on the Election in the State of Florida in 1876," report no. 611, 44th Cong, 2nd Sess., 256, 261–262.
36. *Journal of the Senate of Virginia, 1876* (Richmond: R. F. Walker, 1876), 113.
37. *Journal of the Constitutional Convention of the State of North Carolina, 1868 Session*, Electronic Edition. http://docsouth.unc.edu/nc/conv1868/conv1868.html.
38. *Journal of the Constitutional Convention of the State of Virginia* (Richmond: Office of the New Nation, 1867), 99–100. On William H. Andrews see Richard G. Lowe, "Virginia's Reconstruction Convention. General Schofield Rates the Delegates" (Part One), *The Virginia Magazine of History and Biography* 80:3 (July 1972), 358.
39. *Journal of the Constitutional Convention of the State of Virginia*, 92.
40. *Official Journal of the Constitutional Convention of the State of Alabama* (Montgomery, AL: Barrett & Brown, 1868), 81–85; McMillan, *Constitutional Development in Alabama*, 121 n. 57.
41. *Official Journal of the Constitutional Convention of the State of Alabama*, 84–85; McMillan, *Constitutional Development in Alabama*, 117 n. 32.
42. Florida Constitution (1865), art. VI, sect. 2; Florida Constitution (1868), art. XV, sect. 2, 4. Michael Perman, *Road To Redemption* (Chapel Hill: University of North Carolina Press, 1984), 27–28.
43. For a comparison of the political composition of 1868 state constitutional conventions see Foner, *Reconstruction*, 316–333; quote on 322.
44. On splits over suffrage in the Republican party in this period see Perman, *Road to Redemption*, 24–31.

45. *Official Journal of the Constitutional Convention of the State of Alabama*, 17, 42–47, quote on 17.
46. *Proceedings of the Constitutional Convention of South Carolina*, 326–337.
47. Alabama Constitution (1865), art. VIII, sect. 1; Alabama Constitution (1868), art. VII, sect. 3; Arkansas Constitution (1864), art. IV, sect. 2; Arkansas Constitution (1868), art. VIII, sect. 2, part 5; Louisiana Constitution (1864), title III, art. 14; Louisiana Constitution (1868), title VI, art. 99; South Carolina Constitution (1865), art. IV, sect 1.; South Carolina Constitution (1868), art. VII, sect. 8; Virginia Constitution (1864), art. III, sect. 1; Virginia Constitution (1870), art. III, sect. 1, part 3.
48. Mississippi Constitution (1868), art. IV, sect. 17; Florida Constitution (1868), art. XIV, sect. 1.
49. *Official Journal of the Constitutional Convention of the State of Alabama*, 41–47, quote on 42.
50. Louisiana Constitution (1868), title IV, art. 99.
51. *Journal of the Constitutional Convention of the State of North Carolina, at Its Session 1868*, 234.
52. For example, W. J. Mixson, who had held office in the Confederacy, petitioned to have his political rights restored, *Journal of the Constitutional Convention of the State of North Carolina, at Its Session 1868*, 179, 234. Other petitions, 627.
53. *Journal of the Constitutional Convention of the State of North Carolina, at Its Session 1868*, 539–540.
54. *Journal of the Constitutional Convention of the State of North Carolina, at Its Session 1868*, 540.
55. *Journal of the Constitutional Convention of the State of North Carolina, at Its Session 1868*, 605.
56. Among the most common changes made in the many southern conventions of 1868 were laws disfranchising for crimes committed by elected officials. Many states also replaced legally ambiguous terms like high crimes and misdemeanors or infamy, with "felony" or penitentiary time. Both of these changes can be considered part of efforts to modernize government and clarify constitutions.
57. Alabama Constitution (1868), art. VII, sect. 3.
58. Virginia Constitution (1868), art. 3, sect. 1.
59. "An Act to Admit the State of Arkansas to Representation in Congress, June 22, 1868," chap. 69, *United States Statutes At Large*, vol. 15, 72; "An Act to Admit the States of North Carolina, South Carolina, Louisiana, Georgia, Alabama and Florida to Representation in Congress, June 25, 1868," chap. 70, *United States Statutes at Large*, vol. 15, 73. The same language can be found in the 1870 acts admitting Virginia, Mississippi, and Texas.
60. "Neither slavery nor involuntary servitude, except as a punishment for crime whereof the party shall have been duly convicted, shall exist within the United States, or any place subject to their jurisdiction." Constitution of the United States, amend. XIII.
61. The U.S. Supreme Court considered the language of the Fourteenth Amendment and Readmission Acts in *Richardson v. Ramirez*. The court found that the restrictions on southern constitutions contained in the Readmission Acts confirmed their interpretation of congressional intent, that the Reconstruction Congress affirmed the right of states to disfranchise for criminal convictions. The court seemed unimpressed or uninterested in the trend of ever tightening restrictions on southern states outlined in this chapter. *Richardson v. Ramirez*, 418 U.S. 24 (1974).

62. *Congressional Globe*, House of Representatives, 40th Congress, 3rd Sess., 728 (January 29, 1869); On Bingham see Michael Kent Curtis, "The Crisis over The Impending Crisis: Free Speech, Slavery, and the Fourteenth Amendment," in Paul Finkleman, ed., *Slavery and the Law* (Oxford: Rowman and Littlefield, 2002), 161–206.

63. *Journal of the House of Representatives of the United States*, 40th Congress 3rd Session 233–235 (December 7, 1868); *Congressional Globe*, House of Representatives, 40th Congress, 3rd Session, 743 (January 29, 1869). On the other elements of Shellabarger's proposal see Richard Bensel, *Yankee Leviathan: The Origins of Central State Authority in America, 1859–1877* (New York: Cambridge University Press, 1990), 357; Michael Les Benedict, *A Compromise of Principle: Congressional Republicans and Reconstruction, 1863–1869* (New York: W. W. Norton & Co, 1974), 332.

64. *Congressional Globe*, U.S. Senate, 40th Congress, 3rd Sess., 861 (February 4, 1869). *Congressional Globe*, U.S. Senate, 40th Congress, 3rd Sess., 1041 (February 9, 1869). On Warner see Sarah Woolfolk Wiggins, *The Scalawag in Alabama Politics, 1865–1881* (Tuscaloosa: University of Alabama Press, 1977), 39.

65. *Journal of the Senate of the United States of America*, December 7, 1868, 40th Congress, 3rd Sess., 222, 226, 230.

66. On the relationship of the Fifteenth Amendment to the disfranchisement provisions in the Reconstruction Act and Readmission Acts, see Chin, "Reconstruction, Felon Disenfranchisement, and the Right to Vote," 259–316.

67. *Congressional Globe*, U.S. Senate, 1305 (February 9, 1869); *Journal of the Senate of the United States of America*, December 7, 1868, 290. See also Xi Wang, *Trial of Democracy: Black Suffrage and Northern Republicans, 1860–1910* (Athens: University of Georgia Press, 1997), 45.

68. Wood and Budnitz, *Jim Crow in New York*, 12–13.

69. Kelly Elizabeth Phipps, "Marriage and Redemption: Mormon Polygamy in the Congressional Imagination, 1862–1887," *Virginia Law Review* 95:2 (April 2009), 437–487.

70. On the role of violence in Reconstruction politics see, George C. Rable, *But There Was No Peace: The Role of Violence in the Politics of Reconstruction* (Athens: University of Georgia Press, 1984).

71. *United States v. Reese*, 92 U.S. 214 (1875); *United States v. Cruikshank*, 92 U.S. 542 (1875); William Gillette, *Retreat from Reconstruction: 1869–1879* (Baton Rouge: Louisiana State University Press, 1979), 280–299.

CHAPTER 3

1. *House Miscellaneous Documents*, 47 Cong., 1 Sess., No. 11: *Testimony in the Contested Election Case of Horatio Bisbee, Jr. vs. Jesse J. Finley, from the Second Congressional District of Florida* (Serial 2037, Washington, DC, 1881), 414–415, quote on 415; hereinafter cited as *Testimony in the Case of Horatio Bisbee, Jr. vs. Jesse J. Finley.*

2. *Ibid.*, 416, 419–420, 458, 469–470, 498, 510, 914, quote on 469.

3. *House Miscellaneous Documents*, 47 Cong., 1 Sess., No. 16: *Testimony and Papers in the Contested Election Case of James Gillette vs. Thomas H. Herndon, from the First Congressional District of Alabama* (Serial 2039, Washington, DC, 1881), 75–77, quote on 76; hereinafter cited as *Testimony in the Case of James Gillette vs. Thomas H. Herndon.*

4. *House Miscellaneous Documents*, 48 Cong., 1 Sess., No. 16: *Papers and Testimony in the Contested Election Case of C. T. O'Ferrall vs. John Paul, from the Seventh Congressional District of Virginia* (Serial 2220, Washington, DC, 1884), 135, 136, 171, 172, 180, 181; hereinafter cited as *Testimony in the Case of C. T. O'Ferrall vs. John Paul.*

5. *House Miscellaneous Documents*, 48 Cong., 1 Sess., No. 27, Pt. 2: *Papers and Testimony in the Contested-Election Case of John E. Massey vs. John S. Wise, from the State of Virginia at Large* (Serial 2227, Washington, DC, 1884), 309–310; hereinafter cited as *Testimony in the Case of John E. Massey vs. John S. Wise.*

6. Perman, *Struggle for Mastery*, 9–36.

7. Foner, *Reconstruction*, 587–591.

8. Texas's 1875 constitution had simply disfranchised all with felony convictions, and this section of the constitution remained unchanged through this period. Texas Constitution (1875), art. VI, sect. 1. See also *The Constitution of the State of Texas: An Annotated Comparative Analysis* by George D. Braden et al. (1977), 483. On suffrage restriction in Texas in this period and some of the factors that made the political situation there distinctive, see Patrick G. Williams, "Suffrage Restriction in Post-Reconstruction Texas: Urban Politics and the Specter of the Commune," *Journal of Southern History* 68 (February 2002), 31–64. For an overview of devices employed to restrict suffrage in this period see Kousser, *Colorblind Injustice*, 25–37.

9. Alec C. Ewald, "'Civil Death': The Ideological Paradox of Criminal Disenfranchisement Law in the United States," *Wisconsin Law Review* 5:2002 (2002), 1088; Andrew L. Shapiro, "Challenging Criminal Disenfranchisement Under the Voting Rights Act: A New Strategy," *Yale Law Journal* 103 (November 1993), 537–566, quote on 540. Scholarship that focuses on the history of "felon disenfranchisement," such as the work of Angela Behrens, Christopher Uggen, and Jeff Manza, also underestimates the significance of provisions passed prior to the 1890s that also disfranchised individuals convicted of misdemeanors. Angela Behrens, Christopher Uggen, and Jeff Manza, "Ballot Manipulation and the 'Menace of Negro Domination': Racial Threat and Felon Disenfranchisement in the United States, 1850–2002," *American Journal of Sociology* 109 (November 2003), 559–605.

10. J. Morgan Kousser notes that the 1870s saw passage of disfranchisement for petty larceny in Virginia and observes that Mississippi's Pig Law had implications for suffrage, but does not identify these laws as part of a larger regional pattern of disfranchising for petty theft in the 1870s. He also considers racially targeted provisions covering a variety of offenses passed at constitutional conventions in Alabama and South Carolina in the 1890s. J. Morgan Kousser, *Colorblind Injustice*, 36. See also Keyssar, *Right to Vote*, 111–113, 162–163.

11. Such was the case of most disfranchisement techniques used by Democrats in the South during the late nineteenth century. Laws were formally neutral with regard to race, but policy makers intended for such laws to have a disproportionate racial impact. Although the most important goal of disfranchisement was to end black suffrage, historians have agreed that in some cases these laws offered a secondary benefit to Democrats by denying the vote to lower-class whites, who were more likely to vote Republican. Kousser, *Shaping of Southern Politics*, 57–59, 68–72; Perman, *Struggle for Mastery*, 31, 326–327.

12. Michael Perman encourages historians of southern voting to distinguish between statutory and constitutional law. According to Perman, "disfranchisement always involved constitutional revision, unlike reducing the vote through laws governing how elections are conducted, which are...statutory in form." Perman, *Struggle for Mastery*, 5. The disfranchisement provisions under study here, however, blur this distinction. Various combinations of statutory and constitutional changes in different states produced similar outcomes—the expansion of disfranchisement to include ever-smaller petty thefts. While distinguishing between statutes and constitutions is indeed important, considering them in coordination is also valuable.

13. Perman, *Road to Redemption*, 27–28.

14. Chap. 57, *Laws of the State of Mississippi, 1876* (Jackson: Power and Barksdale, 1876), 51–52; *Mississippi Senate Journal* (Jackson: Power and Barksdale, 1876), 495.

15. The Mississippi code of 1871 defined "infamous crime" as synonymous with "felony": "offences punished with death or confinement in the penitentiary." Chap. 59, sect. 2855, *The Revised Code of the Statute Laws of the State of Mississippi* (Jackson: Alcorn and Fisher, 1871), 618. See also the testimony of James Lee, later in the chapter, saying that election officials in Alabama disfranchised for many small offenses, thereby interpreting infamy as almost any crime.

16. Alabama Constitution (1868), art. 7, sect. 3.

17. *Acts of the General Assembly of Alabama Passed at the Session of 1874–5* (Montgomery: W. W. Screws, State Printer, 1875), 260.

18. *Acts of the General Assembly of Alabama Passed at the Session of 1874–5*, 258.

19. Alabama Constitution (1875), art. 8, sect. 3

20. Perman, *Road to Redemption*, 243; *Acts of the General Assembly of the State of Arkansas* (Little Rock: Gazette Book and Job Printing, 1874), 112. See also *Ware v. State*, 33 Ark. 567 (Ark. 1878).

21. Arkansas Constitution (1868), art. 8, sect. 3.

22. *Acts and Resolutions of the General Assembly of the State of Arkansas* (Little Rock: Pilot Printing Company, 1881), 144–145. See also *Southworth v. State*, 42 Ark. 270 (Ark. 1883).

23. Act of February 12, 1883, p. 10, cited in *Shepherd v. State*, 44 Ark. 39 (Ark. 1884).

24. Georgia Constitution (1868), art. II, sect. 6.

25. "An Act to Amend Section 4401 of the Code of Georgia, Defining the Punishment for Hog-Stealing," *Acts and Resolutions of the General Assembly of the State of Georgia, Passed at the Regular January Session, 1875* (Atlanta: James P. Harrison, State Printer, 1875), 26.

26. Moral turpitude was a more flexible term than infamy to the extent that judges could decide whether the crime met this standard on a case-by-case basis. Use of the term "moral turpitude" was growing in popularity in this period. In 1891 Congress amended the Immigration Act to exclude individuals convicted of crimes "involving moral turpitude." At the time this term was undefined in the immigration statute, other statutes, or the courts. Scholarship on immigration indicates that this ambiguity allowed officials to discriminate against immigrants based on race, class, sexuality, and gender identity. Kirk Porter's 1918 work, *History of Suffrage in the United States*, suggests that the vagueness of the term allowed it to be used to disfranchise African American's specifically. Kirk Harold Porter, *A History of Suffrage in the United States* (Chicago: University of Chicago Press, 1918), 205.

27. Georgia Constitution (1877), art. II, sect. 2. On the Georgia poll tax, see Kousser, *Shaping of Southern Politics*, 66–68, 71–72, 211–213; and Frederic D. Ogden, *The Poll Tax in the South* (Tuscaloosa: University of Alabama Press, 1958), 34–35.

28. Kousser is alone in noting the electoral implications of these 1870s laws. Kousser, *Colorblind Injustice*, 36.

29. Accounts of the crackdown on petty theft in the 1870s see the protection of property and the control over labor as the two primary motivations. See Perman, *Road to Redemption*, 242–244; Foner, *Reconstruction*, 593–595; Vernon Lane Wharton, *The Negro in Mississippi, 1865–1900* (Chapel Hill: University of North Carolina Press, 1947), 234–242; and Steven Hahn, "Hunting, Fishing, and Foraging: Common Rights and Class Relations in the Postbellum South," *Radical History Review* 26 (October 1982), 37–64.

30. Wharton, *Negro in Mississippi*, 237–238, quote on 237. See a similar analysis in C. Vann Woodward, *Origins of the New South, 1877–1913* (Baton Rouge: Louisiana State University Press, 1951), 212–213.

31. See, for example, David M. Oshinsky, *"Worse Than Slavery": Parchman Farm and the Ordeal of Jim Crow Justice* (New York: The Free Press, 1996), 40–41; and Stephen Cresswell, *Rednecks, Redeemers, and Race: Mississippi after Reconstruction, 1877–1917* (Jackson: University Press of Mississippi, 2006), 46, 108. Mary Ellen Curtin challenges the suggestion that African American convicts were actually guilty of these petty crimes. Curtin, *Black Prisoners and Their World*, 43–44.

32. Matthew J. Mancini, *One Dies, Get Another: Convict Leasing in the American South, 1866–1928* (Columbia: University of South Carolina Press, 1996), 135–136. The fact that the Pig Law was repealed in the wake of complaints about the vast abuses in the convict lease system may have perpetuated its association with convict lease and not disfranchisement. On the repeal of the law see Cresswell, *Rednecks, Redeemers, and Race*, 108.

33. Hazlehurst (Miss.) *Copiahan*, March 11, 1876, p. 3.

34. As discussed in chapter 2, the Readmission Acts forbade the amending of constitutions to deprive citizens of the right to vote except as punishment for crimes that were felonies at common law.

35. It is possible that Georgia is the exception here since Georgia did not disfranchise for any crimes in 1875 when the larceny penalties were expanded. Nonetheless, this statutory change may have been part of a long-term plan by Democrats that would not be implemented until the constitution was changed.

36. Veto Message, in *Journal of the House of Representatives of the State Mississippi, 1876* (Jackson, Miss.: C. M. Price, State Printer, 1876), 358–359.

37. Ames vetoed the law March 2 and resigned March 29. *Ibid.*; William Archibald Dunning, *Reconstruction, Political and Economic, 1865–1877* (New York: Harper and Brothers Publishers, 1907), 280.

38. "Legislative," Greenville (Miss.) *Times*, March 18, 1876, p. 2.

39. Chap. 57, *Laws of the State of Mississippi, 1876*, 51–52.

40. "Memorial of the Republican Members of the Legislature of Alabama to the Congress of the United States," in *Senate Reports*, 44 Cong., 2 Sess., No. 704: *Report of the Subcommittee of the Committee on Privileges and Elections to Inquire and Report whether in Any Elections in the State of Alabama in the Elections of 1874, 1875, and 1876 the Right of Male Inhabitants of Said State . . . to Vote Had Been Denied or Abridged* (Serial 1732, Washington, DC, 1877), 662–669, first quote on 662, second and third quotes on 664; hereinafter cited as *Committee on Privileges and Elections . . . Alabama, Report*.

41. Richard L. Morton, *The Negro in Virginia Politics, 1865–1902* (Charlottesville: University of Virginia Press, 1919), 91–92.

42. "Political Affairs in Virginia," New York *Times*, November 28, 1876, p. 1; "The Constitutional Amendments," Richmond *Daily Dispatch*, November 8, 1876, p. 3. Virginia Constitution (1870, amended 1876), art. 3, sect. 1.

43. "To Northern Democrats," Richmond *Daily Dispatch*, November 1, 1876, p. 2.

44. Untitled article, *ibid.*, October 31, 1876, p. 2. For more on Van Lew, see Elizabeth R. Varon, *Southern Lady, Yankee Spy: The True Story of Elizabeth Van Lew, a Union Agent in the Heart of the Confederacy* (New York: Oxford University Press, 2003).

45. Technically the document produced in 1875 was not a new constitution but an amended version of the 1868 constitution. John V. Orth, *The North Carolina State Constitution, with History and Commentary* (Chapel Hill: University of North Carolina Press, 1995), 16.

46. For a discussion of statutory evidence for the history of disfranchisement for infamy in North Carolina prior to 1875 see note 9 chapter 1.

47. In 1872 the North Carolina General Assembly provided that any of the "chief officers" in cities and towns could serve as justices of the peace. This gave a high degree of local control to this judicial function. Chap. CXCV, *Public Laws of the State of North Carolina, Passed by the General Assembly at Its Session 1871–'72 . . .* (Raleigh: Theo N. Ramsay, State Printer, 1872), 344. In 1877 the General Assembly changed the law, so that justices of the peace were elected by the General Assembly, consolidating control of this judicial office in Raleigh. Chap. CLXI, sect. 4, *Laws and Resolutions of the State of North Carolina...1876–7* (Raleigh: Theo N. Ramsay, State Printer, 1877), 227.

48. Several of these judicial changes were reversed in the 1890s when the "Fusion" coalition of Populists and Republicans took power in the legislature. Phillip J. Wood, *Southern Capitalism: The Political Economy of North Carolina, 1880–1980* (Durham, N.C.: Duke University Press, 1986), 113–114.

49. "Notes from the Capital," *New York Times*, October 11, 1875, p. 5. This article is one of the very few sources that identifies poor whites as a possible target of these laws.

50. Louisiana Constitution (1868), title 6, art. 99; Louisiana Constitution (1879), art. 187.

51. J. A. P. Campbell, *The Revised Code of the Statute Laws of the State of Mississippi*, sect. 108 (Jackson: J. L. Power, 1880), 75.

52. South Carolina Constitution (1868), art. 8.

53. Act of March 22, 1878, cited as 16 Stat. 631 in *State v. Corley*, 13 S.C. 1 (S.C. 1880). Foner also points out that South Carolina tightened penalties for petty theft in this period. Foner, *Reconstruction*, 593–594.

54. *Acts and Joint Resolutions of the General Assembly of the State of South Carolina Passed at the Regular Session of 1882* (Columbia, SC: Charles A. Calvo, State Printer, 1882), 3. This change was part of a larger set of revisions, aimed at African Americans, that restricted access to the franchise. See William J. Cooper Jr., *The Conservative Regime: South Carolina, 1877–1890* (Baltimore: Johns Hopkins Press, 1968), 99–103; and George Brown Tindall, *South Carolina Negroes, 1877–1900* (Columbia: University of South Carolina Press, 1952), 68–71.

55. *Committee on Privileges and Elections Report*, 388, 401, quote on 401.

56. *Report of Pardons, Commutations and Reprieves 1882–1884* (Montgomery, Ala.: W. W. Screws, State Printer, 1887), 8; F. B. Clark to E. A. O'Neal, May 31, 1883, Alabama Board of Pardons, Applications for Pardons, Paroles, or Remission

of Fines, 1846–1915, SG 10283 (Alabama Department of Archives and History, Montgomery). Washington was subsequently pardoned by Governor O'Neal.

57. Untitled article, New Orleans *Southwestern Christian Advocate*, July 5, 1883, p. 1; Mobile *Gazette*, quoted *ibid*. On the *Southwestern Christian Advocate* see James B. Bennett, *Religion and the Rise of Jim Crow in New Orleans* (Princeton: Princeton University Press, 2005), 50–51. The Mobile *Gazette* was edited at this time by an African American man named Philip Joseph. See William Warren Rogers and Robert David Ward, "'Jack Turnerism': A Political Phenomenon of the Deep South," *Journal of Negro History* 57 (October 1972), 313–332, esp. 319.

58. Raney also argued that since Florida law considered all grades of larceny to be infamous crimes, then the provision disfranchising for infamous crimes disqualified those convicted of petit larceny as well. Opinion of the Attorney General of Florida, October 2, 1880, *Attorney General Opinions, 1859-1913*, vol. 1, ser. 632, State Archives of Florida, Tallahassee, FL; *Appletons' Annual Cyclopaedia . . . 1880*, 274.

59. *State v. Buckman*, 18 Fla. 267 (1881).

60. Many in the debate referred to "penitentiary crimes" which was essentially synonymous with "felonies."

61. *A Stenographic Report of the Proceedings Held at the Constitutional Convention held in Atlanta Georgia, 1877* (Atlanta: Constitution Publishing Company, 1877), 70.

62. Ulrich Bonnell Phillips, *The Life of Robert Toombs* (1913; reprint, New York: B. Franklin, 1968).

63. *A Stenographic Report of the Proceedings Held at the Constitutional Convention held in Atlanta Georgia, 1877* (Atlanta: Constitution Publishing Company, 1877), 73.

64. *A Stenographic Report of the Proceedings Held at the Constitutional Convention held in Atlanta Georgia, 1877*, 71.

65. *A Stenographic Report of the Proceedings Held at the Constitutional Convention held in Atlanta Georgia, 1877*, 67.

66. Georgia Constitution (1877), art. II, sect. 2.

67. *Senate Reports*, 46 Cong., 2 Sess., No. 693: *Report and Testimony of the Select Committee of the United States Senate to Investigate the Causes of the Removal of Negroes from the Southern States to the Northern States* (Serial 1899, Washington, DC, 1880), 101; hereinafter cited as *Causes of the Removal of Negroes*.

68. *Ibid.*, 117.

69. *Ibid.*, 130–132.

70. The only instance I have found of a white Republican being charged with larceny in an attempt to disfranchise him is a report from a deputy U.S. Marshal named Reuben S. Mitchell in 1881. Testifying that the justice of the peace courts in Florida had a partisan bias that led them to convict Republicans disproportionately, he described how he had been accused of stealing another man's coat. According to Mitchell, the local magistrate "convicts every person so charged who has the least resemblance of nigger or Republicanism." *Testimony in the Case of Horatio Bisbee, Jr. vs. Jesse J. Finley*, 505.

71. *Senate Miscellaneous Documents*, 44 Cong., 2 Sess., No. 45: *Testimony as to Denial of Elective Franchise in Mississippi at the Elections of 1875 and 1876, Taken under the Resolution of the Senate of December 5, 1876* (Serial 1725, Washington, DC, 1876), 324; hereinafter cited as *Testimony as to Denial of Elective Franchise in Mississippi*. Racial disparities in the enforcement of election laws of all kinds were, of course, quite common. See, for example, Tindall, *South Carolina Negroes*, 71.

72. *Testimony in the Case of James Gillette vs. Thomas H. Herndon*, 76.

73. Neither list is dated, but the Granville county document lists convictions through 1894, whereas the Iredell county list ends in 1888. So, it is likely those are the years that these two documents were compiled and used.
74. "List of Persons Convicted of Felony or Other Infamous Crimes in Granville County, Since March 12, 1877," (undated), and "Iredell County List of Persons Convicted of Felony and Disqualified from Voting," (undated), North Carolina Collection, Wilson Library, University of North Carolina, Chapel Hill, NC. Iredell and Granville counties are adjacent so it is possible these lists reflect some kind of coordinated effort.
75. "Official list of colored persons convicted of felony or petit larceny in the Hustings Court of the city of Richmond, and thereby disfranchised, from 1870 to October 1892" and "Official list of colored persons convicted of petit larceny in the police court of the city of Richmond and are thereby disfranchised, from April 2, 1877 to January 12, 1892," in *Official Lists of Dead, Lunatic, and Convicted Colored Males Who Are Thereby Disfranchised* (Richmond, 1892), copy in Albert and Shirley Small Special Collections Library (University of Virginia Library, Charlottesville). Of course it is also possible that a separate volume of white convicts existed as well and was not preserved. Population data from Steven J. Hoffman, *Race, Class and Power in the Building of Richmond, 1870-1920*, (Jefferson, NC: McFarland and Company, 2004), 71.
76. Six of these elections are analyzed in this chapter. Two additional contested elections in which Congress considered claims of improper enforcement of laws disfranchising for crime are *House Miscellaneous Documents*, 48 Cong., 1 Sess., No. 18: *Testimony and Papers in the Contested-Election Case of George T. Garrison vs. Robert M. Mayo, from the First Congressional District of Virginia* (Serial 2221, Washington, DC, 1884); and *House Miscellaneous Documents*, 47 Cong., 1 Sess., No. 29: *Papers and Testimony in the Contested-Election Case of J. T. Stovall vs. George C. Cabell, from the Fifth Congressional District of Virginia* (Serial 2046, Washington, DC, 1882).
77. *Testimony in the Case of Horatio Bisbee, Jr. vs. Jesse J. Finley*, 469.
78. Green B. Raum, *The Existing Conflict between Republican Government and Southern Oligarchy* (New York: Charles M. Green, 1884), 449.
79. *Testimony as to Denial of Elective Franchise in Mississippi*, 323.
80. *Committee on Privileges and Elections Report*, 202.
81. *Testimony in the Case of John E. Massey vs. John S. Wise*, 309–310.
82. *House Miscellaneous Documents*, 47 Cong., 1 Sess., No. 22: *Testimony and Papers in the Contested Election Case of William M. Lowe vs. Joseph Wheeler, from the Eighth Congressional District of Alabama* (Serial 2041, Washington, DC, 1882), 888.
83. *Testimony in the Case of C. T. O'Ferrall vs. John Paul*, 122, 123, 585, 592.
84. "Voting in Virginia: How Negro Republican Voters Were Disfranchised at Lynchburg," Bangor (Maine) *Daily Whig and Courier*, December 16, 1883, p. 2.
85. *House Reports*, 51 Cong., 1 Sess., No. 1182, [Pt. 1]: *Edmund Waddill vs. George D. Wise* (Serial 2810, Washington, DC, 1890), 1–4; hereinafter cited as *Edmund Waddill vs. George D. Wise*.
86. *Ibid.*, 1–21. See also "Before the Courts," Richmond *Daily Dispatch*, November 8, 1888, p. 1.
87. *Edmund Waddill vs. George D. Wise*, 13.
88. *Ibid.*, 10.
89. *Ibid.*, 8.
90. "Congressman Bisbee," New York *Globe*, January 26, 1884, p. 2.
91. *Appletons' Annual Cyclopaedia and Register of Important Events of the Year 1875 . . .* (New York, 1876), 752. See also "The Colored Virginians," New York *Times*,

August 22, 1875, p. 1; and "The Colored Convention," Richmond *Daily Dispatch*, August 20, 1875, p. 1. One speaker at the meeting observed, "They have filled up the jails and penitentiary with our race. What State would make petit larceny a penitentiary offence?" *Ibid.*

92. "The Old Dominion—How the Negroes Are Persecuted—The Colored People Leaving the State—Decrease in the Value of Real Estate," Richmond *Daily Dispatch*, January 5, 1872, p. 3.

93. "The Amendments," Alexandria (Va.) *Sentinel*, reprinted in Richmond *Daily Dispatch*, November 3, 1876, p. 2.

94. "The Constitutional Amendments," Richmond *Daily Whig*, November 2, 1876, p. 2.

95. "To the Voters of Virginia," *ibid.*, November 4, 1874, p. 2.

96. "The Amendments," Alexandria *Sentinel*, reprinted in Richmond *Daily Dispatch*, November 3, 1876, p. 2. Italics in the original.

97. On the idea that possessing bourgeois values demonstrated fitness for citizenship in the late nineteenth century, see Kevin K. Gaines, *Uplifting the Race: Black Leadership, Politics, and Culture in the Twentieth Century* (Chapel Hill: University of North Carolina Press, 1996), 4, 34–46.

98. For a discussion of the role that chicken has played in African American culture and, in particular, the lives of African American women, see Psyche A. Williams-Forson, *Building Houses out of Chicken Legs: Black Women, Food, and Power* (Chapel Hill: University of North Carolina Press, 2006).

99. "The Colored Convention," Richmond *Daily Dispatch*, August 20, 1875, p. 1.

100. "To Northern Democrats," *ibid.*, November 1, 1876, p. 2.

101. On masculine citizenship in the nineteenth-century South see Stephen Kantrowitz, *Ben Tillman and the Reconstruction of White Supremacy* (Chapel Hill: University of North Carolina Press, 2000), 11, 189–190; Peter W. Bardaglio, *Reconstructing the Household: Families, Sex, and the Law in the Nineteenth-Century South* (Chapel Hill: University of North Carolina Press, 1995); and Stephanie McCurry, *Masters of Small Worlds: Yeoman Households, Gender Relations, and the Political Culture of the Antebellum South Carolina Low Country* (New York: Oxford University Press, 1995). On self-restraint, masculine citizenship, race, and class see Gail Bederman, *Manliness and Civilization: A Cultural History of Gender and Race in the United States, 1880–1917* (Chicago: University of Chicago Press, 1995), esp. 45–52.

102. *Judicial and Statutory Definitions of Words and Phrases*, vol. 4, edited and compiled by the members of the editorial staff of the National Reporter System (St. Paul: West Publishing Company, 1910), 3577.

103. On the debate over this issue in Connecticut for example, see John J. McCook, "Some New Phases of the Tramp Problem," *The Charities Review* 1:8 (June 1892), 355–364.

104. "Chicken-Stealers," Richmond *Daily Dispatch*, August 23, 1875, p. 2.

105. "Exactly Right," *ibid.*, November 4, 1876, p. 2.

106. Kantrowitz, *Ben Tillman and the Reconstruction of White Supremacy*, 45.

107. "Comments on this Act," Greenville *Times*, April 15, 1876, p. 1.

108. Allen Johnston Going, *Bourbon Democracy in Alabama, 1874–1890* (Tuscaloosa: University of Alabama Press, 1951), 34–35.

109. McCurry, *Masters of Small Worlds*, 198.

110. George Campbell, *White and Black: The Outcome of a Visit to the United States* (London: Chatto and Windus, 1879), 170–171.

111. Booker T. Washington, *Up from Slavery: An Autobiography* (Garden City, New York: Doubleday and Company, 1901), 4–5.

112. *New National Era*, January 26, 1871, reprinted in Dorothy Sterling, ed., *The Trouble They Seen: The Story of Reconstruction in the Words of African Americans* (New York: Da Capo Press, 1994), 155.
113. Mobile *Gazette*, quoted in untitled article, New Orleans *Southwestern Christian Advocate*, July 5, 1883, p. 1.
114. Untitled article, Richmond *Virginia Star*, November 11, 1882, p. 1. The reference to robbing "star routes"—postal routes—was likely due to the fact that when the article was written, the existence of fraudulent contracts for western mail service was being exposed. See J. Martin Klotsche, "The Star Route Cases," *Mississippi Valley Historical Review* 22 (December 1935), 407–418.
115. *Causes of the Removal of Negroes*, 244–245, 250, quote on 250.
116. Gaines, *Uplifting the Race*, xv, first quote on 4, second quote on 6.
117. *Ibid.*, 1–10, 20–22.

CHAPTER 4

1. *Ratliff v. Beale*, 74 Miss. 247 (1896). For a thorough discussion of this case see R. Volney Riser, *Defying Disfranchisement: Black Voting Rights Activism in the Jim Crow South, 1890–1908* (Baton Rouge: Louisiana State University Press, 2010), 55–60.
2. *Ratliff v. Beale*, 74 Miss. 247 (1896).
3. Edward Ayers argues that African Americans in the South in this period were more likely to be accused of property crimes than whites, while rural whites who found themselves in court were nearly always accused of violent crimes. He writes "black thefts and white assaults received first attention" from the courts. Furthermore, individuals convicted of property crime were more likely to be convicted than those who were prosecuted for other types of crime. Edward Ayers, *Vengeance and Justice: Crime and Punishment in the Nineteenth-Century American South* (London: Oxford University Press, 1984), 179–181. While these patterns might partially account for the belief by constitution writers that they could select disfranchising crimes to impact the races differently, there is a significant element of a self-fulfilling prophesy that needs to be explained. Why were most thefts attributed to African Americans? Why were many instances of white violence minimized, justified, or forgiven?
4. On the motivations for southern constitutional conventions in the 1890s see Perman, *Struggle for Mastery*.
5. Alexander Keyssar, *The Right to Vote: The Contested History of Democracy in the United States* (New York: Basic Books: 2000), 117–171.
6. For example, in 1974, a U.S. House of Representatives committee held hearings on a bill to restore voting rights to ex-offenders after incarceration, at which committee chair Peter Rodino identified Mississippi's 1890 constitution and South Carolina's 1895 constitution as prime examples of the racially motivated criminal disfranchisement provisions adopted across the region. John Buggs, the Staff Director of the U.S. Commission on Civil Rights echoed Rodino's comments, quoting extensively from *Ratliff v. Beale*. Statement of Hon. Peter W. Rodino Jr. and Testimony of John A. Buggs, U.S. Commission on Civil Rights, Hearings before the Subcommittee on Courts, Civil Liberties, and the Administration of Justice of the Committee on the Judiciary, House of Representatives 93rd Cong., 2nd Sess., January 30, 1974, 6–7, 11–12. In 1984 the Eleventh Circuit Court of Appeals, in *Underwood v. Hunter* (which the U.S. Supreme Court would decide as *Hunter v. Underwood*) also emphasized the

importance of Mississippi's leadership in the region with regard to criminal disfranchisement. *Underwood v. Hunter,* 730 F.2d 614 (11th Cir. 1984). A 2002 report from the Americans For Democratic Action fund asserted, "Mississippi became the first state to tailor its pre-existing laws to target black offenders. At a state convention, it was decided to replace a law disenfranchising those who had committed 'any crime' with one that disenfranchised only those convicted of certain petty crimes such as bribery, perjury, and bigamy, all considered to be far more prevalent among black offenders than white." Elizabeth Simson, *Justice Denied: How Felon Disfranchisement Laws Undermine American Democracy* (Washington, D.C.: Americans For Democratic Action Education Fund, 2002), 6. For examples of legal scholarship that endorses Mississippi's leadership on this issue see Andrew Shapiro, "Challenging Criminal Disenfranchisement Under the Voting Rights Act: A New Strategy," *Yale Law Journal* 103 (November 1993), 540–541; Alec C. Ewald, "'Civil Death': The Ideological Paradox of Criminal Disenfranchisement Law in the United States," *Wisconsin Law Review* 5:2002 (2002), 1088. The phrase "Second Mississippi Plan" has been used to refer to the disfranchisement scheme of the 1890 convention generally and the racially targeted list of crimes in particular.

7. The significance of the Second Mississippi Plan in general is indisputable, but I take issue here with the idea that Mississippi's provision disfranchising for certain crimes served as a model for the majority of southern states.

8. McMillan, *Constitutional Development in Alabama,* 275 n76. McMillan was cited by the U.S. Supreme Court in *Hunter v. Underwood,* 471 U.S. 222 (1985). See also Virginia E. Hench, "The Death of Voting Rights: The Legal Disfranchisement of Minority Voters," *Case Western Law Review* 48 (1998), n50; Kousser, *Colorblind Injustice,* 353; John Dinan, "The Adoption of Criminal Disenfranchisement Provisions in the United States: Lessons from the State Constitutional Convention Debates," *Journal of Policy History* 19:3 (Fall 2007), 296; Ewald, "'Civil Death,'"1089.

9. Perman, *Struggle for Mastery.*

10. On the Mississippi convention see Kousser, *The Shaping of Southern Politics,* 139–145; Albert Kirwan, *Revolt of the Rednecks: Mississippi Politics 1876–1925* (Lexington: University of Kentucky Press, 1951); Perman, *Struggle for Mastery,* 70–90.

11. Mississippi Constitution (1868), art. IV, sect. 17. Felony and infamous crime soon became interchangeable terms in the state. The 1871 Mississippi Code contained the following definition of felony: "The terms 'felony,' or 'infamous crime,' when used in this code, shall be construed to mean offences punished with death, or confinement in the penitentiary." Chap. 59, sect. 2855, *The Revised Code of the Statute Laws of the State of Mississippi* (1871), 618. The 1868 constitution also instructed the legislature to pass laws excluding from office and suffrage, those convicted of "bribery, perjury, forgery, or other high crimes or misdemeanors." Mississippi Constitution (1868). art. XII, sect 2.

12. *Journal of the Proceedings in the Constitutional Convention of the State of Mississippi* (Jackson, Miss.: E. J. Martin, 1890), 37–38.

13. *Journal of the Proceedings in the Constitutional Convention of the State of Mississippi,* 52.

14. *Journal of the Proceedings in the Constitutional Convention of the State of Mississippi,* 38, 52.

15. *Journal of the Proceedings in the Constitutional Convention of the State of Mississippi*, 66.

16. Elizabeth Pleck, "Wife Beating in Nineteenth-Century America," *Victimology* 4:1 (1979), 60–74.

17. Philippine Tariff, Hearings before the Committee on Ways and Means, 59th Cong., 1st Sess., December 1905 (Washington: GPO 1906), 75, 234. Welborn was testifying before Congress in his capacity as Chief of the Bureau of Agriculture in the Philippines. On Welborn see John Knox Bettersworth, *People's College: A History of Mississippi State* (Tuscaloosa: University of Alabama Press, 1953), 118.

18. Mississippi Constitution (1890), sect. 241; *Journal of the Proceedings in the Constitutional Convention of the State of Mississippi*, 135.

19. Minute book of the Committee on Elective Franchise, Apportionment, and Elections, kept by Clerk H. M. Quin, Aug. 15–Sept. 11, 1890, box 1, vol. 4, Charles K. Reagan Papers, Mississippi Department of Archives and History.

20. *Journal of the Proceedings in the Constitutional Convention of the State of Mississippi*, 271.

21. The term "infamous offense" in the 1868 constitution had by the 1870s included murder and any felony-level assault. See n. 11 above. According to Michael Perman, murder was listed as a disfranchising offense in the final report of the Committee on Elective Franchise, but I cannot find this in the convention minutes, only in the draft in the minute book. Perman, *Struggle for Mastery*, 83.

22. On the goals of the convention in protecting white voters while targeting African American voters see Perman, *Struggle for Mastery*, 22–23, 87–90.

23. Jack Bass, "South Carolina's Borrowing from Mississippi," *Charleston Law Review* 3 (Spring 2009), 525–533.

24. South Carolina Constitution (1868), art. VIII.

25. *Acts and Joint Resolutions of the General Assembly of the State of South Carolina Passed at the Regular Session of 1882* (Columbia, S.C.: James Woodrow, 1882), 3.

26. *Journal of the Constitutional Convention of the State of South Carolina, 1895* (Columbia, SC: Charles Calvo, 1895), 101.

27. *Journal of the Constitutional Convention of the State of South Carolina, 1895*, 70.

28. *Journal of the Constitutional Convention of the State of South Carolina, 1895*, 121. On Wilson see James L. Underwood, *The Constitution of South Carolina: The Struggle for Political Equality* (Columbia: University of South Carolina Press, 1986), 65–66.

29. Underwood, *The Constitution of South Carolina*, 64–65.

30. *Journal of the Constitutional Convention of the State of South Carolina, 1895*, 111–112.

31. *Journal of the Constitutional Convention of the State of South Carolina, 1895*, 268.

32. Disfranchising prisoners disqualified individuals prior to conviction if they were being held before a trial.

33. It is not completely clear why the convention chose to target "assault with intent to ravish" rather than rape, though this may have had a racial subtext.

34. *Journal of the Constitutional Convention of the state of South Carolina, 1895*, 487. Underwood, *The Constitution of South Carolina*, 109–110.

35. On the goals of the South Carolina convention see Perman, *Struggle for Mastery*, 92–93.

36. According to J. Morgan Kousser this move at the South Carolina convention was racially motivated, since embezzlement was a "middle class" crime—i.e., a crime

of whites since blacks were rarely if ever middle class. Kousser, "Undermining the First Reconstruction," 35.

37. On the history of definitions of theft see George Wilfred Stumberg, "Criminal Appropriation of Movables—A Need for Legislative Reform," *Texas Law Review* 19:2 (February 1941), 117–140.

38. Illinois Constitution 1848, art. III, sect. 32; *Revised Statutes of the State of Illinois, 1844–1845*, division XV, sect. 174 (Springfield: William Walters, 1845), 182.

39. Tennessee Acts of 1829, chap. 23, sect. 71, 253. Tennessee Constitution (1835) art. IV sect. 2.

40. Tennessee Constitution (1835), art. IV, sect. 1; Illinois Constitution (1848), art. VI, sect. 1.

41. Carroll is quoted in the introduction to this book.

42. *Official Report of the Proceedings....Kentucky* (1890), 1866–1867.

43. *Official Report of the Proceedings....Kentucky* (1890), 1866.

44. *Official Report of the Proceedings....Kentucky* (1890), 2333. *Anderson v. Winfree*, 85 Ky. 597 (Ky. App. 1887). This idea was not without precedent, nor was it unique to the South. When John Carroll said that those acting in "heat and passion" lacked depravity, he evoked the legal distinction between murder and manslaughter. Historically, unlawful killing was classified as manslaughter, not murder, if the assailant was provoked to the extent that he or she lost self-control. In 1862 the Michigan Supreme Court described the differentiation this way: "But if the act of killing, though intentional, be committed under the influence of passion or in heat of blood, produced by an adequate or reasonable provocation, and before a reasonable time has elapsed for the blood to cool and reason to resume its habitual control, and is the result of the temporary excitement, by which the control of reason was disturbed, rather than of any wickedness of heart or cruelty or recklessness of disposition; then the law, out of indulgence to the frailty of human nature, or rather, in recognition of the laws upon which human nature is constituted, very properly regards the offense as of a less heinous character than murder, and gives it the designation of manslaughter." *Maher v. People*, 10 Mich. 212 (1862). See also *Young v. State*, 30 Tenn. 200 (Tenn. 1850); *Smith v. State*, 83 Ala. 26 (1887).

45. Louisiana Constitution (1879), art. 148, 187.

46. Louisiana Constitution (1898), art. 202. Louisiana's constitution also disfranchised individuals in prison.

47. North Carolina Constitution (1899), art. VI, sect. 8.

48. On the specific dynamics of disfranchising conventions in these states see Perman, *Struggle for Mastery*, 70–172. He summarizes the Mississippi and South Carolina conventions by saying that in these states "the call for a constitutional convention arose from a contest within the Democratic Party, and in each state, disfranchisement was the means for unifying the party and ensuring its dominance," quote on 124.

49. Quoted in Perman, *Struggle for Mastery*, 141.

50. Perman, *Struggle for Mastery*, 135–136, 145–147.

51. George Rountree quoted in Perman, *Struggle for Mastery*, 165.

52. Perman, *Struggle for Mastery*, 148–149.

53. On racial disparities in southern justice in this era see Edward Ayers, *Vengeance and Justice: Crime and Punishment in the 19th-Century American South* (New York: Oxford University Press, 1984), 179–181, 223.

54. See n. 8 above.

55. Burns's role in the constitutional history of felon disfranchisement is frequently cited, to an extent I find disproportionate given his relatively minor historical role. See, for example, *Hunter v. Underwood,* 471 U. S. 222 (1985); *Underwood v. Hunter,* 730 F.2d 614 (2d Cir., 1984); Manza and Uggen, *Locked Out,* 58; Brian Pinaire, "Barred from the Vote: Public Attitudes Toward the Disenfranchisement of Felons," *Fordham Urban Law Journal* 30:5 (July 2003), n. 38; Shapiro, "Challenging Criminal Disenfranchisement," n. 23; Dinan, "The Adoption of Criminal Disenfranchisement Provisions," 296.

56. Montgomery *Advertiser,* cited in Birmingham *Age Herald,* July 3, 1901, cited in Perman, *Struggle for Mastery,* 184.

57. Constitution of Alabama (1875), art. 8, sect. 3.

58. *Official Proceedings of the Constitutional Convention of the State of Alabama* (Wetumpka: Wetumpka Printing Co., 1940), vol. 1, 349; "Vagrancy" had shifting racial implications in post-Civil War South. Laura Edwards points out that Black Codes targeted African Americans under vagrancy laws, but over the course of the post-war decades some whites began to see a danger in vagrancy among lower-class whites as well. Laura F. Edwards, *Gendered Strife and Confusion: The Political Culture of Reconstruction* (Champaign: University of Illinois Press, 1997) 77, 95–96.

59. *Official Proceedings of the Constitutional Convention of the State of Alabama,* vol. 1, 276.

60. *Official Proceedings of the Constitutional Convention of the State of Alabama,* vol. 1, 301.

61. Perman, *Struggle for Mastery,* 184–186, quote on 186.

62. *Official Proceedings of the Constitutional Convention of the State of Alabama,* vol. 1, 301, 313.

63. *Official Proceedings of the Constitutional Convention of the State of Alabama,* vol. 1, 511.

64. *Official Proceedings of the Constitutional Convention of the State of Alabama,* vol. 1, 511.

65. *Washington v. State,* 75 Ala 582 (Ala. 1884).

66. On reluctance on the part of other convention members to provoke a court ruling on the grandfather clause, see Perman, *Struggle for Mastery,* 184–185.

67. *Official Proceedings of the Constitutional Convention of the State of Alabama,* vol. 2, 1259–1260.

68. *Official Proceedings of the Constitutional Convention of the State of Alabama,* vol. 3, 3276–3277.

69. *Official Proceedings of the Constitutional Convention of the State of Alabama,* vol. 3, 3276–3277.

70. *Official Proceedings of the Constitutional Convention of the State of Alabama,* vol. 3, 3276–3277.

71. *Official Proceedings of the Constitutional Convention of the State of Alabama,* vol. 3, 3276–3277.

72. *Official Proceedings of the Constitutional Convention of the State of Alabama,* vol. 3, 3277.

73. *Official Proceedings of the Constitutional Convention of the State of Alabama,* vol. 3, 3277.

74. *Official Proceedings of the Constitutional Convention of the State of Alabama,* vol. 3, 4003.

75. *Official Proceedings of the Constitutional Convention of the State of Alabama*, vol. 3, 3164–3173.
76. See n. 8 above.
77. Perman, *Struggle for Mastery*, 180–181; Kousser, *The Shaping of Southern Politics*, 46–47.
78. Including crimes of "moral turpitude" was perhaps the only real stroke of creative genius evidenced by the convention. Unlike infamy, "moral turpitude" had a vague legal meaning that could be interpreted by the courts and state attorney general as necessary in decades to come. In 1985 in *Hunter v. Underwood* the U.S. Supreme Court heard testimony on how "moral turpitude" had come to be defined in Alabama and concluded that this provision had been enacted with racially discriminatory intent and interpreted in a racially discriminatory way. *Hunter v. Underwood*, 471 U. S. 222 (1985). "The enumerated crimes contain within them many misdemeanors. If a specific crime does not fall within one of the enumerated offenses, the Alabama Boards of Registrars consult Alabama case law or, in absence of a court precedent, opinions of the Alabama Attorney General to determine whether it is covered by § 182. Various minor nonfelony offenses such as presenting a worthless check and petty larceny fall within the sweep of § 182, while more serious nonfelony offenses such as second-degree manslaughter, assault on a police officer, mailing pornography, and aiding the escape of a misdemeanant do not because they are neither enumerated in § 182 nor considered crimes involving moral turpitude. It is alleged, and the Court of Appeals found, that the crimes selected for inclusion in § 182 were believed by the delegates to be more frequently committed by blacks."
79. Alabama Constitution (1901), sect. 124.
80. Perman, *Struggle for Mastery*, 191–194. Alabama offered poor whites loopholes through the grandfather clause and other temporary measures, but they had little commitment to protecting the suffrage of lower-class whites. Perman, *Struggle for Mastery*, 183–190.
81. Virginia Constitution (1850), art. 3, sect. 1; Virginia Constitution (1864), art. 3, sect. 1; Virginia Constitution (1870), art. 3, sect. 1.
82. Virginia Constitution 1870 (amended 1876), art. III, sect. 1.
83. Virginia Constitution (1902), art. II, sect. 23.
84. See V. O. Key, *Southern Politics in State and Nation* (New York: Alfred A. Knopf, 1949), 19–20.
85. Perman, *Struggle for Mastery*, 204.
86. Perman, *Struggle for Mastery*, 271. See also Braden, *The Constitution of the State of Texas*, 483.
87. Georgia's 1908 amendment replaced the previous section of the constitution, art. II, sect. 1. Tennessee and Arkansas also follow a different historical trajectory that puts them outside the bounds of the framework of this chapter. Both states revised their constitutions *before* Mississippi, so they were not influenced by the "Mississippi Plan." These states did not alter their provisions disfranchising for crime, relying instead primarily on the secret ballot and the poll tax to diminish electoral participation. Perman, *Struggle for Mastery*, 68–69. Arkansas's first constitution, established in 1836, had disfranchised for bribery, perjury, or other infamous crimes. In 1868 the state's constitutional convention changed this to treason, embezzlement of public funds, malfeasance in office, crimes punishable by law with imprisonment in the penitentiary or bribery. As in the Alabama constitution, Arkansas replaced the "infamy" standard with one

based on penitentiary time—in other words, a felony. This followed the federal standard—the Reconstruction Act—that specified that felony was the standard for disfranchisement. And, like Alabama, Arkansas disfranchised for electoral offenses. Arkansas Constitution (1836), sect. 12; Arkansas Constitution (1868), art. VIII, sect. 3.

88. Perman, 67–68; Florida Constitution (1885), art. VI, sect. 8.
89. "Congressman Bisbee," New York *Globe*, January 26, 1884, p. 2.
90. Quoted in Walter W. Manley, E. Canter Brown, Eric W. Rise, *The Supreme Court of Florida and Its Predecessor Courts, 1821–1917* (Gainesville: University of Florida Press, 1998), 272.
91. Florida Constitution (1885), art. VI, sect. 4. "No person under guardianship, *non compos mentis* or insane shall be qualified to vote at any election, nor shall any person convicted of felony by a court of record be qualified to vote at any election unless restored to civil rights."
92. *The Revised Code of the Statute Laws of the State of Mississippi*, chap. 59, sect. 2855 (Jackson: Alcorn and Fisher, 1871), 618.
93. Div. XV, sect. 220, *A Compilation of the Statutes of Illinois of a General Nature, in Force January 1, 1856* (Chicago: Keen and Lee, 1856), 399; Chap. 38, sect. 279, *The Revised Statutes of the State of Illinois, 1874* (Springfield, IL: Illinois Journal Company, 1874), 394.
94. Also in this period, a number of court cases considered the legal standard for infamy due to debates over the validity of denying infamous individuals the court testimony. See Paul G. Stemm, "The Role of Common Law Concepts in Modern Criminal Jurisprudence (A Symposium) II. Infamy and the Officeholder," *The Journal of Criminal Law, Criminology and Political Science* 49:3 (Sep.–Oct., 1958), 250–255.
95. *Ex Parte Wilson*, 114 U.S. 417 (1885).
96. *Mackin v. United States*, 117 U.S. 348 (1886).
97. *United States v. Coppersmith*, 4 Fed. 199 (C. C. Tenn., 1880).
98. *Official Report of the Proceedings . . . .Kentucky* (1890), 1864.
99. *Official Report of the Proceedings . . . .Kentucky* (1890), 1808.
100. Official Proceedings . . . .Kentucky, 1880; 1865–1866.
101. *State v. Earnhardt*, 86 SE 960 (N.C. 1915).
102. For overviews on the system of convict leasing in the South in this period, as well as the specific issue of lack of segregation in convict labor systems, see Mancini, *One Dies, Get Another*, esp. 104; Lichtenstein, *Twice the Work of Free Labor*, esp. 189–190.
103. Opponents of convict labor pointed out its degrading aspect as well. Workers, particularly in coal country, who sought to block wage competition from convicts pointed out that competing with convicts "degraded" and "polluted" their trade. Karin Shapiro, *A New South Rebellion: The Battle against Convict Labor in the Tennessee Coalfields, 1871–1897* (Chapel Hill: University of North Carolina Press, 1998), 6, 50, 73. From this perspective, competing with degraded white men lowered these workers to this degraded level. Just as voting alongside a convict could degrade, so might competing with convicted men for work.
104. The rejection of this ideal of "pure" southern white male violence and the acceptance that violent criminals should be viewed and punished like other felons did not occur immediately and it did not happen without debate in the South. For example, Alabama courts sought to protect the "higher order of men" from infamy into the twentieth century. Alabama's constitution of 1901 disfranchised for felonies, as well as for infamous crimes and crimes of

moral turpitude. This raised the question as to whether misdemeanor acts of violence constituted moral turpitude. In 1910 the Alabama Supreme Court explained, "A mere assault and battery does not involve moral turpitude. Moral turpitude signifies an inherent quality of baseness, vileness, depravity. Assaults and batteries are frequently the result of transient ebullitions of passion, to which a high order of men are liable, and do not necessarily involve any inherent element of moral turpitude." *Gillman v. State*, 165 Ala. 135 (Ala. 1910).

CHAPTER 5

1. *Commonwealth v. Fugate*, 2 Leigh 724 (Va. Gen. 1830).
2. *Ex Parte Garland*, 71 U. S. 333 (1866). The Court's language echoed that of William Blackstone on pardons: "Lastly, the *effect* of such pardon by the king, is to make the offender a new man; to acquit him of all corporal penalties and forfeitures annexed to that offence for which he obtains his pardon; and not so much to restore his former, as to give him a new, credit and capacity." William Blackstone, *Commentaries on the Laws of England: A Facsimile of the First Edition of 1765–1769*, vol. 4 (Chicago: University of Chicago Press, 1979), 16.
3. Pardons could be issued by a board made up of "The Governor, Justices of the Supreme Court, and Attorney General, or a major part of them, of whom the Governor shall be one." Florida Constitution (1868), art. V, sect. 12; art. XIV, sect. 2.
4. Mississippi Constitution (1868), art. 5, sect. 10.
5. Alabama Constitution (1868), art. V, sect. 11.
6. South Carolina Constitution (1868), art. 3, sect. 11.
7. At issue in this case was whether a pardon relieved the civil disability barring court testimony. In Louisiana, as in several other states, convictions impacted a number of civil rights, not just the right to vote. *State v. Baptiste*, 26 La. Ann. 134 (La. 1874).
8. Virginia Constitution (1870), art. IV, sect. 5; A. E. Dick Howard, *Commentaries on the Constitution of Virginia*, vol. 2 (Charlottesville, VA: University Press of Virginia, 1974), 643.
9. *Edwards v. The Commonwealth*, 78 Va. 39 (Va. 1883).
10. Confusion over the various kinds of pardons and their functions extended well into the twentieth century in Virginia. In 1969, William F. Stone Jr. noted in the *Washington and Lee Law Review* that "there is apparently some confusion in Virginia as to the types of pardons and their legal effects." Part of the problem, the author found, was that different governors had interpreted the pardon power in different ways. Furthermore, Virginia courts had used one set of classifications for pardons—labeling them "full" and "full and complete"—whereas governors had used terms such as "absolute," "simple without conditions,'" and "conditional" over the years. William F. Stone Jr., "Pardons in Virginia," *Washington and Lee Law Review* 26:307 (1969), 307–322. A 1993 article on pardons in Virginia, written by the then-serving executive assistant to the governor of Virginia, chief of policy, and chief counsel who handled all clemency petitions, described the distinction between a restoration of political rights and an absolute pardon as "illogical." Walter A McFarlane, "The Clemency Process in Virginia," *University of Richmond Law Review* 27:241 (1993), 241–280. For a longer discussion of pardons, including the diverse terms used to refer to this

action, see Leslie Sebba, "The Pardoning Power—A World Survey," *Journal of Criminal Law and Criminology* 68:83 (1977), 83–121 esp. 116.

11. Chapter XI, sect. 31, *Acts of the General Assembly of Virginia* (Richmond: Samuel Shepherd, 1848), 124.

12. *Journal of the Senate of the Commonwealth of Virginia, 1914* (Richmond: Davis Bottom, 1914), 47; *Journal of the Senate of the Commonwealth of Virginia, 1916* (Richmond: Davis Bottom, 1914), 37.

13. Virginia Code of 1919, Section 4779. This section of the 1919 code was cited in a 1920 Attorney General's Opinion on whether escaped convicts could testify against each other, and if the prison was permitted to pay convicts for such testimony. *Annual Report of the Attorney General to the Governor of Virginia* (Richmond: Davis Bottom, 1921), 140–141; D. W. Woodbridge, "The Effect in Virginia of Conviction of Crime on Competency and Credibility of Witnesses," *Virginia Law Review* 23:470 (1937), 470–471.

14. The 1830 constitution barred individuals who had participated in a duel from holding public office. Virginia Constitution (1830), art. 3, sect. 12. The 1870 constitution also barred such individuals from voting. Virginia Constitution (1870), art. 3, sect. 1.

15. Chapter 84, "An Act for the Relief of P. G. Coghlan and Others," *Acts and Joint Resolutions Passed by the General Assembly of the State of Virginia, 1876–1877* (Richmond: F. Walker, 1877), 68. This act restored the citizenship rights of P. G. Coghlan, John B. Donovan, John R. Moss, and James Barron Hope. The act restoring citizenship to these men preceded the passage of the act allowing the General Assembly to do so. It is possible that the restorations were interpreted as coming under the category of special legislative acts, but in the aftermath of this the legislature soon decided that a statute allowing such restorations was necessary. Hope was a well-known poet and the founder of the Norfolk *Landmark* newspaper. W. P. Trent, ed. *Southern Writers: Selections in Prose and Verse* (New York: MacMillan Company, 1905), 295–296.

16. Chapter 271, *Acts and Joint Resolutions Passed by the General Assembly of the State of Virginia, 1876–1877*, 280–281.

17. In the Matter of the Executive Communication of the 23rd of September 1872, *In Re Opinion of Justices*, 14 Fla. 318 (Fla. 1872); *Ex Parte Garland*, 4 Wallace 380 (1866). In 1896, the Florida Supreme Court ruled that this power resides exclusively in the executive and that the legislature could not pardon individuals through individual acts. *Singleton v. State*, 38 Fla. 297 (Fla. 1896).

18. Another issue raised in the post-election controversy was whether a Republican candidate could run for office if he had been convicted of bribery at an earlier date. Since he had been pardoned, Congress considered whether pardons restored the right to vote and the right to hold office. Majority Report, *Senate Report*, 44th Cong., 2nd Sess., no. 611, "Report of the Senate Committee on Privileges and Elections with the Testimony and Documentary Evidence on the Election in the State of Florida in 1876," 28.

19. *Foreman v. Baldwin*, 24 Ill. 298 (Ill. 1860); Majority Report, "Report of the Senate Committee on Privileges and Elections with the Testimony and Documentary Evidence on the Election in the State of Florida in 1876," 28; Minority Report, "Report of the Senate Committee on Privileges and Elections with the Testimony and Documentary Evidence on the Election in the State of Florida in 1876," 14.

20. *Journal of the Constitutional Convention of the State of Alabama* (Montgomery: W. W. Screws, 1875), 70.

21. Alabama Constitution (1875), art. V, sect. 12.

22. "Private Secretary" to J. T. Hey, August 4, 1904, file of K. S. Villipigue, box 14, Papers of Governor Martin F. Ansel, Pardons, Paroles, and Commutations, S531014, South Carolina Department of Archives and History, Columbia, SC. (Hereafter SCDAH.) Villipigue's file is contained in Governor Ansel's papers because Ansel eventually granted him the restoration.

23. File of J. M. Cortez, box 3, Papers of Governor Martin F. Ansel, Pardons, Paroles, and Commutations, SCDAH.

24. File of J. M. Cortez (box 3); Lige Simpson (box 11); E. B. Roberts (box 11); Kirby Lark (box 7), W. T. Mims (box 9); W. B. Lightfoot (box 8); H. W. Byrd (box 2); Matthew Atkinson (box 1); John Belk (box 1); K. S. Villipigue (box 14), Papers Governor Martin F. Ansel, Pardons, Paroles, and Commutations, SCDAH.

25. Georgia Constitution (1877), art. V, para. xii.

26. *Report and Opinions of the Attorney General of Georgia, 1915–1916* (Atlanta: Index Printing Company, 1916), 72–74.

27. In most states disfranchisement is a consequence of conviction; the judge assigns the sanction of the conviction, but the other punishments follow the conviction. In Tennessee and North Carolina, however, disfranchisement and other civil disabilities were part of the punishment assigned by the judge. This explains why convicted individuals in these two states must petition the court for restoration of civil rights, not the governor or legislature as is usually the case. Infamy that comes from the court must be lifted by the court. In either situation, though, pardons may not remove all collateral consequences of conviction. Denial of gun ownership, deportation (for non-citizens), denial of certain state benefits (such as federally assisted housing or student loans), and denial of access to certain professional licenses might follow even if an individual is pardoned. These collateral consequences have been held to be separate from those disabilities of citizenship imposed by law and therefore may not be mitigated by a pardon.

28. Chapter 152, *Acts Passed at the First Session of the Twenty-Third General Assembly of the State of Tennessee* (Nashville: J. Geo. Harris, 1840), 245. The 1840 Act required a ten-year period before rights could be restored. In 1851 the legislature amended the act in a variety of ways, including changing the waiting period to six months or three years, depending on the crime. Chap. 30, sect. 1, *Acts of the State of Tennessee, 1851–1852* (Nashville: Bang & McKennie, 1852). 37.

29. North Carolina Statutes of 1840, Chapter 36, Section 1, Iredell, *A Digested Manual of the Acts of the General Assembly of North Carolina*, 21.

30. *Evans v. State*, 66 Tenn. 12 (Tenn. 1872).

31. Texas Constitution (1875), art. VI, sect. 1; Seth Shepard McKay, ed. *Debates in the Texas Constitutional Convention of 1875* (Austin: University of Texas, 1930), 260–261.

32. Mississippi Constitution (1868), art. 5, sect. 10.

33. Mississippi Constitution (1890), art. 12, sect. 253.

34. *Official Report of the Proceedings and Debates in the Convention Assembled at Frankfort, on the Eighth Day of September, 1890, to Adapt, Amend, or Change the Constitution of the State of Kentucky* (Frankfort, KY: E. P. Johnson, 1890), 1876. Hereafter cited as *Official Report of the Proceedings....Kentucky* (1890).

35. *Official Report of the Proceedings....Kentucky* (1890), 1880.

36. Kentucky Constitution (1890), sect. 145.

37. Act 85, April 19, 1873, *Acts passed by the General Assembly of the State of Louisiana at the First Session of the Third Legislature* (New Orleans: Republican Office, 1873), 157–158.

38. On development and standardization of pardon procedures in this period and observations about the increase in pardons in this era see Vivien M. L. Miller, *Crime, Sexual Violence, and Clemency: Florida's Pardon Board and Penal System in the Progressive Era* (Gainesville: University Press of Florida, 2000), 134–137. William Novak, *The People's Welfare: Law and Regulation in Nineteenth Century America* (Chapel Hill: University of North Carolina Press, 1996), 246–278.

39. The records of these pardons are incomplete, and the available data varies. I have collected and reviewed summaries of approximately 1,400 applications for restoration from individuals convicted of crimes. For many of these cases little information is available except for name, crime, date of offense, and date of restoration, but some case files also include related correspondence, court minutes, and copies of the actual petitions restoring citizenship rights. Although it is impossible to make any quantitative conclusions from this data, it does illuminate the value and function of pardons as well as the motivations of petitioners and officials. Some of the materials in the pardon files or criminal cases identify the petitioner by race, but racial identity is inconsistently available in court records. Most of those who are identified by race are African American, because it was rare for whites to be identified as such. Accordingly, it is likely that most of the individuals whose race is unidentified were white. When I have been able to identify petitioners by race I have indicated this.

40. Alabama established a Board of Pardons as required under the 1901 constitution; Florida established such a board in 1868. Pardon boards were established in many states and charged with reviewing cases and making recommendations for pardons (including restoration of citizenship rights) to the governor. See for example, Alabama Constitution (1901), sect. 124; South Carolina Constitution (1895), art. IV, sect. 11.

41. Access to pardon records in Florida is limited by statute, and I have not been able to view complete files in that state. (A full discussion of this is in the acknowledgements to this book.) I have not been able to locate any communication between those seeking rights restoration and legislators in Mississippi.

42. Petitions of R. Fagan Erwin, August 25, 1894, roll 34; Henry Murray, August 6, 1888, roll 33, Giles County Circuit Court Records, TSLA.

43. Though the court documents do not indicate Ratliff's race, the fact that the victim was African American and that African American witnesses testified against Ratliff suggest strongly that he, too, was African American. It would have been quite unlikely for a white man to be convicted of stealing a hog from a white man based on African American testimony in this period. File of Jefferson Rattliff, box CR005.928.3, Anson County, North Carolina, Miscellaneous Records 1758–1960, North Carolina State Archives (hereafter, NCSA), Raleigh, NC.

44. Petition of Alfred Exum, box CR103.928.1, Wayne County Miscellaneous Records, 1788–1936, NCSA.

45. Petition of James Weaver, box CR044.928.26, Granville County Miscellaneous Records 1848–1929, NCSA.

46. Individuals seeking release from incarceration through pardons also faced significant costs, and often employed attorneys to facilitate their application. Miller, *Crime, Sexual Violence, and Clemency*, 135–136.

47. O. V. F. Blythe to R. L. Green, December 19, 1908, file of R. L. Green, box CR080.928.1, Polk County Miscellaneous Records, 1856–1921, NCSA.

48. Petition of Alex Smith, unlabeled boxes, Giles County Circuit Court Records, 1893–1900, Old Records Office, Giles County Court House, Pulaski, Tennessee.

49. Lewis Price to Governor William Atkinson, February 19, 1895, file of Lewis Price, box 98, file #2856-10, Convict and Fugitive Records—Applications for Clemency, 1858–1942, Georgia State Archives, Morrow, Georgia. (Hereafter, GSA.)

50. Often laws disqualifying former convicts from testifying permitted testimony in one's own criminal case. See Tennessee Acts of 1829, chap. 23, sect. 71.

51. Letter to prison commission of Georgia from E. L. Herndon (undated, c. 1905), file of Samuel A Pickens, box 95, Convict and Fugitive Records—Applications for Clemency, 1858–1942, GSA; *Journal of the House of Representatives of the State of Georgia* (Atlanta: Franklin Printing and Publishing Company, 1906), 57.

52. *Journal of the Senate of the Commonwealth of Virginia, 1916*, 42.

53. J. H. McGuire to Edward A. O'Neal, Feb. 27, 1883, file of L. Adkins Baker, box SG10305, Alabama Board of Pardons, Applications for Pardons, Paroles, or Remission of Fines, 1846–1915, Alabama Department of Archives and History, Montgomery, Alabama. (Hereafter, ADAH).

54. File of Kirby Lark, box 7, Governor Martin F. Ansel, Pardons, Paroles, and Commutations, SCDAH.

55. Petition of James J. Worsham, May 9, 1876, roll 11, Maury County Circuit Court Civil Minutes, Tennessee State Library and Archives, Nashville, Tenn. (Hereafter, TSLA.); Conviction of James J. Worsham, January 8, 1872, roll 26, Maury County Circuit Court Criminal Minutes, TSLA.

56. Petition of H. T. Turner, January 6, 1908, roll 50, Knox County Circuit Court, Civil Minutes, East Tennessee Historical Society, Knoxville, Tenn. (Hereafter, ETHS.)

57. Fred Stephenson to Goodlow Yancey, December 21, 1905, file of Fred L. Stephenson, box 114, file #2864-04, GSA.

58. Petition of Thomas Cobb, file of Thomas Cobb, box 24, file #2849-12, Convict and Fugitive Records—Applications for Clemency, 1858–1942, GSA.

59. On pardon strategies more generally, see Miller, *Crime, Sexual Violence, and Clemency*, 137–262.

60. W. J. Creery to Andrew J. Montague, January 20, 1902, file of W. J. Creery, box 16, folder 5, Applications for Reinstatement of Citizenship, Executive Papers of Governor Andrew J. Montague, Acc. # 23349, State Government Records Collection, The Library of Virginia, Richmond, Virginia. (Hereafter, LVA.)

61. Petition of W. E. Terrell, August 11, 1947, roll 15, Maury County Circuit Court, Civil Minutes, TSLA.

62. *Journal of the House of Representatives of the State of Mississippi, 1904* (Jackson: Clarion-Ledger, 1904), 758–759.

63. *Journal of the House of Delegates of the Commonwealth of Virginia, 1912* (Richmond: Davis Bottom, 1912), 45.

64. Petition of James Weaver, file of James Weaver, box CR044.928.26, Granville County Miscellaneous Records, 1848–1929, NCSA.

65. Chapter 152, *Acts Passed at the First Session of the Twenty-Third General Assembly of the State of Tennessee*, 245.

66. Restoration of Charles Lyle, Knox County Circuit Court Minutes, roll I-29, ETHS.

67. Restoration of Robert Vick, June 11, 1910, roll I-29, Knox County Circuit Court Minutes, ETHS; Restoration of Sam McMickens, November 27, 1911, roll I-29, Knox County Circuit Court Minutes, ETHS.

68. Petition of Francis Marion Henderson, January 21, 1949, film A4236, Crocket County Circuit Court Minutes, TSLA.

69. Petition of Henry Colvin, box SG 15.429, Alabama Secretary of State Convict Pardon Docket, February 3, 1887–July 1, 1891, ADAH.

70. T. L. Galloway to William Atkinson, August 2, 1897, file of Jack Goldsmith, box 46, #2851-11, GSA.

71. Petition of Jefferson Ratliff, file of Jefferson Ratliff, box CR005.928.3, Anson County, North Carolina, Miscellaneous Records 1758–1960, NCSA.

72. William W. Osborne to Prison Commission, January 2, 1903, file of Simon J. O'Neal, box 90 #2855-11, GSA.

73. Chambers Goode to Andrew J. Montague, February 21, 1905, file of J. W. Baisey, box 16, folder 5, Applications for Reinstatement of Citizenship, Executive Papers of Governor Andrew J. Montague, LVA.

74. Restoration of citizenship for George Payne Jr., John D. Brown, and Billie Bright, *Journal of the House of Representatives of the State of Mississippi, 1900* (Jackson: Clarion-Ledger, 1900), 491, 492, 549, 581.

75. *Journal of the Senate of the Commonwealth of Virginia, 1924* (Richmond: Davis Bottom, 1924), 79.

76. J. T. Casey to Whom it May Concern, April 9, 1906, file of Tommie Burns, box 17, #4202-12, Convict and Fugitive Records—Applications for Clemency, 1858–1942, GSA.

77. Restoration of citizenship of D. B. Vess, Oct. 30, 1922, Knox County Circuit Court Minutes, roll I-36, ETHS.

78. *In re: Curtis*, 6 Tenn. Civ. App. (Tenn. Civ. App. 1915).

79. James W. English to William Atkinson, Feb. 25, 1895, file of Thomas Cobb, Convict and Fugitive Records—Applications for Clemency, 1858–1942, GSA.

80. C. E. Hill to William Atkinson, Feb. 25, 1895, Convict and Fugitive Records— Applications for Clemency, 1858–1942, GSA. On the Chattahoochee Brick Company see Blackmon, *Slavery by Another Name*, 343–345; Charles Berry, "Free Labor He Found Unsatisfactory: James W. English and Convict Lease Labor at the Chattahoochee Brick Company" (master's thesis, Georgia State University, 1991).

81. *Journal of the Senate of the Commonwealth of Virginia, 1908* (Richmond: Davis Bottom, 1908), 50.

82. *Journal of the Senate of the State of Georgia, 1899* (Atlanta: Franklin Print and Publishing, 1899), 89.

83. *Report of Pardons, Commutations and Reprieves 1884–1886* (Montgomery, AL: W. D. Brown and Co. State Printers, 1887), 54; *Journal of the Senate of the Commonwealth of Virginia, 1924*, 79, 83.

84. Group indictments, March 12, 1875, Maury County Circuit Court, Criminal Minutes, vol. ix, TSLA; Petitions of Toney Long and Frank Lawrence, May 25, 1896, Maury County Circuit Court, Civil Minutes, roll 12, TSLA; petition of Eli Bowen, May 2, 1892, Maury County Circuit Court, Civil Minutes, roll 12, TSLA. For a similar grouping of three African American tenant farmers in the middle Tennessee area, see petitions of John Henry Starks, Ebert "Ebb" Fitzpatrick, and Felix Wilkerson, May 15, 1902, Giles County Circuit Court, Civil Minutes, roll 1418, TSLA.

85. A. G. Gordon to Rufus W. Cobb, July 20, 1880, file of J. H. Culver, box SG 10311, Alabama Board of Pardons, Applications for Pardons, Paroles, or Remission of Fines, 1846–1915, 19.

86. File of Berry Burt, J. E. Gardner to William Atkinson, Dec. 28, 1894, Convict and Fugitive Records—Applications for Clemency, 1858–1942, GSA.

87. Petition of Jack Goldsmith, file of Jack Goldsmith, box 46, file #2851-11, Convict and Fugitive Records—Applications for Clemency, 1858-1942, GSA.

88. *Report of State Officers, Board and Committees to the General Assembly of the State of South Carolina*, vol. II (Columbia, SC: Gonzales and Bryan, 1922), 6.

89. W. J. Dozier to Nat E. Harris, June 30, 1916, file of Will Giles, box 45 #2851-10, Convict and Fugitive Records—Applications for Clemency, 1858–1942, GSA.

90. Martin Tipton to William H. Mann, October 6, 1910, file of M. S. Guynn, box 42, Rejected Applications for Pardons and Removal of Political Disabilities, Executive Papers of Governor William H. Mann, 1899–1914, Acc. # 23349 & 41428, State Government Records Collection, LVA.

91. R. E. McElmore to William H. Mann, November 22, 1910, file of R. E. McElmore, box 44, Rejected Applications for Pardons and Removal of Political Disabilities, Executive Papers of Governor William H. Mann, LVA.

92. "Statement of Pardons and Commutations," in *Reports and Resolutions of the General Assembly of South Carolina*, vol. 2 (Columbia, SC: The State Company, 1903), 236.

93. Claude Beverly to Henry Carter Stuart, March 19, 1917, file of Noah L. Vanover, box 45, Political Disabilities, Executive Papers of Governor Henry Carter Stuart, Acc. # 28722, State Government Records Collection, LVA.

94. Petition of Abe Brown, file of Abe Brown, box 14, #2849-02, Convict and Fugitive Records—Applications for Clemency, 1858–1942, GSA. See also *Journal of the Senate of the State of Georgia, 1897* (Atlanta: Franklin Printing and Publishing Company, 1897), 87.

95. *Official Report of the Proceedings and Debates in the Convention Assembled at Frankfort, on the Eighth Day of September, 1890, to Adapt, Amend, Or Change the Constitution of the State of Kentucky* (Frankfort, Kentucky: E. P. Johnson, 1890), 2332–2333.

96. Petition of Fred Stephenson, file of Fred Stephenson, box 114, #2864-04, Convict and Fugitive Records—Applications for Clemency, 1858–1942, GSA.

97. Lewis Hill to William H. Mann, Nov. 22, 1910, Lewis Hill file, box 42, Rejected Applications for Pardons and Removal of Political Disabilities, Executive Papers of Governor William H. Mann, LVA.

98. Robert Bennett to Joseph M. Terrell, December 13, 1902, file of Henry Manning, box 78, #2854-17, Convict and Fugitive Records—Applications for Clemency, 1858–1942, GSA; *Journal of the Senate of the State of Georgia, 1905* (Atlanta: Franklin Print and Publishing, 1905), 86.

99. Pardon, file of J. F. Jarman, June 1, 1887, box SG 15.429, Alabama Secretary of State, Convict Pardon docket, Feb 3 1887–July 1, 1891, ADAH.

100. *Journal of the Senate of the Commonwealth of Virginia, 1910* (Richmond: Davis Bottom, 1910), 67.

101. *Journal of the Senate of the Commonwealth of Virginia, 1908* (Richmond: Davis Bottom, 1910), 49.

102. Keyssar, *The Right to Vote*, 14–15.

103. P. G. Hubbard to Andrew Montague, November 22, 1910, box 16, folder 5, Applications for Reinstatement of Citizenship, Executive Papers of Governor Andrew J. Montague, LVA.

104. J. L. Lypps to Henry H. Stuart, January 2, 1918, box 48, Pardons, Executive Papers of Governor Westmoreland Davis, Acc. # 21567a, State Government Records Collection, LVA.

105. R. E. McLemore to William H. Mann, November 22, 1910, file of R. E. McLemore, box 44, Rejected Applications for Pardons and Removal of Political Disabilities, Executive Papers of Governor William H. Mann, LVA.

106. *Report of the Alabama Board of Pardons, 1917* (Montgomery: Brown Printing Co., 1917), 23.

107. "Vets Mass on Housing Issue," *Jackson Clarion Ledger*, March 2, 1948, 1, 10. The local press did not comment on the connection between the veterans rally and the legislation, though I suspect these events were not simply coincidental.

108. HB 275, "Restore Right of Suffrage Under Certain Conditions," *Journal of the House of Representatives of the State of Mississippi 1948* (Jackson: State of Mississippi, 1948), 196; A similar statute had been enacted after World War I. Sect. 2563.5, *Mississippi Code 1942, Annotated*, vol. 8 (Jackson: Harrison Company, 1943), 150.

109. G. W. Mullins to E. Lee Trinkle, July 22, 1923, box 630, Applications for Pardons, Executive Papers of Governor E. Lee Trinkle, State Government Records Collection, Acc. #21567b, LVA; *Journal of the Senate of the Commonwealth of Virginia, 1924,* 90.

110. State Archives of Florida, Minutes of the State Pardon Board, RG690, Series 187, vol. D, p. 75–76.

111. State Archives of Florida, Minutes of the State Pardon Board, Series 187, vol. D, p. 103.

112. Conviction of Hay Long Wall, 28 November 1930, Maury County Circuit Court, Criminal Minutes, roll 23; Restoration of Hay Long Wall, June 22, 1945, Maury County Circuit Court, Civil Minutes, roll 17.

113. Conviction of Louise Douglas, January 7, 1932; March 23, 1932; June 4, 1932, Knox County Circuit Court Minutes, roll I-245.

114. Restoration of Louise [Douglas] Glass, Knox County Circuit Court Minutes, roll I-49.

115. *Report of the Alabama Board of Pardons, 1915* (Montgomery: Brown Printing Co., 1915), 28. I have been unable to locate Clark's file in the loose records of the pardon board, so the information in the published report of the pardon board is all I have about this case.

116. *Report of the Alabama Board of Pardons, 1915,* 22.

117. Petition of L. C. Lovett, 29 November 1926, Knox County Circuit Court Minutes, roll I-39.

118. See, for example, files on George Flannery and George Richardson, box 45, Political Disabilities, Executive Papers of Governor Henry Carter Stuart, LVA.

119. H. A. W. Skeen to Claude A. Swanson, April 16, 1907, and W. W. G. Dobson to Claude A. Swanson, April 10, 1907, box 5, Rejected Applications for Pardons and Removal of Political Disabilities, Executive Papers of Governor Claude A. Swanson, Acc. # 29593, State Government Records Collection, LVA.

120. J. P. Schneller to Westmore [sic] Davis, box 21567, Pardons, Executive Papers of Governor Westmoreland Davis, LVA.

121. William H. Mann to Samuel L. Adams, Jan 27, 1913, and E. J. Prescott to William H. Mann, July 17, 1913, box 40, Rejected Applications for Pardons

and Removal of Political Disabilities, Executive Papers of Governor William H. Mann, LVA.

122. I am reluctant to make any quantitative claims at all about restorations of citizenship rights because the available records varied so much from state to state. However, it does seem that Virginia stands out in terms of racial and partisan claims in petitions for restoration and in the number of rejected applications from African Americans.

123. Petition of Doc Edwards, no month, 1904 and D. E. Edwards to A. J. Montague, April 11, 1905, box 16, folder 5, Applications for Reinstatement of Citizenship, Executive Papers of Governor Andrew J. Montague, LVA.

124. *Journal of the House of Representatives of the State of Mississippi, 1896* (Jackson: R. H. Henry, 1896), 357; "The State Elections," *New York Times*, November 5, 1899, p. 4.

125. The only other opposition in Mississippi to legislative restoration of citizenship rights came from Representative M. Harwell of Meridian who voted against six such restorations in 1913 *Journal of the House of Representatives of the State of Mississippi, 1913* (Jackson: Tucker Printing House, 1913), 872, 1002, 1196, 1270, 1272, 1308; A few bills for restoration garnered a handful of "no" votes. Chester Carroll of Webster County had three members of the Mississippi House oppose his restoration, and Robert Pender received one no vote. The records offer no explanation for any of this opposition. *Journal of the House of Representatives of the State of Mississippi, 1900* (Jackson: Clarion-Ledger, 1900), 170–171 (Carroll); *Journal of the House of Representatives of the State of Mississippi, 1904* (Jackson: Clarion-Ledger, 1904), 757–758 (Pender).

126. T. A. Lynch to D. A. Ritchie, September 29, 1903, box 16, folder 5, Applications for Reinstatement of Citizenship, Executive Papers of Governor Andrew J. Montague, LVA.

127. T. A. Lynch to Governor Swanson, 26 May 1906, box 10, Applications for Pardons and Removal of Political Disabilities, Executive Papers of Governor Claude A. Swanson, LVA.

128. F. G. Woodson to Governor Swanson, July 31, 1907, box 6, Applications for Pardons and Removal of Political Disabilities, Executive Papers of Governor Claude A. Swanson, LVA.

129. "Disorders Mark Florida Election," *Baltimore Afro-American*, November 5, 1920, p. 1.

130. On the extent of disfranchisement in Virginia under the 1902 constitution see Key, *Southern Politics in State and Nation*, 19–20.

131. See, for example, George R. Shinn, who carried his pardon with him to the polls in Virginia in 1883. *Testimony in the Case of John E. Massey vs. John S. Wise*, 45.

132. Testimony, "Report of the Senate Committee on Privileges and Elections with the Testimony and Documentary Evidence on the Election in the State of Florida in 1876," 263–265.

133. *Testimony and Papers in the Contested-Election Case of George T. Garrison vs. Robert M. Mayo*, 37, 38, 90, 91–94, 102. On the "oyster wars" see John R. Wennersten, *The Oyster Wars of Chesapeake Bay* (Centreville, Md.: Tidewater Press, 1981).

134. Virginia did not have a system of probation or parole at this date. One congressman suggested that the other possibility was that the five had escaped from jail, but if the Democrats had actually thought that they should have "lodged a complaint against [him] as an escape-convict [sic]" (92). *Testimony and Papers in*

the Contested-Election Case of George T. Garrison vs. Robert M. Mayo, 90–92. The five men did indeed receive pardons. *Journal of the Senate of the Commonwealth of Virginia, 1883–1884* (Richmond: R. F. Walker, 1884), 2.

135. *Report of the Alabama Board of Pardons, 1915,* 22.
136. Whitman, *Harsh Justice,* 12.

CHAPTER 6

1. "Statements Made by Democrats on Vote Controversy," *St. Louis Star,* n.d., Tuskegee News Clippings File.
2. "Bring the Vote Thieves to Judgment," *St. Louis Argus,* November 10, 1916, p. 1.
3. Matthew Lakin, "'A Dark Night': The Knoxville Race Riot of 1919," *Journal of East Tennessee History* 72 (2000): 1–29.
4. Rayford Logan, *The Negro in American Life and Thought: The Nadir, 1877–1901* (New York: Collier Books, 1965).
5. On these legal defeats for black voting rights activists in this earlier period, see Riser, *Defying Disfranchisement.*
6. *Guinn v. United States* 238 U.S. 347 (1915).
7. *In re: Curtis,* 6 Tenn. Civ. App. (Tenn. Civ. App. 1915); Knox County Criminal Court Minute Book, vol. 53, December 19, 1907, ETHS; Knox County Criminal Court Minute Book, vol. 53, December 20, 1907, ETHS; Knox County Criminal Court Minute Book, vol. 57, April 20, 1910, ETHS; "Grand Jury Didn't Finish," *The Daily Journal and Tribune* (Knoxville, TN), December 21, 1907, p. 8. Curtis is listed as a prisoner at Brushy Mountain Penitentiary in the 1910 census, U.S. Census of 1910, Tennessee District No. 2, Brushy Mountain.
8. Tennessee Acts of 1829, chap. 23, sect. 71.
9. Tennessee Constitution (1835), art. IV, sect. 2; Keyssar, *The Right to Vote,* 61–63.
10. Chap. 30, sect. 1, *Acts of the State of Tennessee, 1851–1852.* The 1858 Tennessee code added the penalty of disfranchisement for infamy, as the 1834 constitution had required, stipulating that infamous individuals lost the vote for the remainder of their lives, unless they petitioned the court for restoration; Tennessee Code of 1858, art. IV, sect. 834, *The Code of Tennessee: Enacted by the General Assembly of 1857–'8,* 225.
11. I found seventy-six petitions for restoration in the Knox County Court minutes between 1881 and 1940. I have confined my search for restorations of citizenship to the years after 1865.
12. Court records do not indicate restorations of citizenship for African American men in Knoxville in the next few decades. The fact that none of the individuals who had their citizenship restored are identified as African American is not a guarantee that none were African American. The recording of race was inconsistent and varied from court to court and year to year. It is possible that some black men did succeed at this but were not identified by race in the civil or criminal court minutes. The court rejected two more petitions for restoration in the years after the Curtis case, though a cross check with the criminal court records (which did identify by race in those particular years) indicated that both were white men. Both appear to have been rejected on reasonable grounds. One man's petition was dismissed because he failed to appear at his own court hearing and one man's petition was denied because the court determined that crime for which he was convicted—violation of the age of consent laws—was not an infamous offense. Petition of L. C. Lovett, Knox County Circuit Court Minutes,

November 29, 1926, ETHS; Petition of Ben Carroll, Knox County Circuit Court Minutes, September 6, 1938, roll I-47.

13. Ogden, *The Poll Tax in the South*, 96–98; Joseph H. Cartwright, *The Triumph of Jim Crow: Tennessee Race Relations in the 1880's* (Knoxville: The University of Tennessee Press, 1976), 242–250; Key, *Southern Politics*, 74–75; J. Morgan Kousser, *The Shaping of Southern Politics*, 104–123.

14. The terms "honesty, respectability, and veracity" come from the statute. Chap. 30, sect. 1, *Acts of the State of Tennessee, 1851–1852*.

15. In 1915 Roscoe Eakes of Giles County, Tennessee had served nearly a year of a three- to five-year sentence for unlawful carnal knowledge when Governor Tom Rye pardoned him; eight months later he successfully filed for restoration. In Anderson County, Tennessee Bruce Pemberton worked even faster. Rendered infamous in January 1933 on an arson charge (he and two accomplices were accused of setting fire to three automobiles and a barn belonging to one of the three for an insurance claim), he was sentenced to a year in prison but successfully petitioned for a suspended sentence. His rights were restored five months later. Petition of Roscoe Eakes, October 19, 1915, Giles County Circuit Court, Civil Minutes, roll A-1419; Conviction of Bruce Pemberton, Anderson County Circuit Court Criminal Minutes, roll A-4095.

16. *In re: Curtis*, 6 Tenn. Civ. App. (Tenn. Civ. App. 1915).

17. These issues are discussed at length in chapter 5.

18. Jack Neely, "The Chill In the Air: One Century Ago, the Traditional Christmas Disaster," *Metro Pulse* (Knoxville, TN), December 21, 2006, http://www.metro-pulse.com/news/2006/Dec/21/secret_history-2006-51/. Accessed February 18, 2010.

19. Vivien M. L. Miller finds that African American men serving prison sentences often sought assistance from white men—including former employers—in seeking pardons releasing them from incarceration. She notes that "Race, gender, and class relations were marked by personal, interclass, and interracial ties which could be paternalistic and patronizing, but which at the same time could yield the desired outcome for social inferiors and offenders. Indifference or hostility was exhibited toward assertive and threatening black and lower-class white men and women, but paternalism was demonstrated toward 'good negroes' and 'model prisoners' of both races." Miller, *Crime Sexual Violence and Clemency*, 159.

20. File of Allonzo Jones, Convict and Fugitive Records—Applications for Clemency, 1858–1942, GSA.

21. Files of Daniel Butler and Elias Peavy, box SG 10274, Alabama Board of Pardons, Applications for Pardons, Paroles, or Remission of Fines, 1846–1915, ADAH.

22. On the social and personal ties between African American and whites in the rural South see Mark Schultz, *The Rural Face of White Supremacy: Beyond Jim Crow* (Urbana: University of Illinois Press, 2005).

23. On the 1915 election in Knoxville see Lakin, "'A Dark Night,'" 1–29.

24. *In re: Curtis*, 6 Tenn. Civ. App. (Tenn. Civ. App. 1915).

25. *In re: Curtis*, 6 Tenn. Civ. App. (Tenn. Civ. App. 1915).

26. On McDermott see *Law Notes* (Long Island, NY: Edward Thompson, Company, 1921), 96.

27. *In re: Curtis*, 6 Tenn. Civ. App. (Tenn. Civ. App. 1915).

28. Missouri Constitution (1820), sect. 14, art. 3; Missouri Constitution (1865), sect. 26, art. 2; Missouri Constitution (1875), art. 8 sect. 10.

29. *The Revised Statutes of the State of Missouri* (St. Louis: J. W. Dougherty, 1845), chap. 47, art. II, sect 45; chap. 47, art. III, sect. 65; chap. 47, art. IV, sect. 35; chap. 47, art. V, sect. 46; chap. 47, art. VI, sect. 18.

30. *Hartwig v. Hartwig*, 160 Mo. App. 284 (Mo. App. 1912).

31. Chicago Commission on Race Relations, *The Negro in Chicago: A Study of Race Relations and a Race Riot* (Chicago: University of Chicago Press, 1922), 80.

32. Lana Stein, *St. Louis Politics: The Triumph of Tradition* (St. Louis: Missouri Historical Society Press, 2002), 13–20.

33. *Gass v. Evans* 244 Mo. 329 (Mo. 1912).

34. *Gass v. Evans* 244 Mo. 329 (Mo. 1912).

35. *Gass v. Evans* 244 Mo. 329 (Mo. 1912).

36. Stephen Grant Meyer, *As Long as They Don't Move Next Door: Segregation and Racial Conflict in American Neighborhoods* (Lanham: Rowman and Littlefield, 2000), 20–22.

37. Richard Breitman and Alan M. Kraut, *American Refugee Policy and European Jewry, 1933–1945* (Bloomington: Indiana University Press), 126–145.

38. "Injunctions to Stop Arrest of Negroes Refused," St. Louis *Post Dispatch* (hereafter *STLPD*), November 7, 1916, p. 1; "Long Declares Glenn Planned Wholesale Arrest of Negroes," St. Louis *Daily Globe Democrat* (hereafter *STLDGD*), December 3, 1916, p. 6.

39. "Election Board Admits Wholesale Fraud in St. Louis," *STLDGD*, November 17, 1916, p. 1; "Lawyers Say They Gave Lists to Long in Election Probe," *STLDGD*, November 24, 1916, p. 4.

40. "Long Declares Glenn Planned Wholesale Arrest of Negroes," *STLDGD*, December 3, 1916, p. 6.

41. "Election Board Admits Wholesale Fraud in St. Louis," *STLDGD*, November 17, 1916, p. 1.

42. "Intimidated Voter Files $10,000 Suit against Democrats," *STLDGD*, November 18, 1916, p. 1, 2. Capital letters in original announcement.

43. William Young, General Order No. 228, November 2, 1916, reprinted in *St. Louis Police Journal* Volume 5, No. 32, p. 1, 8.

44. "Warning to Negro Voters," St. Louis *Argus*, 3 November 1916, p. 1.

45. "Statements Made by Democrats on Vote Controversy," St. Louis *Star*, n.d., in Tuskegee News Clipping File, reel 5.

46. "Circuit Attorney to Prosecute," *St. Louis Police Journal* (Official Organ of the Board of Police Commissioners and Police Department of St. Louis), Volume 5, no. 3, 3.

47. Elliott M. Rudwick, *Race Riot at East St. Louis, July 2, 1917* (Carbondale: Southern Illinois Press, 1964).

48. "Bring the Vote Thieves to Judgment," *St. Louis Argus*, November 10, 1916, p. 1.

49. This is discussed in chapter 3.

50. "Police Keep 3000 Voters from Polls," *STLDGD*, November 8, 1916, p. 2, 8.

51. "Officer tells of Arrest of Man at Polls," *STLDGD*, November 23, 1916, p. 2.

52. "Steps to Contest the Election of Gardner Taken," *STLPD*, November 17, 1916, p. 3.

53. "Checking Registration Laws," *STLDGD*, December 3, 1916, 12. This article also supported the contention that challengers merely used last names to match convicts to voters.

54. "Against Rejected St. Louis Ballots," St. Louis *Argus*, November 24, 1916, Tuskegee News Clipping File, reel 5.

55. "Injunctions to stop arrest of Negroes Refused," *STLPD*, November 7, 1916, 1; "Negroes Arrested Election Day Are All Discharged," *STLPD*, November 10, 1916, p. 1.

56. "Grand Jury Has Kiel and Election Board Summoned," *STLPD*, November 24, 1916, p. 1.

57. "Police Keep 3000 Voters from Polls," *STLDGD*, November 8, 1916, p. 2, 8.

58. "Election Board Admits Wholesale Fraud in St. Louis," *STLDGD*, November 17, 1916, p. 1.

59. "Grand Jury Has Kiel and Election Board Summoned," *STLPD*, November 24, 1916, p. 1.

60. "Intimidation Charge False, says Democrats," n.d., St. Louis *Star*, reprinted in Tuskegee News Clipping File, reel 5.

61. "Police Keep 3000 Voters from Polls," *STLDGD*, November 8, 1916, p. 2, 8.

62. In St. Louis the majority of the Police Board members are appointed by the governor, so the city police are effectively under state, not local, control. This was true in 1916 and remains true today.

63. "Police Keep 3000 Voters from Polls," *STLDGD*, November 8, 1916, p. 2, 8.

64. "Negro Democrat is Arrested by Mistake," *STLDGD*, November 8, 1916, p. 1.

65. "Injunctions to Stop Arrest of Negroes Refused," *STLPD*, November 7, 1916, 1.

66. "Police Keep 3000 Voters from Polls," *STLDGD*, November 8, 1916, p. 2, 8.

67. "Intimidated Voter Files $10,000 Suit against Democrats," *STLDGD*, November 18, 1916, p. 1.

68. "Injunctions to Stop Arrest of Negroes Refused," *STLPD*, November 7, 1916, p. 1.

69. "Police Keep 3000 Voters from Polls," *STLDGD*, November 8, 1916, p. 2, 8.

70. "Three indicted after Election Fraud Inquiry," *STLDGD*, December 3, 1916, p. 6.

71. Ages and occupations were listed for most but not all of the arrested men. "GOP Voters Arrested in Police Intimidation," *STLDGD*, November 8, 1916, p. 2.

72. "Negros Arrested on Election Day are All Discharged," *STLPD*, November 10, 1916, p. 1.

73. "Move Started to Get Election Law Amended," *STLPD*, November 22, 1916, p. 3.

74. "Against Rejected St. Louis Ballots," St. Louis *Argus*, Tuskegee News Clipping File, reel 5.

75. "Indictments Returned in Vote Inquiry," November 30, 1916, p. 1; "Three Indicted after Election Fraud Inquiry," *STLDGD*, December 3, 1916, p. 6.

76. "Nonpartisan Committee Urges Co-operation to Punish Frauds," *STLGD*, November 26, p. 1.

77. For age and occupation of Lucas see Register of Voters, Record Retention, Office of the Comptroller, Microfilm DA 581, St. Louis City Hall, St. Louis, Missouri.

78. "Officer Tells of Arrest of Man at Polls," *STLDGD*, November 23, 1916, p. 2.

79. "Officer Tells of Arrest of Man at Polls," *STLDGD*, November 23, 1916, p. 2.

80. Plaintiff's Petition, file for *Henry Lucas v. Theodore Sandman et al*, December 1916, file 6916, Circuit Court Case Files, Office of the Circuit Clerk-St. Louis, Missouri State Archives-St. Louis, Office of the Secretary of State. Hereafter "*Lucas v. Sandman* file."

81. Plaintiff's petition, *Lucas v. Sandman* file. On Ferris and Rosskpof, see Walter B. Stevens, *Centennial History of Missouri (the Center State): One Hundred Years in the Union, 1820–1921* (St. Louis: Clarke Publishing, 1921), 201.

82. List of witnesses and charges, April 7, 1920, *Lucas v. Sandman* file; Minutes of Proceedings 1916-1919, *Lucas v. Sandman* file.

83. Memorandum for Clerk, March 10, 1920, *Lucas v. Sandman* file.

84. Memorandum for Clerk, March 10, 1920, *Lucas v. Sandman* file.

85. "Intimidated Voter files $10,000 Suit against Democrats," *STLDGD*, November 18, 1916, p. 1, 2.

86. Plaintiff's petition, *Lucas v. Sandman* file.

87. "Second Amended Answer" of the defendant, *Lucas v. Sandman* file.

88. Handwritten jury verdict, *Lucas v. Sandman* file.

89. Minutes of Proceedings 1916–1919, *Lucas v. Sandman* file.

90. "Intimidated Voter Files $10,000 Suit against Democrats," *STLDGD*, November 18, 1916, p. 1, 2.

91. "Negro Files $11,000 Damage Suit against Democratic Officials," *STLDGD*, November 29, 1916, 2; "Indictments Returned in Vote Inquiry," *STLDGD*, November 30, 1916, p. 1.

92. Amended petition, File for *John L. Sullivan vs. Breckinridge Long et al.*, December 1916, file 7075, Circuit Court Files, Office of the Circuit Clerk-St. Louis, Missouri State Archives-St. Louis, Office of the Secretary of State. Hereafter, "*Sullivan v. Long* file."

93. "Officer Tells of Arrest of Man at Polls," *STLDGD*, November 23, 1916, 2; Amended petition, *Sullivan v. Long* file.

94. Motion for Security for Costs, January 1917, *Sullivan v. Long* file.

95. Memorandum for Clerk, February 17, 1917, *Sullivan v. Long* file.

96. Motion to dismiss, February 1918, *Sullivan v. Long* file; Memorandum for Clerk, March 30, 1918, *Sullivan v. Long* file.

97. Minutes of proceedings, *Sullivan v. Long* file.

98. Report of Chair of Board of Directors, 1916, NAACP Papers, quoted in Susan D. Carle, "Race, Class, and Legal Ethics in the Early NAACP (1910–1920)," *Law and History Review*, 20:97 (2002), 118.

99. Eric Foner writes that most states had eliminated the bans on court testimony by 1867 though they did this reluctantly and primarily to bring such cases back to local jurisdiction and out of Freedmen's Bureau control. See Foner, *Reconstruction*, 149, 204. Kentucky, having avoided the federal authority of Reconstruction, barred blacks from testifying in court until the 1870s. Lowell Hayes Harrison and James C. Klotter, *A New History of Kentucky* (Lexington: University Press of Kentucky, 1997), 247.

100. "G.O.P. Voters Arrested in Police Intimidation," *STLDGD*, November 8, 1916, 2; "Police Keep 3000 Voters from Polls," *STLDGD*, November 8, 1916, p. 2, 8.

101. *In re: Curtis*, 6 Tenn. Civ. App. (Tenn. Civ. App. 1915).

102. See footnote 12 above.

103. 1920 Census, Belmont, Ohio; 1930 Census, Cleveland Ohio.

CONCLUSION

1. *Laws of Virginia*, 1748, quoted in D.W. Woodbridge, "The Effect in Virginia of Conviction of Crime on Competency and Credibility of Witnesses," *Virginia Law Review* 23:470 (1937), 470–471.

2. *Proceedings and Debates of the Virginia State Convention of 1829–1830*, 433.

3. *State v. Earnhardt*, 86 S.E. 960 (N.C. 1915).

4. See Perkinson, *Texas Tough*.

5. North Dakota Constitution (1889), art. V, sect. 127; South Dakota Constitution (1889), art. VII, sect. 9; Washington Constitution (1889), art. VI, sect. 3; Montana Constitution (1889), art. IX, sect. 2; Idaho Constitution (1889), art. VI, sect. 3; Wyoming Constitution (1889), art. VI, sect. 6; Oklahoma

Constitution (1907), art. 2, sect. 43; New Mexico Constitution (1912), art. VII, sect. 1; Arizona Constitution (1912), art. VII, sect. 2.

6. Disfranchisement for criminal conviction in Pennsylvania stemmed from the stipulation that incarcerated people could not vote absentee. *Com. ex rel. Walden v. Brown*, 85 Pa. D. & C. 581 (Pa. Com. Pl. 1953); *Ray v. Com. of Pa.*, 263 F. Supp. 630 (D.C. Pa. 1967).

7. Alaska Constitution (1956), art. V. sect. 2; Hawaii Constitution (1959), art. II, sect. 2. Manza and Uggen identify a liberalizing trend in the second half of the twentieth century, whereby a number of states allowed for suffrage by some or all ex-felons. Manza and Uggen, *Locked Out*, 50–55.

8. Sentencing Project, *Felony Disfranchisement Laws in the United States 2010*, 1.

9. For an overview of the racial component of the system of mass incarceration in the United States, see Heather Ann Thompson, "Why Mass Incarceration Matters: Rethinking Crisis, Decline, and Transformation in Postwar American History," *The Journal of American History* 97, no. 3 (December 2010): 703–734.

10. Constitution of the Kingdom of Hawaii (1887), art. 73. "The following persons shall not be permitted to register for voting, to vote, or to hold office under any department of the Government, or to sit in the Legislature, namely: Any person who is insane or an idiot, or any person who shall have been convicted of any of the following named offenses, viz: Arson, Barratry, Bribery, Burglary, Counterfeiting, Embezzlement, Felonious Branding of Cattle, Forgery, Gross Cheat, Incest, Kidnapping, Larceny, Malicious Burning, Manslaughter in the First Degree, Murder, Perjury, Rape, Robbery, Sodomy, Treason, Subordination of Perjury, and Malfeasance in Office, unless he shall have been pardoned by the King and restored to his Civil Rights, and by the express terms of his pardon declared to be eligible to offices of Trust, Honor and Profit."

11. *Acts of the General Assembly of the Commonwealth of Kentucky 1904* (Louisville: Geo. G. Fetter Co., 1904), 83 This act was repealed by chap. 406, sect. 336, *Kentucky Acts of 1974*.

12. *The Washington Post*, March 1, 1904, p. 6; Samuel J. Barrows, "Crimes and Offenses," New York State Library, Bulletin 91, Comparative Summary and Index of Legislation 1904 (Albany: New York State Education Department, 1905), d5-d6.

13. Quoted in *The Bourbon News* (Paris, Kentucky) March 18, 1904, p. 4.

14. *Washington Post*, March 1, 1904, p. 6.

15. *The Bourbon News*, July 8, 1904, 5. Daniel Sharfstein has written that "The tragedy befalling negro suffrage was played as a farce." Though he was referring specifically to revocation of African American suffrage in Washington D.C. in the 1870s, this is an apt description of many episodes in the disfranchisement campaigns of this era. Sharfestein, *The Invisible Line*, 107.

16. James C. Klotter, *Kentucky: Portrait in Paradox, 1900–1950* (Frankfort: Kentucky Historical Society 1996), 207. Kentucky's public schools had been segregated by law since 1866. The 1904 segregation law prohibiting racially integrated education at private schools was aimed at the one site of interracial education remaining in Kentucky, privately run Berea College. John A. Hardin, *Fifty Years of Segregation. Black Higher Education in Kentucky, 1904–1954* (Lexington: University Press of Kentucky 1997), 11–15.

17. Idaho Constitution (1889), art. VI, sect. 3; *Proceedings and Debates of the Constitutional Convention of Idaho, 1889*, vol. 2 (Caldwell, Idaho: Caxton Printers, 1912), 1033. The convention also voted to permanently disfranchise

all individuals convicted of treason, felony, election offenses, embezzlement, or infamous crimes. Manza and Uggen write that Idaho's constitution only disfranchised individuals for the duration of their prison sentence, but I read the document differently. Manza and Uggen, *Locked Out,* 56.

18. Wood, *Restoring the Right to Vote;* King, *Expanding the Vote.*
19. Richard M. Re and Christopher M. Re, "Voting and Vice: Criminal Disenfranchisement and the Reconstruction Amendments," *Yale Law Journal* 121 (2012): 1584–1670.
20. Arguments that "crime" was a word with some implied limitation has been put forth by others as well. For other explorations of this issue, see Cosgrove, "Four New Arguments," 175–181; Pettus, *Felony Disenfranchisement,* 120–121; Manza and Uggen, *Locked Out,* 44; Re and Re, "Voting and Vice," 1648–1655.
21. *Official Journal of the Constitutional Convention of the State of Alabama,* 42; Louisiana Constitution (1868), title IV, art. 99.
22. Re and Re, "Voting and Vice," 1593–1597.
23. Quoted in Re and Re, "Voting and Vice," 1621–1622.
24. Re and Re, "Voting and Vice," 1594; Appendix to the *Congressional Globe,* House of Representatives, 40th Congress, 3rd Sess., 200 (January 29, 1869).

BIBLIOGRAPHY

ARCHIVAL SOURCES

Alabama Board of Pardons, Applications for Pardons, Paroles, or Remission of Fines, 1846–1915, Alabama Department of Archives and History, Montgomery, Alabama.

Anson County, North Carolina, Miscellaneous Records 1758–1960, North Carolina State Archives, Raleigh, North Carolina.

Charles K. Reagan Papers, Mississippi Department of Archives and History, Jackson, Mississippi.

Convict and Fugitive Records—Applications for Clemency, 1858–1942, Georgia State Archives, Morrow, Georgia.

Crockett County Circuit Court Records, Tennessee State Library and Archives, Nashville, Tennessee.

Executive Papers of Governor Westmoreland Davis, Acc. # 21567a. State Government Records Collection, The Library of Virginia, Richmond, Virginia.

Executive Papers of Governor William H. Mann, 1899–1914, Acc. # 23349 & 41428, State Government Records Collection, The Library of Virginia, Richmond, Virginia.

Executive Papers of Governor Andrew J. Montague, Acc. # 23349, State Government Records Collection, The Library of Virginia, Richmond, Virginia.

Executive Papers of Governor Henry Carter Stuart, Acc. # 28722, State Government Records Collection, The Library of Virginia, Richmond, Virginia.

Executive Papers of Governor Claude A. Swanson, Acc. # 29593, State Government Records Collection, The Library of Virginia, Richmond, Virginia.

Executive Papers of Governor E. Lee Trinkle, Acc. #21567b, State Government Records Collection, The Library of Virginia, Richmond, Virginia.

Giles County Circuit Court Records, Tennessee State Library and Archives, Nashville, Tennessee.

Giles County Circuit Court Records, 1893–1900, Old Records Office, Giles County Court House, Pulaski, Tennessee.

Granville County Miscellaneous Records 1848–1929, North Carolina State Archives, Raleigh, North Carolina.

Henry Lucas v. Theodore Sandman et al., December 1916, file 6916, Circuit Court Case Files, Office of the Circuit Clerk–St. Louis, Missouri State Archives, St. Louis, Office of the Secretary of State.

"Iredell County List of Persons Convicted of Felony and Disqualified from Voting." Undated. North Carolina Collection, Wilson Library, University of North Carolina, Chapel Hill, North Carolina.

John L. Sullivan vs. Breckinridge Long et al., December 1916, file 7075, Circuit Court Files, Office of the Circuit Clerk–St. Louis, Missouri State Archives, St. Louis, Office of the Secretary of State.

Knox County Circuit Court, Civil Minutes, East Tennessee Historical Society, Knoxville, Tennessee.

"List of Persons Convicted of Felony or Other Infamous Crimes in Granville County, Since March 12, 1877." Undated. North Carolina Collection, Wilson Library, University of North Carolina, Chapel Hill, North Carolina.

Maury County Circuit Court Records, Tennessee State Library and Archives, Nashville, Tennessee.

Official Lists of Dead, Lunatic, and Convicted Colored Males Who Are Thereby Disfranchised. Richmond, 1892. Copy in Albert and Shirley Small Special Collections Library. University of Virginia Library, Charlottesville.

Papers of Governor Martin F. Ansel, South Carolina Department of Archives and History, Columbia, South Carolina.

Polk County Miscellaneous Records, 1856–1921, North Carolina State Archives, Raleigh, North Carolina.

Wayne County Miscellaneous Records, 1788–1936, North Carolina State Archives, Raleigh, North Carolina.

PERIODICALS

Atlantic Monthly, 1867

Baltimore *Afro American*, November 5, 1920

The Bourbon News (Paris, Kentucky), March 18, 1904

Bangor (Maine) *Daily Whig and Courier*, December 16, 1883

The Daily Journal and Tribune (Knoxville TN), December 21, 1907

Greenville (Miss.) *Times*, March 18, 1876; April 15, 1876

Harpers Weekly, 1867

Hazlehurst (Miss.) *Copiahan*, March 11, 1876

Jackson *Clarion Ledger*, March 2, 1948

The Nation April 30, 2001

New Orleans *Southwestern Christian Advocate*, July 5, 1883

New York *Globe*, January 26, 1884

New York Times, November 28, 1876; October 11, 1875; August 22, 1875; Feb. 15, 2004; March 28, 2004

Palm Beach *Post*, May 27, 2001

Richmond *Daily Dispatch*, October 31, 1876; November 1, 1876; November 3, 1876; November 8, 1876; August 23, 1875; November 4, 1876; November 8, 1888; August 20, 1875; August 20, 1875

Richmond *Daily Whig*, November 2, 1876; November 4, 1874

Richmond *Virginia Star*, November 11, 1882

St. Louis *Argus,* November–December, 1916

St. Louis *Daily Globe Democrat*, November–December 1916

St. Louis Police Journal

St Louis *Post Dispatch,* November–December, 1916

Tuskegee News Clipping File, 1899–1966 on Microfilm, Tuskegee Institute, Tuskegee, Ala.

Washington Post, March 1, 1904

COURT CASES

Allen v. Ellisor, 664 F.2d 391 (4th Cir., 1981)

Anderson v. Winfree, 85 Ky. 597 (Ky. App. 1887)

Commonwealth v. Fugate, (Va. Gen. 1830)

Commonwealth v. Fugate, 2 Leigh 724 (Va. Gen. 1830)

Cotton v. Fordice, 157 F.3d 388 (5th Cir. 1998)

Edwards v. The Commonwealth, 78 Va. 39 (Va. 1883)

Evans v. State, 66 Tenn. 12 (Tenn. 1872)

Ex Parte Garland, 71 U. S. 333 (1866)

Ex Parte Wilson, 114 U. S. 417 (1885)

Gass v. Evans, 244 Mo. 329 (Mo. 1912)

Gillman v. State, 165 Ala. 135 (Ala. 1910)

Guinn v. United States 238 U.S. 347 (1915)

Hartwig v. Hartwig, 160 Mo. App. 284 (Mo. App. 1912)

Hunter v. Underwood, 471 U.S. 222 (1985)

In re: Curtis, 6 Tenn. Civ. App. (Tenn. Civ. App. 1915)

In Re Opinion of Justices, 14 Fla. 318 (Fla. 1872)

Johnson v. Bush, 214 F. Supp. 2d 1333 (S.D. Fla. 2002)

Jones v. Robbins 8 Gray 329 (Mass. S.J.C., 1857)

Mackin v. United States, 117 U.S. 348 (1886).

Maher v. People, 10 Mich. 212 (Mich. 1862)

McGlaughlin v. City of Canton, Mississippi, 947 F. Supp 954 (S.D. Miss., 1995)

Ratliff v. Beale, 74 Miss. 247 (Miss. 1896)

Richardson v. Ramirez, 418 U.S. 24 (1974)

Shepherd v. State, 44 Ark. 39 (Ark. 1884)

Singleton v. State, 38 Fla. 297 (Fla. 1896).

Smith v. State, 83 Ala. 26 (Ala. 1887)

Southworth v. State, 42 Ark. 270 (Ark. 1883)

State v. Baptiste, 26 La. Ann. 134 (La. 1874)

State v. Buckman, 18 Fla. 267 (1881)

State v. Cantey 50 S.C.L. (S.C. Ct. App. 1835)

State v. Corley, 13 S.C. 1 (S.C. 1880).

State v. Earnhardt, 86 SE 960 (N.C. 1915)

State v. Keyes, 8 Vt. 57 (Vt. 1836)

Underwood v. Hunter, 730 F.2d 614 (11th Cir. 1984)

United States v. Coppersmith, 4 Fed. 199 (C. C. Tenn., 1880).

United States v. Cruikshank, 92 U.S. 542 (1875)

United States v. Reese, 92 U.S. 214 (1875)

Ware v. State, 33 Ark. 567 (Ark. 1878)

Williams v. Taylor, 677 F.2d 510 (5th Cir., 1982)

Young v. State 30 Tenn. 200 (Tenn. 1850)

Washington v. State, 75 Ala. 582 (Ala. 1884)

PUBLISHED LEGAL RESOURCES
Alabama

Alabama Constitution (1819).

Alabama Constitution (1865).

Alabama Constitution (1868).

Alabama Constitution (1875).

Alabama Constitution (1901).

Acts of the General Assembly of the State of Alabama, 1819. Huntsville: John Boardman, 1820.

Acts of the General Assembly of Alabama Passed at the Session of 1874–5. Montgomery: W. W. Screws, State Printer, 1875.

Aiken, John G., compiler. *A Digest of the Laws of the State of Alabama.* Philadelphia: Alexander Towar, 1833.

Journal of the Constitutional Convention of the State of Alabama. Montgomery: W. W. Screws, 1875.

Official Journal of the Constitutional Convention of the State of Alabama. Montgomery, AL: Barrett & Brown, 1868.

Official Proceedings of the Constitutional Convention of the State of Alabama. 4 vols. Wetumpka: Wetumpka Printing Co., 1940.

Report of Pardons, Commutations and Reprieves 1882–1884. Montgomery, Ala.: W. W. Screws, State Printer, 1887.

Report of Pardons, Commutations and Reprieves, 1884–1886. Montgomery, AL: WD Brown and Co. State Printers, 1887.

Report of the Alabama Board of Pardons, 1915. Montgomery: Brown Printing Co., 1915.

Report of the Alabama Board of Pardons, 1917. Montgomery: Brown Printing Co., 1917.

ALASKA

Alaska Constitution (1956).

ARIZONA

Arizona Constitution (1912).

ARKANSAS

Arkansas Constitution (1836).

Arkansas Constitution (1864).

Arkansas Constitution (1868).

Acts and Resolutions of the General Assembly of the State of Arkansas. Little Rock: Pilot Printing Company, 1881.

Acts of the General Assembly of the State of Arkansas. Little Rock: Gazette Book and Job Printing, 1874.

CONNECTICUT

Connecticut Constitution (1818).

The Public Statute Laws of Connecticut. Volume 1. Hartford: Hudson and Goodwin, 1808.

FLORIDA

Florida Constitution (1838).

Florida Constitution (1865).

Florida Constitution (1868).

Florida Statutes (2000).

Thompson, Leslie A. *A Manual or Digest of the Statute Law of the State of Florida.* Boston: C. C. Little and J. Brown, 1847.

GEORGIA

Georgia Constitution (1868).

Georgia Constitution (1877).

Acts and Resolutions of the General Assembly of the State of Georgia, Passed at the Regular January Session, 1875. Atlanta: James P. Harrison, State Printer, 1875.

A Stenographic Report of the Proceedings Held at the Constitutional Convention held in Atlanta Georgia, 1877. Atlanta: Constitution Publishing Company, 1877.

Journal of the House of Representatives of the State of Georgia. Atlanta: Franklin Printing and Publishing Company, 1906.

Journal of the Senate of the State of Georgia, 1897. Atlanta: Franklin Printing and Publishing Company, 1897.

Journal of the Senate of the State of Georgia, 1899. Atlanta: Franklin Print and Publishing, 1899.

Journal of the Senate of the State of Georgia, 1905. Atlanta: Franklin Print and Publishing, 1905.

Report and Opinions of the Attorney General of Georgia, 1915 1916. Atlanta: Index Printing Company, 1916.

HAWAII

Constitution of the Kingdom of Hawaii (1887).

Hawaii Constitution (1959).

IDAHO

Idaho Constitution (1889).

Proceedings and Debates of the Constitutional Convention of Idaho, 1889, vol. 2. Caldwell, Idaho: Caxton Printers, 1912.

ILLINOIS

Illinois Constitution (1848).

A Compilation of the Statutes of Illinois of a General Nature, in Force January 1, 1856. Chicago: Keen and Lee, 1856.

Revised Statutes of the State of Illinois, 1844–1845. Springfield, Ill.: William Walters, 1845.

Revised Statutes of the State of Illinois, 1874. Springfield, Ill.: Illinois Journal Company, 1874.

KENTUCKY

Kentucky Constitution (1792).

Kentucky Constitution (1890).

Acts of the General Assembly of the Commonwealth of Kentucky 1904. Louisville: Geo. G. Fetter Co., 1904.

Official Report of the Proceedings and Debates in the Convention Assembled at Frankfort, on the Eighth Day of September, 1890, to Adapt, Amend, Or Change the Constitution of the State of Kentucky. Frankfort, Kentucky: E. P. Johnson, 1890.

LOUISIANA

Louisiana Constitution (1812).

Louisiana Constitution (1845).

Louisiana Constitution (1864).

Louisiana Constitution (1868).

Louisiana Constitution (1879).

Louisiana Constitution (1898).

Acts passed by the General Assembly of the State of Louisiana at the First Session of the Third Legislature. New Orleans: Republican Office, 1873.

Acts Passed at the First Session of the Seventh Legislature of the State of Louisiana. New Orleans: M. Cruzat, 1824–1825.

MAINE

The Debates, Resolutions, and other Proceedings, of the Convention of Delegates. Portland, Maine: A. Shirley, 1820.

MARYLAND

Maryland Constitution (1851).

Debates and Proceedings of the Maryland Reform Convention to Revise the State Constitution. Annapolis: William McNeir Printer, 1851.

The Debates of the Constitutional Convention of the State of Maryland, Assembled at the City of Annapolis, Wednesday, April 27, 1864. Volume II. Annapolis: Richard P. Bayly 1864.

MICHIGAN

Michigan Constitution (1850).

The Debates and Proceedings of the Constitutional Convention of the State of Michigan. Volume II. Lansing: John A. Kerr, 1867.

Report of the Proceedings and Debates in the Convention to Revise the Constitution of the State of Michigan, 1850. Lansing: R.W. Ingals, 1850.

MISSISSIPPI

Mississippi Constitution (1817).

Mississippi Constitution (1868).

Mississippi Constitution (1890).

Campbell, J. A. P. *The Revised Code of the Statute Laws of the State of Mississippi.* Jackson, Miss: J. L. Power, 1880.

Journal of the House of Representatives of the State of Mississippi, 1896. Jackson: R. H. Henry, State Printer, 1896.

Journal of the House of Representatives of the State of Mississippi, 1900. Jackson: Clarion–Ledger, 1900.

Journal of the House of Representatives of the State of Mississippi, 1904. Jackson: Clarion–Ledger, 1904.

Journal of the House of Representatives of the State of Mississippi, 1948. Jackson: State of Mississippi, 1948.

Journal of the House of Representatives of the State of Mississippi, 1876. Jackson: C. M. Price, State Printer, 1876.

Journal of the House of Representatives of the State of Mississippi, 1913. Jackson: Tucker Printing House, 1913.

Journal of the Proceedings in the Constitutional Convention of the State of Mississippi. Jackson: E. J. Martin, 1890.

Laws of the State of Mississippi. Jackson: State of Mississippi, 1838.

Laws of the State of Mississippi, 1876. Jackson: Power and Barksdale, 1876.

Mississippi Code 1942, Annotated. Volume 8. Jackson: Harrison Company, 1943.

Mississippi Senate Journal (Jackson: Power and Barksdale, 1876).

The Revised Code of the Statute Laws of the State of Mississippi. Jackson: Alcorn and Fisher, 1871.

MISSOURI
Missouri Constitution (1820).
Missouri Constitution (1865).
Missouri Constitution (1875).
The Revised Statutes of the State of Missouri. St. Louis: J. W. Dougherty, 1845.

MONTANA
Montana Constitution (1889).

NEW MEXICO
New Mexico Constitution (1912).

NEW YORK
New York Constitution (1821).
A Report of the Debates and Proceedings of the Convention of the State of New York; Held at the Capitol, in the City of Albany, on the 28th Day of August, 1821. New York: J. Seymour, 1821.
Debates and Proceedings in the New York State Convention for the Revision of the Constitution. Albany: Albany Argus, 1846.
New York (State) Commissioners of the Code. *First Report of the Commissioners of the Code*. Book 1. Albany: Weed, Parson, and Co., 1849.

NORTH CAROLINA
North Carolina Constitution (1776, amended 1835).
North Carolina Constitution (1899).
Iredell, James. *A Digested Manual of the Acts of the General Assembly of North Carolina*. Raleigh: Weston R. Gales, 1847.
Journal of the Constitutional Convention of the State of North Carolina, 1868 Session, Electronic Edition. http://docsouth.unc.edu/nc/conv1868/conv1868.html
Laws and Resolutions of the State of North Carolina ... 1876–7. Raleigh: Theo N. Ramsay, State Printer, 1877.
Public Laws of the State of North Carolina, Passed by the General Assembly at Its Session 1871–'72. Raleigh: Theo N. Ramsay, State Printer, 1872.
The State Records of North Carolina, vol. 24. Edited by Walter Clark. Goldsboro, NC: Nash Brothers, 1905.

NORTH DAKOTA
North Dakota Constitution (1889).

OHIO
Ohio Constitution (1802).
Ohio Constitution (1851).
The Public Statutes at Large of the State of Ohio. Cincinnati: Maskell E. Curwen, 1853.

OKLAHOMA
Oklahoma Constitution (1907).

PENNSYLVANIA

Pennsylvania Constitution (1873).

Debates of the Convention to Amend the Constitution of Pennsylvania: Convened at Harrisburg, November 12, 1872. Volume II. Harrisburg, PA: Benjamin Singerly, State Printer, 1873.

Proceedings and Debates of the Convention of the Commonwealth of Pennsylvania to Propose Amendments to the Constitution, Commenced and Held at Harrisburg, on the Second Day of May, 1837. Volume 1–4. Harrisburg: Packer, Barrett, and Parke, 1837.

SOUTH CAROLINA

South Carolina Constitution (1790).

South Carolina Constitution (1790, amended 1810).

South Carolina Constitution (1865).

South Carolina Constitution (1868).

South Carolina Constitution (1895).

Acts and Joint Resolutions of the General Assembly of the State of South Carolina Passed at the Regular Session of 1882. Columbia, SC: Charles A. Calvo, State Printer, 1882.

Acts of the General Assembly of the State of South Carolina, Passed at the Sessions of 1864–1865. Columbia, SC: Julian Selby, 1866.

Journal of the Constitutional Convention of the state of South Carolina, 1895. Columbia, SC: Charles Calvo, 1895.

Proceedings of the Constitutional Convention of South Carolina, 1868. Charleston: Denny and Perry, 1868.

Reports and Resolutions of the General Assembly of South Carolina. Volume 2. Columbia, SC: The State Company, 1903.

Report of State Officers, Board and Committees to the General Assembly of the State of South Carolina. Volume II. Columbia, SC: Gonzales and Bryan, 1922.

SOUTH DAKOTA

South Dakota Constitution (1889).

TENNESSEE

Tennessee Constitution (1835).

Acts of the State of Tennessee, 1851–1852. Nashville: Bang & McKennie, 1852.

Meigs, Return J. and William F. Cooper, compilers. *The Code of Tennessee: Enacted by the General Assembly of 1857–1858.* Nashville: E.G. Eastman, 1858.

Acts Passed at the First Session of the Twenty-Third General Assembly of the State of Tennessee. Nashville: J. Geo. Harris, 1840.

Haywood, John, and Robert L. Cobbs. *The Statute Laws of the State of Tennessee, vol. 1.* Knoxville: F. S. Heiskell, 1831.

Thompson, Seymour D., and Thomas M. Steger. *A Compilation of the Statute Laws of the State of Tennessee.* St. Louis: W. J. Gilbert, 1872.

TEXAS

Texas Constitution (1833).

Texas Constitution (1875).

Braden, George D. *The Constitution of the State of Texas: An Annotated Comparative Analysis.* 2 vols. Austin: Texas Advisory Commission on Intergovernmental Relations, 1977.

VERMONT

The Laws of Vermont of a Publick and Permanent Nature. Windsor, Vermont: Simeon Ide, 1824.

Laws of Vermont of 1832. Montpelier, Vermont: Knapp and Jewitt, 1832.

VIRGINIA

Virginia Constitution (1830).

Virginia Constitution (1850).

Virginia Constitution (1864).

Virginia Constitution (1870, amended 1876).

Virginia Constitution (1902).

Acts of the General Assembly of Virginia. Richmond: Samuel Shepherd, 1848.

Acts and Joint Resolutions Passed by the General Assembly of the State of Virginia, 1876–1877. Richmond: F. Walker, 1877.

Annual Report of the Attorney General to the Governor of Virginia. Richmond: Davis Bottom, 1921.

Journal of the Constitutional Convention of the State of Virginia. Richmond: Office of the New Nation, 1867.

Journal of the House of Delegates of the Commonwealth of Virginia, 1912. Richmond. Davis Bottom, 1912.

Journal of the Senate of the Commonwealth of Virginia, 1876. Richmond: R.F. Walker, 1876.

Journal of the Senate of the Commonwealth of Virginia, 1883–1884. Richmond: R.F. Walker, 1884.

Journal of the Senate of the Commonwealth of Virginia, 1908. Richmond: Davis Bottom, 1908.

Journal of the Senate of the Commonwealth of Virginia, 1910. Richmond: Davis Bottom, 1910.

Journal of the Senate of the Commonwealth of Virginia, 1914. Richmond: Davis Bottom, 1914.

Journal of the Senate of the Commonwealth of Virginia, 1916. Richmond: Davis Bottom, 1916.

Journal of the Senate of the Commonwealth of Virginia, 1924. Richmond: Davis Bottom, 1924.

Proceedings and Debates of the Virginia State Convention of 1829–1830. Richmond: Samuel Shepherd and Company, 1830.

WASHINGTON

Washington Constitution (1889).

WYOMING

Wyoming Constitution (1889).

U.S. GOVERNMENT DOCUMENTS

Congressional Globe. House of Representatives. 39th Congress, 2nd Session.

Congressional Globe. House of Representatives. 40th Congress, 3rd session.

Congressional Globe. U.S. Senate. 40th Congress. 3rd Session.

Edmund Waddill vs. George D. Wise. House Report 1182, 51 Congress, 1st Session.

"General Orders—Reconstruction" House Executive Document 342. 40th Congress, 2nd Session.

Hearings before the Committee on Ways and Means on the Philippine Tariff. 59th Congress, 1st Session, December 1905.

Hearings before the Subcommittee on Courts, Civil Liberties, and the Administration of Justice of the Committee on the Judiciary. House of Representatives. 93rd Cong., 2nd Session, January 30, 1974.

House Miscellaneous Documents, 47th Congress, 1st Session, No. 11: *Testimony in the Contested Election Case of Horatio Bisbee, Jr. vs. Jesse J. Finley, from the Second Congressional District of Florida.*

House Miscellaneous Documents, 47th Congress, 1st Session, No. 16: *Testimony and Papers in the Contested Election Case of James Gillette vs. Thomas H. Herndon, from the First Congressional District of Alabama.*

House Miscellaneous Documents, 47th Congress, 1st Session, No. 22: *Testimony and Papers in the Contested Election Case of William M. Lowe vs. Joseph Wheeler, from the Eighth Congressional District of Alabama.*

House Miscellaneous Documents, 47th Congress, 1st Session, No. 29: *Papers and Testimony in the Contested-Election Case of J. T. Stovall vs. George C. Cabell, from the Fifth Congressional District of Virginia.*

House Miscellaneous Documents, 48th Congress, 1st Session, No. 18: *Testimony and Papers in the Contested-Election Case of George T. Garrison vs. Robert M. Mayo, from the First Congressional District of Virginia.*

House Miscellaneous Documents, 48th Congress, 1st Session, No. 27: Pt. 2: *Papers and Testimony in the Contested-Election Case of John E. Massey vs. John S. Wise, from the State of Virginia at Large.*

"Interpretation of the Reconstruction Acts." House Executive Document 34. 40th Congress, 1st Session.

Journal of the House of Representatives of the United States. 40th Congress, 3rd Session.

Journal of the Senate of the United States. 40th Congress, 3rd Session.

Records of the U.S. Army Continental Commands, RG 393, National Archives of the United States.

Senate Miscellaneous Documents. 44th Congress, 2nd Session, No. 45: *Testimony as to Denial of Elective Franchise in Mississippi at the Elections of 1875 and 1876, Taken under the Resolution of the Senate of December 5, 1876.*

Senate Report. "Report of the Senate Committee on Privileges and Elections with the Testimony and Documentary Evidence on the Election in the State of Florida in 1876." 44th Congress, 2nd Session, No. 611.

Senate Reports. 44th Congress, 2nd Session, No. 704: *Report of the Subcommittee of the Committee on Privileges and Elections to Inquire and Report whether in Any Elections in the State of Alabama in the Elections of 1874, 1875, and 1876 the Right of Male Inhabitants of Said State . . . to Vote Had Been Denied or Abridged.*

Senate Reports. 46th Congress, 2nd Session, No. 693: *Report and Testimony of the Select Committee of the United States Senate to Investigate the Causes of the Removal of Negroes from the Southern States to the Northern States.*

United States Statutes at Large, Volume 14. Boston: Little, Brown, and Company, 1867.

United States Statutes at Large, Volume 15. Boston: Little, Brown, and Company, 1869.

BOOKS AND ARTICLES

Ayers, Edward. *Vengeance and Justice: Crime and Punishment in the Nineteenth-Century American South.* London: Oxford University Press, 1984.

Bardaglio, Peter W. *Reconstructing the Household: Families, Sex, and the Law in the Nineteenth-Century South.* Chapel Hill: University of North Carolina Press, 1995.

Barnes, William Horatio. *History of the Thirty-Ninth Congress of the United States.* New York: Harper & Brothers, 1868.

Bass, Jack. "South Carolina's Borrowing from Mississippi." *Charleston Law Review* 3 (Spring 2009): 525–533.

Bederman, Gail. *Manliness and Civilization: A Cultural History of Gender and Race in the United States, 1880–1917.* Chicago: University of Chicago Press, 1995.

Behrens, Angela, Christopher Uggen, and Jeff Manza. "Ballot Manipulation and the 'Menace of Negro Domination': Racial Threat and Felon Disenfranchisement in the United States, 1850–2002." *American Journal of Sociology* 109 (November 2003): 559–605.

Benedict, Michael Les. *A Compromise of Principle: Congressional Republicans and Reconstruction, 1863–1869.* New York: W.W. Norton & Co, 1974.

Bennett, James B. *Religion and the Rise of Jim Crow in New Orleans.* Princeton: Princeton University Press, 2005.

Bensel, Richard. *Yankee Leviathan: The Origins of Central State Authority in America, 1859–1877.* New York: Cambridge University Press, 1990.

Berlin, Ira. *Slaves Without Masters. The Free Negro in the Antebellum South.* New York: Pantheon Books, 1975.

Berry, Charles. "Free Labor He Found Unsatisfactory: James W. English and Convict Lease Labor at the Chattahoochee Brick Company." M.A. Thesis, Georgia State University, 1991.

Bettersworth, John Knox. *People's College: A History of Mississippi State.* Tuscaloosa: University of Alabama Press, 1953.

Blackmon, Douglas. *Slavery by Another Name: The Re-enslavement of Black People in America from the Civil War to World War II.* New York: Doubleday, 2008.

Blackstone, William. *Commentaries on the Laws of England*, vol. 4. Oxford, UK: Clarendon Press, 1769.

Blackstone, William. *Commentaries on the Laws of England: A Facsimile of the First Edition of 1765–1769.* Volume 4, 5. Chicago: University of Chicago Press, 1979.

Bourne, Richard W. "*Richardson v. Ramirez*: A Motion to Reconsider." *Valparaiso University Law Review* 42 (Fall, 2007): 1–32.

Bouvier, John. *Bouvier's Law Dictionary and Concise Encyclopedia.* 3rd revision, 8th edition. Kansas City: Vernon Law Book Company, 1914.

Bradley, Mark L. *Bluecoats and Tar Heels: Soldiers and Civilians in Reconstruction North Carolina.* Lexington: University Press of Kentucky, 2009.

Breitman, Richard and Alan M. Kraut. *American Refugee Policy and European Jewry, 1933–1945.* Bloomington: Indiana University Press.

Campbell, Sir George. *White and Black: The Outcome of a Visit to the United States.* London, Chatto & Windus, 1879.

Carle, Susan D. "Race, Class, and Legal Ethics in the Early NAACP (1910–1920)." *Law and History Review* 20 (2002): 97–146.

Cartwright, Joseph H. *The Triumph of Jim Crow: Tennessee Race Relations in the 1880's.* Knoxville: The University of Tennessee Press, 1976.

Cecil-Fronsman, Bill. *Common Whites: Class and Culture in Antebellum North Carolina.* Lexington: University Press of Kentucky, 1992.

Chicago Commission on Race Relations. *The Negro in Chicago: A Study of Race Relations and a Race Riot.* Chicago: University of Chicago Press, 1922.

Chin, Gabriel J. "Rehabilitating Unconstitutional Statutes: An Analysis of *Cotton v. Fordice*, 157 F.3d 388 (5th Cir. 1998)." *University of Cincinnati Law Review* 71 (Winter 2003): 421–455.

Chin, Gabriel J. "Reconstruction, Felon Disenfranchisement, and the Right to Vote: Did the Fifteenth Amendment Repeal Section Two of the Fourteenth Amendment?" *Georgetown Law Journal* 92, no. 259 (2004): 259–316.

Cohen, Neil P. "Tennessee Civil Disabilities: A Systemic Approach." *Tennessee Law Review* 41 (1974): 253–267.

Congressional Research Service. *The Constitution of the United States: Analysis and Interpretation*. Washington, DC: GPO, 1972.

Cooper Jr., William J. *The Conservative Regime: South Carolina, 1877–1890*. Baltimore: Johns Hopkins Press, 1968.

Cosgrove, John R. "Four New Arguments Against the Constitutionality of Felony Disenfranchisement." *Thomas Jefferson Law Review* 26 (2004): 157–202.

Cresswell, Stephen. *Rednecks, Redeemers, and Race: Mississippi after Reconstruction, 1877–1917*. Jackson, Miss: University Press of Mississippi, 2006.

Croly, David G. *Seymour and Blair, Their Lives and Services*. New York: Richardson and Company, 1868.

Curtin, Mary Ellen. *Black Prisoners and Their World, Alabama, 1865–1900*. Charlottesville: University of Virginia Press, 2000.

Curtis, Michael Kent. "The Crisis over The Impending Crisis: Free Speech, Slavery, and the Fourteenth Amendment." In *Slavery and the Law*, edited by Paul Finkleman, 161–206. Oxford: Rowman and Littlefield, 2002.

Dane, Nathan. *A General Abridgement and Digest of American Law, With Occasional Notes and Comments*. Volume 2. Boston: Cummings, Hillard, and Company, 1823.

Davis, S. F. "Something about Some of the Justices' Courts of Mississippi." *Case and Comment* 22 (1915): 42–45.

Dayan, Joan. "Legal Slaves and Civil Bodies." In *Materializaing Democracy: Toward a Revitalized Cultural Politics*, edited by Russ Castronovo and Dana D. Nelson, 53–94. Durham, NC: Duke University Press, 2002.

Dinan, John. "The Adoption of Criminal Disenfranchisement Provisions in the United States: Lessons from the State Constitutional Convention Debates." *Journal of Policy History* 19 (Fall 2007): 282–312.

Dunning, William Archibald. *Reconstruction, Political and Economic, 1865–1877*. New York: Harper and Brothers Publishers, 1907.

Eden, William. *Principles of Penal Law*. London: B. White, 1771.

Edwards, Laura F. *Gendered Strife and Confusion: The Political Culture of Reconstruction*. Champaign: University of Illinois Press, 1997.

Edwards, Laura F. "Status without Rights: African Americans and the Tangled History of Law and Governance in the Nineteenth Century U.S. South." *American Historical Review* 112 (2007): 365–393.

Ewald, Alec C. " 'Civil Death': The Ideological Paradox of Criminal Disenfranchisement Law in the United States," *Wisconsin Law Review* 5 (2002): 1045–1138.

Ewald, Alec C., and Brandon Rottinghaus, ed. *Criminal Disenfranchisement in an International Perspective*. New York: Cambridge University Press, 2009.

Foner, Eric. *Reconstruction: America's Unfinished Revolution*. New York: Harper and Row, 1988.

Fredrickson, George M. *The Black Image in the White Mind: The Debate on Afro-American Character and Destiny, 1817–1914*. New York: Harper and Row, 1971.

Friedman, Lawrence M. *Crime and Punishment in American History*. New York: Basic Books, 1993.

Gaines, Kevin K. *Uplifting the Race: Black Leadership, Politics, and Culture in the Twentieth Century*. Chapel Hill: University of North Carolina Press, 1996.

Gilfoyle, Timothy. *A Pickpocket's Tale: The Underworld of Nineteenth-Century New York.* New York: Norton 2006.

Gillette, William. *Retreat from Reconstruction: 1869–1879.* Baton Rouge: Louisiana State University Press, 1979.

Glenn, Myra C. *Campaigns Against Corporal Punishment: Prisoners, Sailors, Women, and Children in Antebellum America.* Albany: State University of New York Press, 1984.

Going, Allen Johnston. *Bourbon Democracy in Alabama, 1874–1890.* Tuscaloosa: University of Alabama Press, 1951.

Hahn, Steven. "Hunting, Fishing, and Foraging: Common Rights and Class Relations in the Postbellum South." *Radical History Review* 26 (October 1982): 37–64.

Halladay, Donald L. "Infamy as Ground of Disqualification in Tennessee." *Tennessee Law Review* 22 (December 1951): 544–557.

Hancock, Brian J. "The Voting Rights of Convicted Felons." *FEC Journal of Election Administration* 17 (1996): 35–42.

Hardin, John A. *Fifty Years of Segregation. Black Higher Education in Kentucky, 1904–1954.* Lexington: University Press of Kentucky, 1997.

Harrison, Lowell Hayes and James C. Klotter. *A New History of Kentucky.* Lexington: University Press of Kentucky, 1997.

Hench, Virginia E. "The Death of Voting Rights: The Legal Disenfranchisement of Minority Voters." *Case Western Reserve University Law Review* 48 (1998): 727–798.

Hinchcliff, Abigail M. "The 'Other' Side of Richardson v. Ramirez: A Textual Challenge to Felon Disenfranchisement." *Yale Law Journal* 121 (2011): 194–236.

Hoffman, Steven J. *Race, Class and Power in the Building of Richmond, 1870–1920.* Jefferson, NC: McFarland and Company, 2004.

Howard, A.E. Dick. *Commentaries on the Constitution of Virginia*, vol. 2. Charlottesville, VA: University of Virginia Press, 1974.

Itzkowitz, Howard, and Oldak, Lauren. "Restoring the Ex-Offender's Right To Vote: Background and Developments." *American Criminal Law Review* 11 (1973): 721–770.

Johnson, Guion Griffis. *Ante-Bellum North Carolina: A Social History.* Chapel Hill: University of North Carolina Press, 1937.

Kann, Mark E. *Punishment, Prisons and Patriarchy: Liberty and Power in the Early American Republic.* New York: New York University Press, 2005.

Kantrowitz, Stephen. *Ben Tillman and the Reconstruction of White Supremacy.* Chapel Hill: University of North Carolina Press, 2000.

Key, V.O. *Southern Politics in State and Nation.* New York: Alfred A. Knopf, 1949.

Keyssar, Alexander. *The Right to Vote: The Contested History of Democracy in the United States.* New York: Basic Books, 2000.

King, Ryan S. *Expanding the Vote: State Felony Disenfranchisement Reform, 1997–2008.* Washington, DC: Sentencing Project, 2008.

Kirwan, Albert. *Revolt of the Rednecks: Mississippi Politics 1876–1925.* Lexington: University of Kentucky Press, 1951.

Klotsche, J. Martin. "The Star Route Cases." *Mississippi Valley Historical Review* 22 (December 1935): 407–418.

Klotter, James C. *Kentucky: Portrait in Paradox, 1900–1950.* Frankfort: KY Historical Society, 1996.

Kousser, J. Morgan. *The Shaping of Southern Politics: Suffrage Restriction and the Establishment of the One-Party South, 1880–1910.* New Haven: Yale University Press, 1974.

Kousser, J. Morgan. *Colorblind Injustice: Minority Voting Rights and the Undoing of the Second Reconstruction*. Chapel Hill: University of North Carolina Press, 1999.

Kousser, J. Morgan. "Disfranchisement Modernized" (book review). *Election Law Journal* 6 (2007): 104–112

Lakin, Matthew. "'A Dark Night': The Knoxville Race Riot of 1919." *Journal of East Tennessee History* 72 (2000): 1–29.

Lamson, Peggy. *The Glorious Failure: Black Congressman Robert Brown Elliott and the Reconstruction of South Carolina*. New York: Norton, 1973.

Lichtenstein, Alex. *Twice the Work of Free Labor: The Political Economy of Convict Labor in the New South*. New York: Verso, 1996.

Liles, William Walton. "Challenges to Felony Disenfranchisement Laws: Past, Present, and Future." *Alabama Law Review* 58 (May 2007): 615–629.

Lockley, Timothy James. *Lines in the Sand: Race and Class in Lowcountry Georgia, 1750–1860*. Athens: University of Georgia Press, 2004.

Logan. Rayford. *The Negro in American Life and Thought: The Nadir, 1877–1901*. New York: Collier Books, 1965.

Lowe, Richard G. "Virginia's Reconstruction Convention. General Schofield Rates the Delegates." *The Virginia Magazine of History and Biography* 80 (July 1972): 341–360.

Mancini, Matthew J. *One Dies, Get Another: Convict Leasing in the American South, 1866–1928*. Columbia, SC: University of South Carolina Press, 1996.

Manley, Walter W., E. Canter Brown, Eric W. Rise, *The Supreme Court of Florida and Its Predecessor Courts, 1821–1917*. Gainesville: University of Florida Press, 1998.

Manza, Jeff and Christopher Uggen. *Locked Out: Felon Disenfranchisement and American Democracy*. New York: Oxford University Press, 2006.

Mauer, Marc. Statement of Marc Mauer, Prepared for the House Judiciary Committee Subcommittee on the Constitution, Civil Rights and Civil Liberties, Hearing on H.R. 3335, "The Democracy Restoration Act of 2009," March 16, 2010.

McCook, John J. "Some New Phases of the Tramp Problem." *The Charities Review* 1, no. 8 (June 1892): 355–364.

McCurry, Stephanie. *Masters of Small Worlds: Yeoman Households, Gender Relations, and the Political Culture of the Antebellum South Carolina Low Country*. New York: Oxford University Press, 1995.

McCurry, Stephanie. *Confederate Reckoning: Power and Politics in the Civil War South*. Cambridge: Harvard University Press, 2010.

McFarlane, Walter A. "The Clemency Process in Virginia." *University of Richmond Law Review* 27 (1993), 241–280.

McKay, Seth Shepard, editor. *Debates in the Texas Constitutional Convention of 1875*. Austin: University of Texas, 1930.

McLennan, Rebecca M. *The Crisis of Imprisonment: Protest, Politics, and the Making of the American Penal State, 1776–1941*. Cambridge: Cambridge University Press, 2008.

McMillan, Malcolm Cook. *Constitutional Development in Alabama, 1798–1901: A Study in Politics, the Negro, and Sectionalism*. Chapel Hill: University of North Carolina Press, 1955.

Meader, Lewis Hamilton. "The Council of Censors in Vermont." *Proceedings of the Vermont Historical Society*. Burlington: Free Press Association, 1898.

Meyer, Stephen Grant. *As Long as They Don't Move Next Door: Segregation and Racial Conflict in American Neighborhoods*. Lanham: Rowman and Littlefield, 2000.

Miller, Vivien M. L. *Crime, Sexual Violence, and Clemency: Florida's Pardon Board and Penal System in the Progressive Era*. Gainesville, FL: University Press of Florida, 2000.

Mondesire, Whyatt. "Felon Disenfranchisement: the Modern Day Poll Tax." *Temple Political and Civil Rights Law Review* 10 (Spring 2001): 435–441.

Morgan-Foster, Jason. "Transnational Judicial Discourse and Felon Disenfranchisement: Re-examining *Richardson v. Ramirez.*" *Tulsa Journal of Comparative and International Law* 13 (Spring 2006): 279–319.

Morris, Richard B. "The Measure of Bondage in the Slave States." *Mississippi Valley Historical Review* 41 (September 1954): 219–240.

Morton, Richard L. *The Negro in Virginia Politics, 1865–1902.* Charlottesville: University of Virginia Press, 1919.

Novak, William. *The People's Welfare: Law and Regulation in Nineteenth Century America.* Chapel Hill: University of North Carolina Press, 1996.

O'Donovan, Susan E., John C. Rodrigue, and Leslie S. Rowland. "Between Emancipation and Enfranchisement: Law and the Political Mobilization of Black Southerners, 1865–1867." *Chicago-Kent Law Review* 70 (1995), 1059–1077.

Ogden, Frederic D. *The Poll Tax in the South.* Tuscaloosa: University of Alabama Press, 1958.

Olbrich, Emil. *The Development of Sentiment on Negro Suffrage to 1860.* Madison: The University of Wisconsin, 1912.

Orth, John V. *The North Carolina State Constitution, with History and Commentary.* Chapel Hill: University of North Carolina Press, 1995.

Oshinsky, David M. *"Worse Than Slavery": Parchman Farm and the Ordeal of Jim Crow Justice.* New York: The Free Press, 1996.

Palast, Gregory. "Florida's Flawed 'Voter-Cleansing' Program." Salon.com, December 4, 2000.

Patterson, Orlando. *Slavery and Social Death: A Comparative Study.* Cambridge, MA: Harvard University Press, 1982.

Perkinson, Robert. *Texas Tough: The Rise of America's Prison Empire.* New York. Metropolitan Books, 2010.

Perman, Michael. *Road To Redemption.* Chapel Hill: University of North Carolina Press, 1984.

Perman, Michael. *Struggle for Mastery: Disfranchisement in the South, 1888–1908.* Chapel Hill: University of North Carolina Press, 2001.

Pettus, Katherine Irene. *Felony Disenfranchisement in America: Historical Origins, Institutional Racism, and Modern Consequences.* New York: LFB Scholarly Publishing, 2005.

Phipps, Kelly Elizabeth. "Marriage and Redemption: Mormon Polygamy in the Congressional Imagination, 1862–1887." *Virginia Law Review* 95 (April 2009): 437–487.

Pinaire, Brian. "Barred from the Vote: Public Attitudes Toward the Disenfranchisement of Felons." *Fordham Urban Law Journal* 30 (July 2003): 519–1550.

Pleck, Elizabeth. "Wife Beating in Nineteenth-Century America." *Victimology* 4 (1979): 60–74.

Porter, Kirk Harold. *A History of Suffrage in the United States.* Chicago: University of Chicago Press, 1918.

Porter, Nicole D. *Expanding the Vote: State Felony Disenfranchisement Reform, 2010.* Washington, DC: Sentencing Project, 2010.

Rable, George C. *But There Was No Peace: The Role of Violence in the Politics of Reconstruction.* Athens: University of Georgia Press, 1984.

Raum, Green B. *The Existing Conflict between Republican Government and Southern Oligarchy.* New York: Charles M. Green, 1884.

Re, Richard M. and Christopher M. Re. "Voting and Vice: Criminal Disenfranchisement and the Reconstruction Amendments." *Yale Law Journal* 121 (2012): 1584–1670.

Riser, R. Volney. *Defying Disfranchisement: Black Voting Rights Activism in the Jim Crow South, 1890–1908*. Baton Rouge: Louisiana State University Press, 2010.

Rogers William Warren and Robert David Ward. "'Jack Turnerism': A Political Phenomenon of the Deep South." *Journal of Negro History* 57 (October 1972): 313–332.

Rudwick, Elliott M. *Race Riot at East St. Louis, July 2, 1917*. Carbondale: Southern Illinois Press, 1964.

Russ, Jr., William A. "The Negro and White Disfranchisement During Radical Reconstruction." *The Journal of Negro History* 19 (April 1934): 171.

Schultz, Mark. *The Rural Face of White Supremacy: Beyond Jim Crow*. Urbana: University of Illinois Press, 2005.

Sebba, Leslie. "The Pardoning Power—A World Survey." *Journal of Criminal Law and Criminology* 68 (1977): 83–121.

The Sentencing Project. *Felony Disfranchisement Laws in the United States, 2010*. Washington, DC: The Sentencing Project, 2010.

The Sentencing Project. *Felony Disenfranchisement Rates for Women*. Washington, DC: The Sentencing Project, March 2008.

Simson, Elizabeth. *Justice Denied: How Felony Disenfranchisement Laws Undermine American Democracy*. Washington, DC: Americans For Democratic Action Education Fund, 2002.

Sharfestein, Daniel. *The Invisible Line: Three Families' Histories of 'Passing' from Black to White*. New York: Penguin Press, 2011.

Shapiro, Andrew L. "Challenging Criminal Disenfranchisement under the Voting Rights Act: A New Strategy." *Yale Law Journal* 103 (November 1993): 537–566.

Shapiro, Karin. *A New South Rebellion: The Battle against Convict Labor in the Tennessee Coalfields, 1871–1897*. Chapel Hill: University of North Carolina Press, 1998.

Smith, Chester H. "The Justice of the Peace System in the United States." *California Law Review* 15 (1927): 118–141.

Stein, Lana. *St. Louis Politics: The Triumph of Tradition*. St. Louis: Missouri Historical Society Press, 2002.

Stemm, Paul G. "The Role of Common Law Concepts in Modern Criminal Jurisprudence (A Symposium) II. Infamy and the Officeholder." *The Journal of Criminal Law, Criminology and Political Science* 49 (Sep.–Oct., 1958): 250–155.

Sterling, Dorothy. Editor. *The Trouble They Seen: The Story of Reconstruction in the Words of African Americans*. New York: Da Capo Press, 1994.

Stevens, Walter B. *Centennial History of Missouri (the Center State): One Hundred Years in the Union, 1820–1921*. St. Louis: Clarke Publishing, 1921.

Stone, William F., Jr. "Pardons in Virginia." *Washington and Lee Law Review* 26 (1969): 307–322.

Stumberg, George Wilfred. "Criminal Appropriation of Movables—A Need for Legislative Reform." *Texas Law Review* 19 (February 1941): 117–140.

Taifa, Nkechi. *Re-Enfranchisement! A Guide for Individual Restoration of Voting Rights in States that Permanently Disenfranchise Former Felons*. Washington, DC: The Advancement Project, 2002.

Thompson, Heather Ann. "Why Mass Incarceration Matters: Rethinking Crisis, Decline, and Transformation in Postwar American History." *The Journal of American History* 97 (December 2010): 703–734.

Tindall, George Brown. *South Carolina Negroes, 1877–1900*. Columbia, SC: University of South Carolina Press, 1952.

Toobin, Jeffrey. *Too Close to Call: The Thirty-Six-Day Battle to Decide the 2000 Election*. New York: Random House, 2002.

Trent, W. P., ed. *Southern Writers: Selections in Prose and Verse*. New York: MacMillan Company, 1905.

Uggen, Christopher, Sarah Shannon, and Jeff Manza. *State-Level Estimates of Felon Disenfranchisement in the United States, 2010*. Washington, DC: The Sentencing Project, 2010.

Underwood, James L. *The Constitution of South Carolina: The Struggle for Political Equality*. Columbia, SC: University of South Carolina Press, 1986.

Underwood, James Lowell, and W. Lewis Burke Jr., editors. *At Freedom's Door: African American Founding Fathers and Lawyers in Reconstruction South Carolina*. Columbia: University of South Carolina Press, 2000.

Varon, Elizabeth R. *Southern Lady, Yankee Spy: The True Story of Elizabeth Van Lew, a Union Agent in the Heart of the Confederacy*. New York: Oxford University Press, 2003.

Wang, Xi. *Trial of Democracy: Black Suffrage and Northern Republicans, 1860–1910*. Athens: University of Georgia Press, 1997.

Washington, Booker T. *Up from Slavery: An Autobiography*. Garden City, New York: Doubleday and Company, 1901.

Wennersten, John R. *The Oyster Wars of Chesapeake Bay*. Centreville, Maryland: Tidewater Press, 1981.

Wharton, Vernon Lane. *The Negro in Mississippi, 1865–1900*. Chapel Hill: University of North Carolina Press, 1947.

Whitman, James Q. *Harsh Justice: Criminal Punishment and the Widening Divide Between America and Europe*. New York: Oxford University Press, 2003.

Wiggins, Sarah Woolfolk. *The Scalawag in Alabama Politics, 1865 1881*. Tuscaloosa: University of Alabama Press, 1977.

Willcox, Walter F. "Negro Criminality." In *Studies in the American Race Problem*, edited by Alfred Holt Stone, 443–476. New York: Doubleday, Page, and Company, 1908.

Williams, Patrick G. "Suffrage Restriction in Post-Reconstruction Texas: Urban Politics and the Specter of the Commune." *Journal of Southern History* 68 (February 2002): 31–64.

Williams-Forson, Psyche A. *Building Houses out of Chicken Legs: Black Women, Food, and Power*. Chapel Hill: University of North Carolina Press, 2006.

Wood, Erika, and Liz Budnitz. *Jim Crow in New York*. New York: Brennan Center for Justice, 2010.

Wood, Erika L., and Neema Trivedi. "The Modern Day Poll Tax: How Economic Sanctions Block Access to the Polls." *Clearinghouse Review: Journal of Poverty Law and Policy* (May–June 2007): 31–45.

Wood, Phillip J. *Southern Capitalism: The Political Economy of North Carolina, 1880–1980*. Durham, NC: Duke University Press, 1986.

Woodbridge, D.W. "The Effect in Virginia of Conviction of Crime on Competency and Credibility of Witnesses." *Virginia Law Review* 23 (1936–1937): 470–480.

Woodward, C. Vann. *Origins of the New South, 1877–1913*. Baton Rouge: Louisiana State University Press, 1951.

Wyatt-Brown, Bertram. *Southern Honor: Ethics and Behavior in the Old South*. New York: Oxford University Press, 1982

Zetlin-Jones, David. "Right to Remain Silent? What the Voting Rights Act Can and Should Say About Felony Disenfranchisement." *Boston College Law Review* 47 (2006): 411–454.

INDEX